FROM SYRIA TO SEMINOLE

From Syria to Seminole

. . .

Memoir of a High Plains Merchant

Ed Aryain

Edited and with an Introduction by
J'Nell L. Pate

. . .

Foreword by
John R. Wunder

Afterword by
Edward Aryain and Jameil Aryain

TEXAS TECH UNIVERSITY PRESS

This book is typeset in Walbaum. The paper used in this book meets the minimum
requirements of ANSI/NISO Z39.48–1992 (R1997). ∞

Designed by Mark McGarry, Texas Type & Book Works

Library of Congress Cataloging-in-Publication Data
Aryain, Ed.
   From Syria to Seminole : memoir of a High Plains merchant / Ed Aryain ;
edited and with an Introduction by J'Nell L. Pate.
          p. cm.—(Plains histories)
   Summary: "Sixty years after his arrival in America in 1913 at age fifteen, Syrian-
American Mohammed (Ed) Aryain recounts his life as first a dry-goods peddler and then
a merchant and family man on the Great Plains, eventually owning a store in Seminole,
Texas. Introduction and notes provide historical context"—Provided by publisher.
Includes bibliographical references and index.
   ISBN-13: 978-0-89672-586-7 (cloth : alk. paper)
   ISBN-10: 0-89672-586-3 (cloth : alk. paper)
   1. Aryain, Ed. 2. Syrian Americans—Texas—Biography. 3. Texas—Biography.
4. Merchants—Texas—Biography. I. Pate, J'Nell L. II. Title. III. Series.
E184.S98A79 2006
976.4'009275691—dc22   2006005512

Printed in the United States of America
06 07 08 09 10 11 12 13 14 | 9 8 7 6 5 4 3 2 1
TS

Texas Tech University Press
Box 41037
Lubbock, Texas 79409–1037 USA
800.832.4042
www.ttup.ttu.edu

To the memory of Ed and Etta Aryain,
To their sons, Eddie and Jameil, and family,
To all the early immigrants who came to America
to work hard and to succeed,
And always to my husband, Kenneth,
who listens to all my excited explanations
when my research has unearthed more
gems of history.

. . .

Contents

. . .

Maps appear on pages xxv and xxxi

Photographs follow page   96

Plainsword

. . .

On the wintry Saturday evening of February 18, 2006, the winning number of the largest lottery jackpot ever—$365 million—was announced. Soon it was revealed that the lucky ticket had been purchased at a U-Stop in Lincoln, Nebraska. Who might this be? Finally, after what seemed like a long wait, but was only five days, the winners stepped forward. They were eight workers at a Lincoln food-processing plant. At a press conference, they claimed an equal share of the prize—$22.2 million each after taxes; and once they stepped forward, they revealed that they were a diverse group of new Plains millionaires.

The lucky eight, as they were immediately labeled, hailed from Lincoln and a few surrounding towns in Nebraska but also from Vietnam and the Congo. The Congolese Alain Maboussou had immigrated to the United States in 1999 as a refugee from an African civil war. He had grown up in Brazzaville and lived in Paris briefly before he arrived on the Great Plains four years ago. Here he married a local woman, and they had a baby daughter. This twenty-six-year-old might have uttered, "What a beautiful country," the day he found out he won the lottery.

The Vietnamese winners included Dung Tran and Quang Dao. Dao, a fifty-six-year-old Lincoln resident left his homeland seventeen years ago. His good fortune could not have come at a better time as he has serious health problems. He also stated that he could afford to visit Vietnam to help some of his relatives who live there. Tran is a more recent immigrant, an Amerasian whose American father disappeared, Tran, his Vietnamese mother, and an aunt arrived in Lincoln in 1990 when he was nineteen. Tran, now age thirty-five, has worked long hours as a mechanic to support his family. His message, delivered first in halting English and then in Vietnamese, was, "I got to say thank you to everybody."

The other five winners—Eric Zornes, Michael Terpstra, Robert Stewart, Chastity Rutjens, and David Gehle—were equally thrilled and similarly diverse. Americans by birth, they represented Dutch, Belgian, Scottish, German, and Irish ancestors. Interestingly, several had already quit their jobs, but all eight created a positive picture for the public. One Lincolnite quoted in the local paper reflected, "It's almost as good as winning yourself."[1]

As demonstrated once again by the recent excitement in the heartland, the Great Plains has been and continues to be perhaps the most ethnic polyglot of any region in all of North America, save the cities of Montreal and New York. Although often deemed a somewhat less inviting region than others, the Great Plains has the distinct advantage of openness and bigness, and is a place where hard work is rewarded and admired. It is the kind of place that an immigrant desires, and that was certainly true for young Mohammed Aryain, a fifteen-year-old Syrian immigrant to the United States in 1913, who shortened his first name to Ed and eventually settled in the West Texas oil town of Seminole. Ed was the only foreign-born resident there. It seemed each small town had one or two. His oldest son Eddie would later reflect that many West Texas towns had a Syrian or Jewish merchant and perhaps a Greek restaurant.

In the memoir that follows, we are treated to a unique story.

Not many immigrants narrate their own autobiography in self-taught English, fewer still are Druze immigrants from the Middle East, and even fewer are permanently settled in the Great Plains. But this is precisely what Ed Aryain, born in 1897 to a Druze family in the small village of Henna, Syria, eighteen miles from Damascus, had done. At the time he began his memoir, Ed was seventy-five years old, and he died just two years later in 1974. In the pages that follow, he tells us of his early years growing up in Greater Syria when Palestine, Lebanon, and modern Syria were administered together under the Turkish Empire. The prelude to World War I was a particularly unstable time that no doubt influenced the young Syrian to leave home for a new land. Aryain remembers that all he wanted to do was work hard, save money, and stay in the United States for about ten years. He would then purchase a gold watch and return to his village so that he could contribute his American money to help his father irrigate their farmland. That, of course, doesn't happen. Instead, Ed remains in the USA, where he becomes a successful American citizen and settles in the land of the "underground rain."

Ed was drawn to commerce and trade. At first he worked with others, selling various goods, traveling as a peddler from town to town. He soon found that boomtowns with instant populations constituted the best markets for his wares, and thus he found himself spending a great deal of time in Texas and Oklahoma as well as the front range of the Rockies in Colorado and New Mexico. But it was West Texas that caught his eye, along with Etta Stone, a Baptist girl from Missouri visiting her aunt and uncle in Lamesa. In 1925 Ed married Etta; in 1939 Ed became a United States citizen; and together Ed and Etta set up dry goods stores in four West Texas towns. Also in 1939 they and their two boys opened one last store in Seminole, Texas, where they would thrive and live the rest of their lives. Ed became a respected and well-to-do citizen, and his son Jameil was eventually elected Seminole's mayor.

Not every experience was positive for Ed Aryain—or for most

other immigrants. Black Tuesday and the onset of the Great Depression wiped out Ed's stores in Littlefield and Sudan. Local law enforcement in Littlefield harassed him. Life wasn't easy. "I took notice," reflected Ed, "that some foreigners were more despised than others. People most disliked in America were Jews, Greeks, Italians, Syrians, Poles, Chinese, Japanese, and Turks." Ed lamented these feelings. "Why should a great country like America," he wrote, "hold so much hate for these immigrant people who were only asking to be allowed to make an honest living?"[2]

Nevertheless, Ed Aryain emphasizes the positive in his memoirs. This volume of reflections on a life lived to the fullest on the southern Plains in the twentieth century, together with a detailed introduction by J'Nell L. Pate, makes for an informative and thoughtful read. It truly expands our knowledge of the immigrant experience in America and their many contributions to society. Ed Aryain's son Jameil, in a personal Afterword, proudly remembers his father's favorite expression, "What a beautiful country!"

John R. Wunder
February 2006
Lincoln, Nebraska

Acknowledgments

. . .

I would not have had the opportunity to edit the wonderful story of Mohammed (Ed) Aryain had Dr. Paul Carlson of the Texas Tech University history department not suggested that I might be interested in the manuscript. My thanks go to him for introducing me to the story.

Getting to know the Aryain family during the course of this project has been a delightful experience. Visits with Jameil Aryain and his wife, Pat, in Seminole and long telephone conversations with Eddie Aryain in Los Angeles have provided me with both a great deal of information and encouragement in my work.

Suggestions and support from Judith Keeling, editor at Texas Tech Press, also have been invaluable. My friend and fellow historian Carol Roark, manager of the Texas/Dallas History and Archives Division at the Dallas Public Library, helped me locate information on the Jewish wholesalers in Dallas who advanced merchandise to Ed on credit. Dr. Arthur J. Ehlmann, professor emeritus and former head of the geology department at Texas Christian University, located information I needed about William Monnig of Fort Worth, who was extremely helpful to Ed during the Depression.

Tom Caldwell of Drumright, Oklahoma, who researched Syrians and Lebanese throughout Oklahoma, answered a lot of my questions about Syrians in oil boomtowns and Drumright in particular. Thanks go to Eileene Russell Huff, who found a photo of Drumright from her father's photography studio near the time Ed Aryain was there.

I also wish to thank the ladies in the Drumright Public Library who steered me to its newspaper on microfilm, to Gail Hopkins at the Sapulpa County Court House, and especially to Tiana Fortney, who did some research for me when I could not make a second trip back to Drumright. Clerks in the Kay County, Oklahoma, Records Office also were helpful. Librarians in Seminole and Brownfield assisted me, as did Shelby Concotelli and Candy Boyer at the Seminole Chamber of Commerce, who provided a photo of Aryain's Dry Goods Company on Main Street. Thanks to Matthew Crawford for the maps.

I would like to thank Professor Yushau Sodiq of the Religion Department of Texas Christian University for translating some passages from Arabic into English for me as I sought information about Ed Aryain's ancestor Shibli al-Aryan. He also answered my questions about the Druze.

Thanks to the Southwest Collection Library, Texas Tech University, for permitting publication. The Aryain family donated Ed's story to them. Working with Katherine Dennis, Managing Editor at Texas Tech University Press, has been a joy.

Thanks also to my husband, Kenneth, who patiently listened.

Introduction

. . .

FIFTEEN-YEAR-OLD MOHAMMED (ED) ARYAIN LEFT HIS HOME, his parents, and two sisters in Greater Syria, still a part of the weakening Ottoman Empire, and in 1913, crossed an ocean to America, hoping to make a better life for himself than he could in the Old Country. Ed dreamed, as many young men did, that he could come to the United States, make money quickly, and return with gold in his pockets to show to his friends and make life easier for his family. Ed was not alone in his dream. "Hundreds go out every year," writes Gertrude Bell, a well-educated Englishwoman who traveled to the Middle East in the early twentieth century.[1]

Nearly fifty years elapsed before Ed Aryain returned to Syria. More than a decade after that, with much urging from his sons, Ed began telling his story to his wife, Etta. She wrote it down and then typed it. "They would cry a while and write a while," remembers their older son, Edward (Eddie) Aryain. The experience of reminiscing brought them closer together, he says. He believes that the manuscript sounds like his father spoke: "He was a born storyteller."[2]

Just as Olive King Dixon wrote the story that her pioneer buffalo hunter husband Billy Dixon told, making him a well-known figure in frontier West Texas history, so too Etta Aryain assisted her husband to what may become greater recognition of the Syrian merchandising community of Texas and the Midwest. Additionally, they tell a great story.

"At the end of the two and one-half years we spent at this work Ed's health had begun to fail rapidly. Had we waited even a year longer, this story never would have been put on paper," Etta wrote Eddie as she sent the finished manuscript to him.[3] The earliest typed copy that exists is in three loose-leaf notebooks in the hands of their son, Jameil Aryain, Seminole, Texas.

Ed told a well-organized, chronological story with only a few pertinent digressions. When he left Syria in 1913, the Turkish domination over his homeland that had lasted for four centuries was nearing its end. The Ottoman Empire conquered Syria in 1516 and administered it until 1918 at the close of World War I. Under decentralized rule the Syrians saw little of the Ottoman Turks, as long as provinces paid their taxes and a head man existed in the province to keep order. Syrian provinces were called *vilayets* and were ruled by a governor, *vali*, with the title of *pasha*. Local governing bodies, called *millets* or *milyets*, organized themselves by faith—Christians, Jews, Druze, Muslims. A *millet* was a uniquely Middle Eastern political and religious institution, very different from the Western idea of states and nations. People of the same religion were considered to belong to the same social order, society, or "nation." The Ottoman Turks formalized the *millet* into a socio-political reality. The people ruled themselves, and the Turks left them alone as long as they did not challenge Ottoman Islamic society.[4]

Under the weakened, still despotic rule of its last sultan, Abdul Hamid (also known as Sultan Abd-al-Hamid), who ruled from 1876 to 1909, the Ottoman Empire began losing territory to Russia and Italy and losing influence to Britain and France. Troops of the Turkish First Army Corps mutinied in Istanbul against the police state, and the Turkish Chamber of Deputies and Senate deposed Abdul Hamid on April 29, 1909. The sultan's brother Reshad temporarily took his place.[5] In Chapter 1, Ed Aryain mentions these events. During the years of Ottoman rule, no borders existed in the six-hundred-mile stretch of Greater Syria, from Alexandretta to Aqaba, but later the smaller states of Syria, Lebanon, Jordan, and Israel emerged with definite boundaries.[6]

Economic motivations for Syrians to leave their homeland were strong. When Ed Aryain left Syria for America in 1913, the per capita income of citizens of the Ottoman Empire was only 5 percent of what British citizens earned and only 10 percent of that of other Europeans. Approximately three automobiles existed in the entire area of what was then Syria, including what later became Lebanon, and all three of them were in the city of Beirut. The Syria dating from the Roman Empire referred to an area from Turkey to Egypt and Iraq to the Mediterranean, including all of Palestine. In fact, Damascus, its capital, is considered to be the "oldest continuously inhabited city in the world."[7] Surrounded on three sides by mountains, Damascus was a city of nearly 300,000 people in 1905.[8]

No Ottoman unity, nor even a cultural Syrian identity, existed when Ed was born on August 22, 1897. Instead, religious division created conflict, and the British, Russians, and French intervened to establish schools. Even American missionaries and educators arrived in Syria early in the nineteenth century. They established elementary and high schools and, in 1866, a college they originally called Syrian Protestant College, now the American University of Beirut.[9]

Syria rarely knew security because of its geographical position between East and West, making it a frontier and a battleground. One could compare it to a bridge connecting Egypt, Mesopotamia, and Asia Minor or, stated another way, the land area where the continents of Africa, Asia, and Europe touched.[10]

Syrians like Ed emigrated because of poor economic conditions, the uncertainty and high taxes of Ottoman rule, and friction between religious groups. Over a period of seventy years, beginning in 1880, these optimistic Syrians sought new opportunities in North America (35 percent), South America (35 percent), and Egypt (10 percent) and scattered through the rest of the world (20 percent).[11]

Ed Aryain mentions his Druze religion several times, explaining that many of its practices were little known. In fact, one historian called the Druze "the great mystery of the Lebanon mountains."[12] As was the case with other religions of the Middle East, a person was born into his or her religion and was expected to remain for life. The total Druze population in the Middle East at the beginning of the twenty-first century is fewer than one million. They live in Syria, Lebanon, and Israel.[13]

The Druze religion, sometimes spelled "Druse," is a sect of Islam founded by the Shiite Caliph Al-Hakim bi-amr Allah of Cairo in the tenth century and thus is a split from Shiite Muslims. Al-Hakim disappeared without a trace in 1021 A.D., four years after proclaiming himself a divinity. Many of his followers believed that he would return like a messiah. The name Druze comes from Darazi, a missionary who encouraged Al-Hakim in his claims of divinity. Early persecution by other Muslims apparently caused the Druze to be secretive about their religious beliefs.[14]

The Druze believe in predestination and reincarnation. They read the Koran and believe that Mohammed was a prophet, but they do not observe Ramadan or take pilgrimages to Mecca. They do not follow the ritual prayers or practice polygamy. Orthodox Muslims consider them heretics.[15] Some accounts of the Druze say that they have no public places of worship and do not require their women to be veiled, but in Ed's experience in early-twentieth-century Syria, they did. Ed's family and fellow Druze met on Friday nights to worship.

Centuries ago the Druze were forced out of Egypt and took refuge in the Lebanon mountains, which now are considered their ancestral homeland. Many live in isolated communities called the Jabal-Druze in the mountains. Most Druze have blue eyes, as did Ed, causing some historians to speculate that they might have been descended from the crusaders from Western Europe.[16]

The Druze accept the Old and New Testaments as divine books. Consequently, they got along with the Maronites (Christians) until Turkish interference created conflict in the mid-nineteenth century.[17] In Chapter 2, Ed refers to the 1860 fighting several times.

Some Druze practices created problems for those who wished to leave their homeland. The Druze communities in Syria, Lebanon, and Palestine were closed because they did not accept intermarriage. Druze elders in Syria forbade Druze women from emigrating to America; thus, Druze men, like Ed, often married outside their faith.[18] Etta Aryain originally was a Baptist.

Some immigrants retained their Druze religion, however. The largest Druze community in the United States in the late twentieth century existed in Los Angeles, California. Many of the California Druze joined the American Druze Public Affairs Committee (ADPAC). An American Druze Society also exists. A current television and radio personality of Druze background is Casey Kasem.[19]

Ed reveals no attempts to pursue his Druze religion in America, and in fact, as a teenager in Syria, he had renounced it as being too strict in outlawing alcohol and cigarettes. Although he does not specifically say that his break with his parents' religion influenced his decision to leave Syria for America, it might have been an unacknowledged influence nevertheless.

Ed Aryain expresses understandable pride in his ancestor Shebly Aryain, also spelled Shibli al-Aryan, who, in the first half of the nineteenth century, had been a chief of the Jabal-Druze. In the mid-1830s Shibli al-Aryan led the Druze in resisting Ibrahim

Pasha, son of Muhammad Ali, governor of Egypt under the Ottoman Empire. Ali turned against the Ottoman sultan and sent Ibrahim to conquer Syria, which he did in 1832–33. Attempts at conscription and various reforms created unrest among the Syrians.[20]

In an attempt to be conciliatory to the Druze, the Ottoman Turks gave local chieftains, such as Ed's ancestor Shibli al-Aryan, "robes of honor." They appointed al-Aryan governor of the Houran and the leader of irregular troops made up of his own men. He told the Turkish government that he would start a revolt in Damascus unless the government made financial concessions. At first they agreed, but later the Turks turned and ambushed al-Aryan and forced him to surrender.[21]

Eventually the British and French brought an end to the hostilities, but the problems were a prelude to the 1860 massacres that Ed mentions. By that time al-Aryan had retired as leader, and Ismail al-Atrash had replaced him in the late 1840s.[22]

By the 1850s the Turks renewed their attempts to take the Jabal-Druze area and reinstituted their conscription demands. This time the Druze and Bedouins combined to defeat them.[23]

Conflict between the Druze and Maronites broke out in 1860, the precipitating factor being a quarrel between a Druze boy and a Maronite boy. Fighting for control of the area and religious differences led to land disputes. In what amounted to a civil war, thousands of people on both sides lost their lives in the brutal fighting in Mount Lebanon. In twenty-two days, 7,771 people lost their lives, 360 villages were destroyed, 560 churches and 43 monasteries were burned, and 28 schools were leveled. Druze were better fighters and inflicted more damage on the Christians than they received themselves, but it is no wonder that Ed Aryain mentions the 1860 massacres often.[24] Relief for the suffering after the 1860 massacres came from various places, including the United States.[25] Again the British and French intervened on opposite sides.

Ed came to the United States during the time period that historians label the "New Immigration" (1880–1920). Nearly thirty million newcomers arrived in the United States during those forty years, while nearly three-quarters of a century was needed for that many immigrants to arrive in what was called the "Old Immigration" (prior to 1880).[26]

Historians have characterized the "Old Immigration" as consisting of immigrants mostly from the British Isles, Germany, Scandinavia, and other parts of western Europe. Except for a few German and Irish Catholics, most of the newcomers were Protestant. They enjoyed a high rate of literacy, melded easily and quickly into American society, and made permanent plans to remain in the United States, usually acquiring land.

In contrast, the "New Immigration" of people coming after 1880 migrated from southern and eastern Europe or the Middle East. They were mostly Orthodox Catholic or Jewish, many of them illiterate and impoverished, and they settled in ethnic ghettos in large cities because no free or cheap land, such as the earlier immigrants found, remained available. Often the newer immigrants wanted to come, make money, and return to their home country, as was Ed's early expressed wish. The new immigrants generally took longer than the earlier ones did to assimilate.[27]

One reason for the increased numbers of immigrants after 1880 was that faster and cheaper travel existed. In 1840 a sailing ship needed an average of forty-four days to sail from Europe to New York. By 1897 the more advanced steamship travel to the United States took five and a half days. To pay his steerage on the ship, train fare in America, and other incidental expenses, an immigrant needed approximately $50. The steerage fares alone were about $22.50.[28]

Making things easier for Ed, the French had built a modern port in Beirut between 1880 and 1895, and by 1914 nine steamship lines made regular stops on a weekly to monthly basis. The cheaper fares and available steamship lines made the trip to America possible for many more people than could afford it a half-century earlier.[29]

Apparently the very first Syrian immigrant family ever to come to America was that of Joseph Arbeely of Damascus, who came in 1878. Upon arrival Arbeely held up a sign proclaiming, "The children and I have happily found liberty."[30] Those of his countrymen who followed him sought the same freedom from Turkish tyranny, from the military draft, and from the poverty that had so plagued their families.[31]

Unlike Ed, who was Druze, the earliest Syrians were "overwhelmingly Christian." Very few Muslims came before 1945. Of Syrian immigrants before World War II, 95 percent were Christian, and only 5 percent were Muslim or Druze.[32]

In contrast to the huge Jewish migration that began in the mid-nineteenth century and increased tremendously by the year 1900, the Syrian immigrants were not regarded as much of a threat because their numbers were few.[33] When they arrived in the wave of immigration at the end of the nineteenth century, the Lebanese-Syrians represented about 1 percent of the total immigration. Even so, between 1900 and 1914 as many as 25 percent of the population of the region called Mount Lebanon, a broad area encompassing Damascus and Beirut at that time, left home to emigrate to America, a total of one hundred thousand people. Of the Arabic speaking Middle Easterners who began to come to America at that time, nearly 90 percent were from this area. They arrived wearing "red fezzes, short open jackets, short, baggy blue trousers to the calves of the legs, and ill fitting shoes."[34]

The year that Ed chose to travel to America was one of two peak years (the other was 1914), when more than 9,000 Syrians arrived each year. He became one of 9,210 in 1913 when he arrived June 17, 1913, on the ship *Niagara*. Ed later could not remember the name of the ship, but his great-grandson Jordan Robins visit-

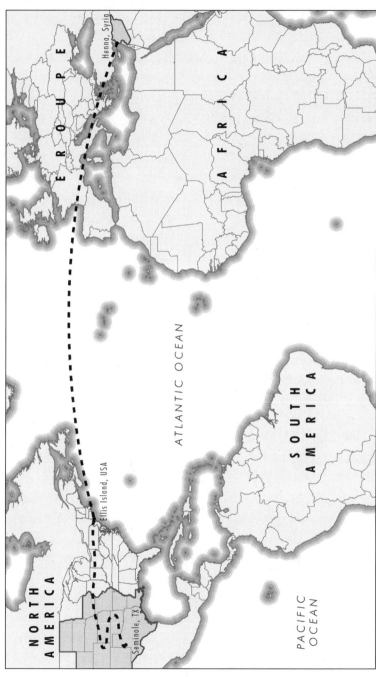

Traveling nearly halfway around the world at fifteen, Mohamed Aryain landed at Ellis Island, found Syrian sponsors on the East Coast, and began peddling merchandise in the Midwest. A quarter of a century later his last stop was Seminole, Texas. Map by Matthew Crawford.

ed Ellis Island on a trip to New York in July 2005 and found the
ship's manifest.[35]

According to Oscar Handlin in *The Uprooted*, emigration from
a homeland was the central life experience of many Americans. It
certainly was for Ed Aryain.[36] Among the first generation Syrian
immigrants who came during the "New Immigration" era, a high
degree of assimilation and Americanization occurred. In addition,
their children adopted American customs and experienced little
ethnic consciousness of their parents' background. Such early
Lebanese and Syrian immigrants often did quite well financially
in the first generation.[37] After a few years in America one Syrian
immigrant returned home with ten thousand dollars, intending to
stay, but he recalls, "I had begun to enjoy some of the American
luxuries such as good sanitation and freedom of movement." He
instead returned to the United States, bringing neighbors and relatives with him.[38]

Ed was fortunate that he came to the United States when he
did. After the 1924 immigration law took effect, limiting the number of immigrants who could enter the United States each year,
Syria became one of the nations with the smallest allotment.
Syrians in large numbers no longer arrived at Ellis Island.[39]

When Ed arrived, Ellis Island had only been in business to
receive immigrants for twenty-one years, since January 1, 1892.
The year the island saw the highest number of human receipts
from all locations was 1907, with 1,004,756 arrivals, but the year
Ed arrived, 1913, saw the second highest total with 892,653. After
war broke out in Europe the following year, the arrivals at Ellis
Island slowed or even ceased for a time because people were afraid
to cross the Atlantic.[40]

As the ship carrying him to America reached what became the
major entry port for most new arrivals for six decades (until its
closing in 1954), Ed and his fellow passengers began craning their
necks, standing on tiptoe, elbowing their way to the rail to get

their first glimpse of the Statue of Liberty. Most, including Ed, became very emotional when they saw Lady Liberty's welcoming torch. Ed tossed his red fez into the water. [41]

With trepidation, Ed and his fellow immigrants entered the red brick main building with its two-story Great Hall. Rumors spread quickly among the hopeful newcomers that many would be turned away if they did not pass a medical inspection. In about four hours, 80 percent of the new arrivals passed through Ellis Island, bought their railroad tickets, and then caught river barges to be ferried to train stations in New York or New Jersey. Ed endured a longer wait. An instruction book for medical examiners on the island warned that trachoma, a contagious eye disease, was prevalent among "Syrians, Greeks, Armenians, Russians, and Finns," so the workers checked people from those countries more closely. The ship's official manifest cites Mohammed Aryain's age as twenty. Either he feared being turned away because of his youth or the recorder made an error. The family never heard from him any age other than fifteen for when he arrived in the United States.[42]

During his detainment Ed ate on the long tables in the Ellis Island dining hall and worried that his money would run out before he got off of Ellis Island. The typical dinner included beef stew, boiled potatoes, and rye bread. He could only speak Arabic, but thankfully, workers at Ellis Island could translate. As Ed notes in Chapter 3, they warned the newcomers to be careful of fraud and deceit, for there were those who would take advantage of the immigrants' lack of knowledge of the language, of prices of food and train tickets, and of American practices.[43]

To help alleviate such problems, a Syrian network had developed by the 1890s. It helped fellow countrymen upon their arrival in America. Syrian wholesale suppliers and Arab language newspapers provided a great boon to young men like Ed Aryain. Suppliers, often former peddlers themselves, would sell on credit the merchandise that a young man needed to get a start in

America as a peddler. Such networks provided psychological as well as financial support and created interdependent relationships. Syrians often encouraged fellow villagers to emigrate and served as mentors to them when they arrived in the United States.[44]

Like the Jewish immigrants who had preceded them, the Syrians were attracted to trade. They disliked working for anyone else and saw being an employee as being exploited. The early Syrian immigrants wanted to succeed and own property; they sought financial security in a free-enterprise America.[45] Additionally, new immigrants often found it difficult to obtain employment or were only offered the most menial or low paying positions.

"When we look at the Syrian peddler/trader, we are looking at the key to the Syrian-Lebanese Americanization process," analysts have concluded.[46] However, the Druze and Muslim Arabs who arrived in the early twentieth century, when peddling was on the decline, were not able to form as large a network as the earlier Christian Arabs had done. Also, there were not as many Druze or Muslims in the United States at that time.

Peddling became "the major factor in explaining the relatively rapid assimilation" of Arabic-speaking immigrants before World War I. "With more courage than capital and more determination than experience, many Syrians had launched into their business-es."[47] Perhaps they all knew the old Arab proverb that "Trade will lead a man far."[48]

Fortunately the 1920s ushered in an age that Samuel Strauss and others have called "consumptionism." Americans began focus-ing on "luxury and security and comfort" that they believed nec-essary to the "good life." Many of the new Syrian immigrants like Ed became convinced that selling consumer goods was the way to make it in America.[49]

Nearly 90 percent of Arab immigrants to the United States before 1914 began earning their living as peddlers. Retailing required no academic credentials. The immigrants realized that success at retailing could be achieved in almost direct proportion to how hard one was willing to work. They could sell their wares while still learning English, for they simply showed their merchandise, named a price, and counted the change. They compensated for their language deficiencies by long hours at their task. In addition, they could enter retailing with a relatively low investment of funds. They took goods on consignment or purchased small, inexpensive trinkets for resale.[50]

Peddling brought the Syrians west to rural areas where housewives would welcome their products. A typical peddler who walked the rural roads of the Midwest strapped a heavy suitcase to his back, hung a small notions case called a *kashshi* on his chest, and carried a full satchel of merchandise in each hand. All of this baggage when full could weigh two hundred pounds. Straps often wore calluses, and much later in life Ed mentioned a permanent scar that remained. In this way a peddler could carry goods worth one hundred to three hundred dollars.[51]

In these suitcases and satchels the Syrian peddlers offered such items as notions, thread, ribbon, handkerchiefs, laces, underwear, garters, and suspenders, plus buttons, costume jewelry, combs, and shoelaces. For three cents a housewife could buy a pattern for a child's dress and one for herself. Specialty items that the Syrian peddlers discovered sold well were wooden crosses, bookmarks, rosaries, or anything from the "Holy Land." Since the young men came from that area of the world anyway, nearly any product made in their home country would suffice. Many of the young men wrote home to their mothers to supply homemade laces and scarves. Ed mentioned several times that he gave fancy items to housewives as thanks for a meal or a bed for the night.[52]

Some Americans, whose ancestors' arrival in America several generations earlier had been forgotten, looked down on peddlers and considered them destitute beggars. Syrians, however, saw door-to-door sales as a temporary means to an end. In fact, through their progression from peddling to renting a storefront to owning a department store, many of them became quite successful in only one generation.[53]

Surprisingly, peddling merchandise in rural areas or new oil boomtowns could be quite lucrative. The average per capita income for an American in 1910 was only $382. The next year a typical income for men over eighteen born in the United States reached $665 annually. Industrious peddlers usually earned from $10 to $12 per week. Ed mentioned earning $40 in a week several times. In fact, most peddlers earned between $200 and $1,500 each year, consistently sending money home to their families in Syria. A writer in 1924 revealed, "The Syrians send, per capita, more money home than almost any other immigrant people."[54]

Living expenses in the beginning remained cheap. Farm families often gave peddlers food and let them sleep in their barns. In an age before rural mail delivery for letters or newspapers, farmers were happy to see a peddler arrive from a large city in order to learn some outside news.[55]

Fiction writer Loula Grace Erdman, whose stories of pioneering West Texas have become classic, described a peddler named Albert Allerdyne in her autobiographical book *Life Was Simpler Then*. Allerdyne came regularly, twice a year, to Erdman's childhood home. The women of the community greeted him cordially, asked about his health, and offered him coffee or lemonade. "Nobody called the Better Business Bureau to check his credentials, and above all, nobody had a sign over the door saying 'no agent, peddlers, or solicitors admitted here.' Everyone accepted him for what he was—a man trying to make an honest living in the one way he knew."[56] Famous people in American history who peddled merchandise door-to-door before their later successes include Levi Straus, Benjamin Altman, Adam Gimball, Marshall Field, Meyer Guggenheim, Richard Sears, and Alvah Roebuck.[57]

Ed Aryain began his peddling career in the Midwest, moved

NORTH DAKOTA
Morristown

Pierre ☆
SOUTH DAKOTA
Sioux Falls

WYOMING

Laramie

NEBRASKA
North Platte
Lincoln ☆
Beatrice

IOWA

Akron Brush
Ft. Morgan
Denver ☆
Wray
COLORADO · Limon
Colorado Springs

Colby
Salina
Topeka ☆
KANSAS
Dodge City

MISSOURI

Tonkawa Three Sands
Drumright
OKLAHOMA Tulsa
Shawnee
Chickasha

ARKANSAS

NEW MEXICO
Sudan Amherst
Littlefield Lubbock
Seagraves Brownfield
Seminole
San Angelo
Big Lake

Sherman
Ft. Worth Dallas
Waxahachie Corsicana
Whitney Tuckertown
Waco Navarro
Temple Westphalia
Heidenheimer
Austin ☆

TEXAS

LOUISIANA

MEXICO

GULF OF MEXICO

Ed Aryain peddled merchandise all over the Midwest from 1913 until the early 1920s when he began to rent storefronts in Oklahoma and Texas oil boomtowns. Then when he married in 1925, he and his wife lived in Littlefield, Sudan, Brownfield, and finally, for the last thirty-five years of his life, in the West Texas community of Seminole. Map by Matthew Crawford.

through Oklahoma and central Texas, and then made repeat trips to many of the same places. He learned that oil boomtowns, first in Oklahoma and then Texas, provided more opportunities and faster growth than continued rural peddling. Tents and cheap wooden buildings appeared quickly, and prospective businessmen started restaurants that stayed open twenty-four hours. Hotels rented not rooms but beds or cots. People rushed in to share the wealth, and peddlers like Ed saw a chance to stay in one place for a while with a grocery store, a confectionary, or a dry goods business. He began renting small storefronts, sometimes with other Syrians.[58]

After their marriage on May 14, 1925, Ed and Etta operated dry goods stores in the West Texas towns of Littlefield, Brownfield, Sudan, and Seminole. Syrian families became important parts of many towns in West Texas: Seminole, Lamesa, O'Donnell, Post, Levelland, Wellington, Spur, Shamrock, Munday, Morton, Plainview, and Lubbock.[59]

Apparently Ed is the only one from these places who sat down to write his story. He probably did not realize that his account would speak for the experiences of many fellow Syrians who did not transcribe their adventures. His manuscript makes a valuable contribution to the published record concerning Syrian immigration to America in the late nineteenth and early twentieth centuries.

Much material exists to document the pattern of Jewish migration with mercantile practices from foot peddler to horse-drawn cart and finally to department store success. Until Ed Aryain chose to tell his story, and his sons urged publication, few published accounts existed about similar Syrian progressions from impoverished immigrant to hardworking peddler to upper-middle-class department store owner.

In most ways Ed's story is typical of the early male Syrian immigrants' experiences in America. Some of them went back to the Old Country, but most stayed in the United States to do as Ed did—Anglicize his name, learn English, marry, raise a family, and take part in the American dream. That transition from frightened, penniless newcomer to proud, prosperous American took place slowly, with many setbacks, a tremendous amount of hard work, and, yes, a few tears.

Ed kept in touch with his fellow Syrian merchants, and they got together periodically to eat Syrian cooking and have just one— almost ceremonial—drink of whiskey. They compared discrimination stories as well as tales of West Texas friendliness and acceptance. Yes, Ed and his friends faced discrimination—not as much as Jewish immigrants but enough that its memory lingered. Sometimes people assumed that Ed was Jewish, and he always corrected them.[60]

During the 1920s and 1930s in America, when Ed faced most of the discrimination problems, at least three factors contributed to outbreaks of anti-foreign sentiment: a fresh wave of immigration (five thousand per day in the 1920s before a 1924 law placed limits); the crimes involved in Prohibition, with the knowledge that most "New Immigrants" saw no sin in alcohol consumption as the Protestant Prohibitionists did; and the eventual economic depression. The supposed influence of the wealthy Jews on the Bolshevik Revolution in Russia shaped American attitudes as well.[61]

In addition, William M. Simmons created the Invisible Empire of the Knights of the Ku Klux Klan (KKK) on October 16, 1915, as a rebirth of the anti-black Reconstruction organization. By the end of the 1920s, between four and five million members of the KKK paraded through the main streets of American cities and small towns in their white robes as a means to intimidate immigrants like Ed.[62] However, because many Syrians were Christians, because they were relatively few in number, and because they spread out rather than congregating in ghettos, they faced less discrimination than Jewish immigrants.[63]

Even so, Ed's younger son, Jameil, was once playing in the alley behind their Brownfield store in the 1930s when he saw men in white hoods coming down a stairway. He remembers that Brownfield had been a difficult town for his family to get their business started, but he attributed it more to a network of old, established families' rejection of newcomers than to any ethnic prejudice.[64]

An incident in Littlefield in Lamb County provided the worst memory and even temporarily influenced the attitude of Ed and Etta toward church attendance. Because they needed to move to a new location and do some work in their store on a Sunday, someone complained to the sheriff, who came to the store. "The sheriff came and beat up Dad for working on Sunday," Jameil explains. Ed notes in Chapter 8 that his family always blamed the members of a nearby church for the complaint. For years the family did not attend worship services; however, later in Seminole they became members of the Methodist Church.[65] Ironically, in the town where Ed felt he was not treated fairly, he was calling his clothing business The Fair Store. In later years it became simply Aryain's.

In the oil boomtown of Seminole, the county seat of Gaines County in far West Texas, Ed found friendliness, welcome, and a permanent home. Seminole's population when he and his family arrived in 1939 was about 1,700, up from 400 a decade earlier. Platted as a town in 1906, the site was donated by New York investors seeking oil. The black gold indeed created the economy that would permit a successful dry goods business for a Syrian immigrant ready to settle down. His sons, Eddie and Jameil, joined the less than 400 students in the 753-square-mile school district that had recently consolidated with its rural outlying communities.[66]

Ed Aryain thus details the journey from Henna, Syria, to Seminole, Texas, where he prospered. He bought his store building on the square, built a small frame house, and in later years constructed a new brick home. His sons did well in high school, Eddie enjoying drama and Jameil (known to his friends as "Dink") lettering three years in sports.

Ed also relates a return trip to Syria after nearly a half century away. Then at the age of seventy-five when he had lived in

America for six decades, he began writing his reminiscences of the long journey that brought him to West Texas.

Until the end of his life, Ed subscribed to Syrian newspapers in Arabic published weekly from New York, and he kept up with what happened in his homeland over the years. Although his education in Syria had been the equivalent of the eighth grade, he had become bilingual. Ed followed events after World War I, when the area of Greater Syria was divided and Britain acquired a mandate over Palestine, Jordan, and Iraq. France took oversight of the now smaller Syria and Lebanon. Two decades later both French-controlled countries obtained their independence. Ed knew when Hafiz Asad seized power in Damascus on November 16, 1970, in a military coup, subjecting his homeland to a dictator.[67]

Ed Aryain died on October 12, 1974, at the age of seventy-seven. Although he had retired nearly twenty years earlier, he had only sold his interest in his Aryain's Department Store two years before his death. His younger son, Jameil, had been running it since 1952. Etta died November 22, 1981, at the age of seventy-eight. Although she and Ed had been Methodists, after Ed's death Etta attended worship services at the First Baptist Church in Seminole with her son Jameil and his wife, Pat, because Pat's father was the minister.[68]

Jameil has traveled twice to Israel and reached sites within thirty miles of his father's Henna birthplace on Mount Hermon, but because of restrictions, he could not cross the border to see it. On one trip he was traveling with his father-in-law, Troy Lee Denton, to fulfill the Baptist preacher's lifelong dream to see the Holy Land.[69]

During the 1986 sesquicentennial year for Texas, Jameil, then mayor of Seminole, asked the local newspaper, the *Seminole Sentinel*, if they would like to publish Ed's manuscript in serial form. The community welcomed Ed's story. In a letter to the editor at the conclusion of the series, Mr. and Mrs. Harvey N. Wallen called Ed an "American-by-choice," appreciated his "courage, resourceful-ness, and fine character," and saw his life as "an American success story." Mrs. Wallen had grown up in Seminole.[70]

Mayor Aryain wrote a letter of thanks in the *Sentinel* at the conclusion of the serialized story, and at the request of numerous clubs and organizations, he made speeches around town about his father's background. "My father loved the United States, perhaps more than many American-born citizens do. He knew what it was like to live in a country that did not have all the blessings and free-dom that America has," he said in his letter and in his speeches.[71]

Ed and Etta lived to see their three grandchildren (children of Jameil and Pat) participate in school activities and even to know that the two oldest entered college. One of them, Linda, became a pediatrician in Lubbock and married Dr. Scott Robins. Another, Amy, became a senior counselor at Estacado High School in Lubbock and married Dennis Carpenter, also a teacher. The third, Dwight (Chip), whose wife is Pam, became a scheduler for an oil-related company in Houston, Texas. Were they living when Ed's story is published, Etta and Ed would have had eight great-grand-children and two great-great-grandchildren.

In preparing the manuscript for publication, the editor made only punctuation, spelling, and capitalization changes for clarity and, with a few short digressions omitted, left the story as Ed dic-tated to Etta over three decades ago. Their son Eddie had earlier broken the long manuscript into untitled chapters and put a few things into better chronological order. As he retyped his mother's pages, he was careful as well to preserve his father's words. He did delete or shorten extremely long passages about Ottoman and Syrian history that his father—who loved history—had included. The story needed to be Ed's.

Shortly after finishing the writing of their story, Etta wrote their son Eddie: "Whatever comes of this transcript is anyone's guess, but it is my honest belief that someday it will be brought to the attention of people who will appreciate its worth." It has.[72]

Readers of the manuscript will notice the frequent times that Ed Aryain, in explaining something different, unusual, or fascinating to him, said, "I thought this was very interesting." Readers will find the story very interesting, too. As you read, imagine a slender, blue-eyed, 5'7" man who speaks with a slight Arabic accent. In later life Ed was balding, with just a little strip of hair around the back. Although not outgoing or showy, and reserved around strangers, he was genuine, enjoyed people, and truly wanted to serve the public who patronized his department store. Those qualities contributed to the success in America that Ed Aryain, at age fifteen, had left Syria to achieve.

FROM SYRIA TO SEMINOLE

1

Growing Up in Henna

. . .

I HAVE BEEN IN THE PEDDLING BUSINESS, THE CONFECTIONERY store business, the grocery store business, the oil field work business, the horse trading business, and, especially, the dry goods store business.

But I never thought I would go into the writing business.

Yet here at my age of seventy-five years I am undertaking the enormous job of writing a true account of my life story for our children and grandchildren, and for our friends and neighbors.

In the very small village of Henna, Syria, eighteen miles from Damascus, I was born August 22, 1897.[1]

As far back as I can remember I wanted to come to America. I had in my mind that I would come to the United States, work hard, and save my money for seven or eight years, ten years at the most, then buy myself a fine gold watch and chain like those I had seen proudly displayed by older men when they had returned to Syrian villages after living in America. Then, as they did, [I would] spend my American money to improve and irrigate my father's land near Henna and buy more land.

But things did not work out as I planned. I came to America in

1913 when I was fifteen years old. It has now been sixty years since I landed in New York City. I married an American woman in 1925, and we have a fine family.

I do not mean to leave you with the impression that a man ever forgets his homeland or his family there when he comes to the United States. But he becomes involved in going into business for himself, making a living, rearing a family, wars, and depressions, and he is hindered from returning to his native land. As much as I love the United States of America, and especially Seminole, Texas, my thoughts often wander back to Syria and the family I left there.

My mother, Jenna Tlhok, was married at an early age to Hassim Aryain, a man several years older than she. To this couple was born a daughter, Safaka Aryain. Following the death of her husband when their daughter was very young, my mother continued to make her home with the Aryain family. It is the custom in Syria that a widow not return to the home of her parents but remain under the roof and protection of the family she has married into.

When the little girl, Safaka, was six years old, my mother married her dead husband's brother, Hussian Aryain, a man more nearly her own age. I, Mohammed Aryain, was the firstborn of this marriage. When I was four years old, my sister Hameedie was born.

My parents watched with great pride and admiration the growth of their children. My sisters and I played with the other children of our village and helped in our small way with the work around the small rock house. It was our daily chore to bring cool drinking water from the freely flowing spring at the foot of the mountain upon which the houses of the village of Henna stood.[2] This bubbling spring provided sparkling pure mountain water for the villagers, and the overflow formed a stream in which the children played and the women did their family washing.

Located near the spring was a community stone oven, which served all the village women for baking bread. As a tribute and a belated "thank-you" to my mother, I would like to tell you how she provided her family with bread. Baking is an ancient art among Syrian women, and long hours are required to prepare the traditional bread.[5] My mother first divided the dough into small balls in her palms then threw them gently from one hand to the other to make them larger and thinner. She continued throwing the dough back and forth until it was large enough to cover her arms and was paper thin. Then she put it into the village oven, where it quickly turned golden brown and crisp. We children always gathered at the oven to snatch hot crusts. The little girls were given small pieces of dough to play with so they would learn early how to toss the bread over their hands until it was thin and thus be better cooks when they grew up.

Old and young alike enjoyed bread baking day. I will always remember the tantalizing odor of fresh bread when I returned from school, for my mother kept her bread boxes well stocked. Even to this day when I pass a commercial bakery in Texas or New Mexico and I get a whiff of freshly baked bread, my thoughts rush back to my early days in Syria.

Again I say, "Thank you, my mother, for the bread which made my body strong."

There were few secrets in Henna, for each day every villager was sure to visit either the spring or the oven, where they exchanged the latest gossip, made inquiries about everyone's health, and advised each other. In the cool of the evening after the day's work was finished, the menfolk gathered at the stream to visit and to discuss their crops and their flocks of sheep and goats. Quite often the men made trips into Damascus to sell their wheat, barley, hummus, and audis and then buy clothes and medicine for their families.[4]

On these trips into Damascus the men listened carefully for news of happenings in other places, for in our village there was no other way of knowing what was happening even just across the mountains unless a traveler spent the day in our midst. In an Arab home, hospitality is extended to all, be he a homeless man with feet sore and bleeding from trudging barefoot over the rough mountain trails or the rich owner of a camel caravan traveling between Damascus and Jerusalem. The men of the village would sit for hours to hear the travelers tell of what they had seen and heard.

To me, any news of the faraway country of America was the most exciting.

Often one hears of the three religions born in the Middle East—Jewish, Christian, and Moslem. But actually there were four. I was born into a Druze religious family, just as here in Texas one may be born into a Baptist or Methodist or Catholic family.[5]

The Druze religion is a secret organization not much known to outsiders. It is very strict and demanding. Its members are never supposed to drink or smoke or use profanity, and they are required to be honest and honorable and upright in all their dealings. A Druze woman wears long dresses down to her ankles and long sleeves. She is required to cover her head with a veil, and when [she] speaks to a man not of her immediate family she must pull this veil over her face so that only her eyes can be seen. Druze men are required to wear a tall hat called a "fez" with a white band to signify their religion. The Druze house of worship is called a *Majlis* in Arabic, and on Friday night they gather there and sit on the floor, covered with tapestry rugs, while they sing, pray, and worship Allah, or our God. They believe that nothing is greater than God. [Throughout his telling of the story, Ed usually said "or God" after using the name Allah.]

On the other hand I have known many men who were born into a Druze family who drank, smoked, used profanity, and were not too careful in their dealings with their fellow men. They only went under the name of being Druze. Perhaps it is not polite for me to tell you this about my own people, but I want you, my readers, to know that Druze are just like all other religions.

But Druze are hospitable and kind. A Druze woman will go to the aid of a sick neighbor, carry food, and help with the doctoring no matter what that neighbor's religion. A Druze man will open his home to anyone, and as long as that person is under the roof of the Druze he will be treated with respect and given food. This respect for strangers and guests is taught to the Druze children from a very early age.[6]

The Druze population in the Middle East is estimated at one million people, and they are considered such good warriors that they are often called the "Sword of the Middle East" or the "Brave Ones of the Middle East." In Syria and Lebanon the Druze and Christians lived together peacefully in the same villages. But it was unheard of for Druze and Moslems to live in the same village. This I could never understand.[7]

In school I studied hard and read American history, which interested me greatly. I also studied Russian history under the czar, and I still remember a few words in the Russian language, for the free schools of Syria were established and maintained by the czar of Russia. These schools were located only in villages where there were Christians, so Henna was qualified. No Russian schools were established in Moslem villages.

The reason for this was that Turkey had ruled the Middle East for hundreds of years, and Russia and Turkey had been enemies all through history. The czar of Russia had in mind that in the future he would take the Middle East away from Turkey, and he wished to have a good relationship with the Christian people there. He knew the Russians would not get any help from the Moslem people since the Turkish people were Moslem also.

So intense was the desire of Russia to take over the Middle East that when the Russian czar died, his son, the new czar, came upon the idea that his father, the dead czar, should be buried in Jerusalem, the Holy City. He then announced that a vast Russian army would politely accompany the body of his father, the dead czar, to Jerusalem, the Holy City.

When the Turkish government heard of this, they immediately enlarged their army facing Russia and notified the new czar that it was okay for the dead czar to pass through Turkey and be buried in Jerusalem, the Holy City, but they would permit an escort of only one hundred Russian soldiers. They also said they would send a large Turkish army to politely escort the dead czar to Jerusalem, the Holy City.

But the new czar of Russia refused this offer and again said he would send a vast Russian army to politely accompany his dead father on the trip to Jerusalem, the Holy City.

News travels fast. When the Turkish government heard this they sent the new Russian czar word that before they would allow such a massive Russian army to pass through their country, they would declare war.[8]

So the Russians backed off for the time being and did not move the body of the dead czar. Instead the body was placed in a glass casket so the people of Moscow could view it. It remained in Moscow until the Bolsheviks took over the country from the czars in 1917. It is anybody's guess what happened to the body at that time.

As far back as I can remember, even before I started to school, I heard stories of the terrible Sultan Abd-al-Hamid (1876–1909).[9]

Sultan Abd-al-Hamid ruled Turkey and all the Middle East with an iron hand. During his thirty-three-year rule no roads were built, no hospitals constructed, and no schools established. Because of this last the people in Moslem villages never had a chance to learn to read and write. The sultan was fearful that if the people, especially the younger generation, learned to think for themselves, they might resent being ruled by Turkey and revolt. The sultan ruled Syria and Lebanon with an iron fist, and the people knew hardships and famine.

Sultan Abd-al-Hamid lived in constant fear of revolution, and all through the Middle East he had spies to listen and then report who were his friends and who were his enemies. If the report came to the sultan of a critical remark or threat against him, the man who made the remark was given a long jail sentence or a hanging. The sultan also had a law forbidding other religious people, such as Christians, Jews, or Druze, from making hard remarks about Mohammed, the founder of the Moslem religion. This was considered the worst crime his subjects could commit, and the punishment was a life term or a hanging. When the people heard of this law, they were very careful not to make the slightest hard remark against either Sultan Abd-al-Hamid or Mohammed, the founder of the Moslem religion.

All through Syria and Lebanon there was no justice. If a man was accused of a crime, he won his case if he could afford to pay off the judges and the officers of the court. But if he was a poor man who could not bribe the judges and officers, his case was lost even before he came to trial. This was just another way for the judges and officers to add to their incomes.

Sultan Abd-al-Hamid lived in a great castle in Constantinople (now Istanbul), and the story goes that he was so fearful of his life being assassinated that he never slept in the same room twice. In this castle was a secret wing that no one had ever seen except Sultan Abd-al-Hamid and his harem women. It was rumored that in this harem he kept twenty women—fourteen Turkish women and six women from Switzerland and Norway. Fine Oriental rugs covered the floor and walls of this wing, and the sultan's rocking chair was made of mother of pearl and had solid gold armrests set with precious gems. Each night the sultan sat in this fancy rocking chair and rocked while the women of his harem paraded before him. This was just his way of selecting a woman to spend the night with.

During Sultan Abd-al-Hamid's rule taxes were more than doubled. My father owned thirty-five head of goats. The reason my father owned goats was because we also owned a milk cow, but when she was feeling in her dry season, we used goat's milk to substitute for the cow milk. At one time the Turkish tax on my father's goats had been fifteen cents a head.

Then out of a clear sky the sultan's men came to our village and informed everyone that from now on the tax would be sixty cents a head. And I want to tell you right now that was a lot of money in that country. But my father, like everyone else, paid the tax and called it highway robbery. There was absolutely nothing my father and the other men in the Middle East could do about this new tax, for everyone was under the iron fist of Sultan Abd-al-Hamid.

It was during this harsh rule that Italy got the idea that they should capture some of the Turkish held land for themselves. So they invaded Libya. Libya is located south of Italy on the Mediterranean Sea with the coastal towns of Tripoli, Surt, and Banghazi.[10]

War started with Italy, and for several months the Turks lost ground, for their army was scattered all through the Middle East engaged in other wars. The Turkish warships were anchored in the harbor of Beirut when an Italian submarine decided to slip up on them and attack them.

The Italian submarine fired some torpedoes, and in a few minutes the Turkish ships sank with all the men and ammunition lost. Nothing came of this sinking, and it just goes to show you how weak the Turkish navy was.

A few foolish Moslems from Beirut gathered at the shore, then rode a fishing boat out in the direction the torpedoes had come from. They were armed only with knives and swords, but they began shaking these weapons in the air and yelling, "You damned Italians, wait and we will fight you!"

But there was no one to wait and fight, for by that time the submarine was many miles away on its way back to Italy.

Speaking of Libya reminds me that right here in Seminole, Texas, which is an oil field community, we have known several men who went to Libya to work in the oil fields there. Wages were larger when working in a foreign country. One particular man we had known for several years left Seminole to work in Libya, but while the poor fellow was there he fell off an oil derrick and was killed. The body was returned to Seminole for burial.

When the body arrived, the funeral home manager called and asked me to come to the funeral parlor and verify the Arabic writing with the English writing on the paper he had received from Libya. Half the paper was written in English and the other half was written in Arabic. After reading the paper I told him the wording was the same, containing the same information. The name of the poor man was the same, and the details of how he had been killed—no violence in the death, just another unavoidable accident. The paper had been signed by King [Sayyid] Idris of Libya. The funeral home manager thanked me for my help in clearing up the paper, and I was glad to oblige him.

A few years ago the health of King Idris failed and he went to Istanbul (formerly Constantinople) to see a doctor there. While he was away, the army chiefs of Libya formed a new and democratic government behind his back.

When King Idris returned to Libya, he was told that this new government had been formed and that he could not remain in the country. So then King Idris returned to Istanbul as a private citizen, and as far as I know he is still alive and making his home there.[11]

Now back to my story.

The year I was born, 1897, the Druze people suffered terribly under the Turks. This is the story I have heard my mother tell many times, then add, "I hope and pray we will never again see such suffering and the destruction of our villages."

In our village of Henna lived a Druze man by the name of Joseph-Al-Hamid. He raised and sold fine Arabian horses for a living. Then he decided he was not making enough money in this line of business, so he came upon the idea of making an outlaw of himself, thus increasing his income at a faster pace.

He began his new line of work by robbing Moslems. I have never heard of him molesting Christians, for, as I said, in Syrian villages Christians and Druze lived together peacefully.

In Syria there was a Gypsy town known as Drhbe not too distant from Damascus. Most of the Gypsies from this town traveled all through the country. The women begged for food, told fortunes, and made tattoo marks on people for money. The men sat in the shade of their tents and played violins and guitars.

At one time when I was a young boy a tribe of Gypsies came to Henna, and one of the women said she was very efficient at doing tattoos. I had in my mind I would like to have a tattoo. All the young men of my acquaintance wore tattoos, and to my way of thinking it was a very distinguished way of making a boy of my age look and feel older than my years. We agreed that for six fresh eggs the Gypsy would do a tattoo for me.

But I told her I did not want the same style tattoo I had seen most people wearing. I wanted to be different and have my name written on my left wrist. I wrote my name on my wrist in black ink and told the Gypsy woman to copy this with her tattoo needles. She began the work with five needles tied together and dipped in heavy black ink.

The blood came from my arm where she had pierced the skin, and there was some pain. But as the work continued I saw she was not following the letters, and I told her she was making a terribly messy job. She apologized and said she was sorry to make such a messy job and so many mistakes, but she could neither read nor write and it was difficult for her to follow the letters.

Since the tattoo was incorrect and I could not even read my own name, I told her just to quit. I still have the badly written tattoo scar on my arm, and I have wished a thousand times I had never seen or heard of this old Gypsy woman.

Now back to my mother's story.

In this Gypsy town of Drhbe lived four wealthy families who

raised sheep, goats, cattle, and fine thoroughbred Arabian horses. There was to be a Gypsy wedding for two young people from these families. The future bride and groom and their parents made a trip to Damascus to buy high priced jewelry and bolts of fine silk, as it was the custom that a Gypsy bride have these fine things in her new home.

On their way back from Damascus to Drhbe these Gypsies met Joseph-Al-Hamid. He introduced himself to them, then robbed and shot them.

In the next few days Joseph-Al-Hamid made a trip to Drhbe, where he called upon the other rich Gypsy families and robbed them of their fine belongings. He killed some of the people. Others escaped into the night.

Joseph-Al-Hamid thought he was doing so good in his new line of business that he decided to call upon some rich Moslem families and do the same with them.

Now the Moslems in that part of the world began making complaints that Joseph-Al-Hamid was raiding their homes and killing the people. They did not like this, and they went so far as to make a trip to Damascus to talk it over with the governor. The governor issued orders to the Druze people to capture Joseph-Al-Hamid and hand him over. Otherwise he would send an army to kill all the Druze and burn their villages.

In the Middle East there is a class of people known as the Kurds.[12] They have their own language, but they also speak and write Arabic and Turkish. At one time in the old days the Kurds lived in Russia, but they were Moslems and they wanted to live in the Moslem world. So they said to heck with it and moved into [what later became] Syria, Lebanon, Iraq, Turkey, and Iran.

One particular Kurdish man and his family lived in a small village about four miles from Henna. I have personally been in this village many times. He owned a large farm and also held a high government office in Damascus. It was a well known fact that this man always wore an expensive diamond ring and a gold watch and chain, so Joseph-Al-Hamid decided to make these things his own.

So the next weekend another innocent man was robbed and killed. By this time robbery and murder were nothing new to Joseph-Al-Hamid.

This made matters worse among the Moslems. The governor again sent word that unless Joseph-Al-Hamid was captured and turned over to him, he would send a big army and kill all the Druze people and burn their homes. Orders also came from the sultan of Turkey to kill all the Druze people. The destruction was to be complete. The governor then gave the Moslem people guns and ammunition and told them to invade the twelve Druze villages in that part of Syria if they felt like it.

The Druze people in these villages made an honest effort to capture Joseph-Al-Hamid and hand him over to the governor. But Joseph-Al-Hamid was sly as a fox and always managed to avoid them. His trips to his home were few and far between and always late at night.

Finally the Turks sent a twenty-thousand-man army to strike the Druze villages. There were also about forty thousand well-armed Moslem men to support the Turks. The Druze met them in battle, but they soon realized it was impossible to defeat such a force.

Many of the Druze men became afraid for the safety of their families, so they took them into the mountains and hid them in caves and behind big rocks so they would be safe from the enemy. In six weeks time the villages were destroyed by the Turkish artillery. Homes had been burned to the ground, and the livestock had been stolen. In my village of Henna, the house of Joseph-Al-Hamid and the surrounding two blocks were burned. It so happened that the home of my parents was close to the Christian district, and so it was not fired upon. But every other Druze home in Henna was destroyed.

In desperation, the Druze people decided among themselves that they must find Joseph-Al-Hamid at any cost. Eighteen or twenty men hid behind the burned walls every night and waited for him to come home. Finally one night he came home to his village to see for himself how much damage had been done. When he rode into the yard, the men hiding behind the burned walls jumped out and surrounded his horse and captured Joseph-Al-Hamid. Then they delivered him to the Turkish officers.

The soldiers started for Damascus with Joseph-Al-Hamid, but when they had gone only a few miles one of the Turkish officers pulled out his sword and completely severed Joseph-Al-Hamid's head from his shoulders.

The head rolled on the ground seven or eight feet before coming to a stop. Then when Joseph-Al-Hamid was good and dead, the other Turkish soldiers began stabbing and cutting at the headless body. When they had finished, there was not enough of the body left to bury.

The sultan of Turkey then gave orders not to molest the Druze people again, for his goal had been accomplished and Joseph-Al-Hamid was dead.

My mother always said, "I hope and pray to Allah, or God, that we will never live through such an ordeal again."

When I was a little boy, I always found this story about Joseph-Al-Hamid very interesting. I hope you enjoyed it.

Soon after the death of Joseph-Al-Hamid, his widow married a neighbor man by the name of Il-Hey-Tab, and they moved to Lebanon, leaving her four children in the care of their aunt. The two girls were older than the boys.

The oldest of the girls was named Bnbir, and she was afflicted with a weak mind. The women of the village called her Crazy Bnbir. When one of their own children was disobedient, they said to them, "You are as crazy as Crazy Bnbir-Al-Hamid." In those days there was no help for a person afflicted with a weak mind, and she was destined to go through life being the laughing stock of the community. I can remember many times when I was a small boy seeing Bnbir standing in the yard holding a piece of bread in both hands and biting off the bread just as fast as she could swallow. In fact, she ate like an animal. At times Bnbir would be screaming and crying, and no one seemed to know or care why she was crying. I always felt so sorry for her.

The second girl was named Nidi. She was a beautiful young woman, and later she married a man of modest means and their family was well respected.

The oldest of the boys was named Hamid-Al-Hamid. I will say he was around ten years old when his father was killed. The younger boy was about my age, and his name was Joseph-Al-Hamid. He was born a short time after his father's death. Therefore he was given the name of Joseph. Had the father been alive, he would not have been named Joseph, for it is very unusual in that part of the world for two men in a family to carry the same name. Joseph was my close friend and playmate during our childhood in Henna.

Joseph-Al-Hamid, the father, had saved the money he had made as an outlaw and invested it in land. So when he died, he left his family large holdings in the irrigated valley around Henna. As is the custom of that country, a man's sons inherit his belongings. The daughters have a share, but the sons have controlling interest. The provision is made that if the daughter marries a stranger, he has no right to the land. Thus Hamid-Al-Hamid and Joseph-Al-Hamid (the son) became the rightful owners of their father's land. In time Hamid-Al-Hamid began selling the land and spending the money. People at the stream advised him to be careful, for soon the land would all be sold and the money spent. But he replied, "I have many acres of land left." Personally, I heard him make this remark many times. Again his friends advised him to go into business for himself, and he would say, "Someday I may go into the sheep and goat ranching business for myself."

I can truthfully say that 90 percent of the land Hamid-Al-Hamid sold was to Syrian men who had lived in America then brought their American money back to Syria and invested it in land.

Seeing these prosperous, well-dressed Syrian men wearing their gold watches and chains and using great rolls of American money to buy land in Henna set me on fire. I said to myself, "I must go to America, work hard and save my money, then return to Henna with a fine gold watch and chain and lots of money to improve my father's land and then buy more land."

But more about that later.

2

A Famous Aryain Ancestor

. . .

TO GIVE MY READERS A CRYSTAL CLEAR PICTURE OF THE HISTORY
of the Middle East I would like to relate to you a story about
Shebly Aryain, I will say 150 years ago, who made the Aryain
name famous.[1] Shebly Aryain, a very brave man and one considered highly educated by the standards of those days, and his sister
Biriki Aryain, a well-educated and a fearless woman, conversed
among themselves and decided that Syria and Lebanon should be
free of Turkish rule.

Shebly Aryain always sought the advice of his sister, for she was
more advanced in her thinking than many men of that day. He
told her he had in mind that he was going to devote his life to freeing Syria and Lebanon from Turkey and establishing a free government with himself as president. He would begin by traveling
all through Syria and Lebanon talking to people and asking them
for all the help they could give. Biriki Aryain listened to her brother's well laid plans, then said she would go along too.

Shebly and Biriki Aryain rode horseback all through the two
countries, giving talks and telling people the advantages of being
under their own government rather than under the rule of Turkey.

They visited all villages where Druze and Christians lived but did not bother with Moslem villages, for they knew the Moslems would never back their plan since the Turks were Moslem also.

People listened, but they gave no help, for they thought the Turkish army was too strong with artillery and had too many horses as a means of transportation. They said there was no way to come face to face with the Turkish army and be successful. But Shebly Aryain was a determined man and not one to be discouraged.

In time about seventy men promised to follow Shebly Aryain in his undertaking, but they refused to be foot soldiers. Shebly Aryain said that was okay and assured them they would all ride fine Arabian horses, for his plan was to fight the enemy in guerilla warfare. He planned to surround the Turkish army when it was camped at night and attack them when they were least expecting him, killing the men and capturing their horses, guns, food, and ammunition.

These guerilla attacks went on for six years, and the damage began to show upon the Turks. Any time Shebly Aryain's small army went through a Druze village, the people cheered them, then gave them enough food to last the men and horses several days. Shebly Aryain decided that fighting with a small army was not so bad after all.

At the time Shebly Aryain was fighting his own war in his own country, the Turkish army was busy fighting on four other fronts—Bulgaria, Egypt, Serbia, and Montenegro. The cause of all this unrest was the same—each country wanted to be free from under Turkish rule. Therefore the Turkish army was divided and scattered around. This was beneficial to Shebly Aryain, for he could strike day or night, and he was always successful.

The uprising in Bulgaria did not last long, for Russia (which had been Turkey's enemy all through history) came to the aid of Bulgaria with men, horses, guns, and ammunition. Soon the sultan of Turkey decided he was wasting his time and men trying to rule this country. So then the sultan said to heck with it, and Bulgaria was a free country with its own form of government.

Then a battle raged in Egypt between Turkey and Egypt over the same difficulty which cursed the Middle East—Turkish rule.

The Egyptian army drove the Turkish army out of Egypt once and for all and established their own government. Egypt was so impressed with its victory that it decided now was the time— while Turkey was so weak—to take Syria and Lebanon.

Shebly Aryain was pleased that his Arab brothers had forced the Turkish army out of Egypt, but he was not too crazy about Egypt taking over Syria and Lebanon, and he said to himself, "Why should the Egyptians not be satisfied with their victory and stay home in their own land?"

Egypt sent General Abraham Bassir with twenty thousand troops to Syria.[2] General Bassir was a well respected man all over the Arab world and an excellent leader of the Egyptian army. But Shebly Aryain said to himself, "After all these years I have fought to clear Syria and Lebanon of the Turks. Now I must fight General Bassir, leader of the Egyptian army, in the same way to save my country from being ruled by Egypt."

But Shebly Aryain had many friends throughout Syria and Lebanon, and these men he used as spies who kept him informed as to each move the Egyptian army made and where they were camped. One of these spies reported that General Bassir's army was to travel through a certain narrow valley. Shebly Aryain knew that a small river ran through this valley and that there were high mountains on each side. And he knew that this would be the best victory he could have, for he had well laid plans.

After an all-night ride Shebly Aryain and his men arrived in this narrow valley ahead of the Egyptians. He informed his small army they were to separate—one-half of the men taking positions on one mountain, the other half taking positions on the opposite mountain, leaving the valley open for the incoming Egyptian army.

After the horses were hidden so they could not be seen, each of Shebly Aryain's men found a good hiding place behind the nice big rocks on the mountains with his gun and plenty of ammunition in front of him. Shebly Aryain had given his men instructions not to fire a shot until he gave them a signal.

Then as the Egyptian army began moving into the valley, dark clouds formed in the sky, and rain began to fall. This slowed down the Egyptian army. By the time the Egyptian army was inside the narrow valley, the rain was coming down in torrents. Now was the time for the battle to begin! The Egyptian army was disorganized, for they could hardly see their hands before them in the rain!

Shebly Aryain fired two quick shots—the prearranged signal for his men to begin firing on the Egyptian army.

Then shots rang through the air from the men hidden behind the nice big rocks! The Egyptian men were bewildered and confused, for they could not see where the flying bullets were coming from because of the rain.

Both men and horses began falling to the ground, and still the rain continued to fall. Water was rising in the valley from the overflow of the river! The aim of Shebly Aryain's men found its mark, for they had only to fire down into the valley to hit the enemy.

The battle lasted for three or four hours, and the Egyptians were losing heavily. They were in a bad way, and they began running to higher ground to escape the rising water!

Finally the Egyptians said to heck with it and began waving white flags and saying in a loud voice, "Shebly Aryain, we cannot see you or your men, but we know only you could be our attackers. Please do not shoot us anymore! We surrender to you! We have lost many men and horses and our food and ammunition has been washed away in the river. Please do not shoot us anymore!"

Shebly Aryain heeded their surrender and gave the signal to his men on the mountainsides to cease firing. This battle broke the back of the Egyptian army. The few remaining Egyptians reorganized and started the long trip back to Damascus, where Egypt had its headquarters.

When General Abraham Bassir arrived in Damascus, he was asked time and again, "Well, what do you think of your battle with Shebly Aryain?"

General Abraham Bassir replied, "I always considered myself a good general, but that sonofagun Shebly Aryain really made a jackass of me. I could not see him or his troops to destroy them in that doggone rain. Of all things to happen! The biggest part of my army of twenty thousand men caught in that narrow flooded valley! That sonofagun!"

News travels fast! When Turkey heard of this battle and that Egypt had lost the biggest part of their army, they decided this was the time for Turkey to send another army into Syria and push the Egyptians back into Egypt. The Turks soon cleared Syria and Lebanon of all Egyptian forces, and again Shebly Aryain was forced to fight the Turkish army.

Two years later the Turkish army captured Shebly Aryain and a big part of his followers and took them to Constantinople (now Istanbul) for trial, then pronounced a hanging death for them.

While Shebly Aryain was in jail awaiting his hanging date, he got the blues. Then he heard that the Turkish army was losing many battles with Serbia and Montenegro, and the talk was that Serbia and Montenegro would capture all Turkey, then drive into Syria and Lebanon.

This worried Shebly Aryain, for if this happened all the fighting he had done to free Syria and Lebanon would have been in vain. He knew nothing about Serbia and Montenegro, and he was afraid if they took Syria and Lebanon things would go from bad to worse. Shebly Aryain talked to his fellow prisoners about what might happen and warned them of the dangers.

It so happened that Shebly Aryain and each of his men had a small amount of money, and he suggested they pool their money and make arrangements with the jailer to release them. This the jailer agreed to do for the money they offered him.

That night when Shebly Aryain and his men were released, they swiped some horses and ammunition and rode to a particular village which Serbia and Montenegro had just captured from Turkey. They attacked this village, killed the men from Serbia and Montenegro, then raised the Turkish flag on a high pole in the village.

On three successive nights Shebly Aryain attacked and captured villages held by Serbia and Montenegro and raised the flag of Turkey over these villages.

News travels fast! When the sultan heard of his flag again flying over the villages formerly held by Serbia and Montenegro, he made inquiry as to who had raised these flags after the Turkish army had given up the villages. He was told that Shebly Aryain had somehow gotten out of jail and had swiped some horse, guns, and ammunition and was now fighting for Turkey.

This certainly surprised the sultan of Turkey, and he sent word for Shebly Aryain to appear before him in his palace in Constantinople.[3] When Shebly Aryain arrived at the palace, the sultan met him at the door, smiled a welcome greeting, shook hands with him, and spoke in Arabic. The sultan asked, "Are you the same man who is now fighting for Turkey after fighting so many years to free Syria and Lebanon from our rule? I had heard you were in jail awaiting your hanging."

Shebly Aryain replied, "I am that man."

Then the sultan asked, "Why have you come over to fight on our side?"

Shebly Aryain replied, "For years I have fought the Turkish army to free my country. I lost the war because your army was just too strong and I had too few men to follow me. Now I know it is impossible to accomplish my goal. Since I have been in your jail, I have heard the talk that your army is retreating before Serbia and

Montenegro. There has been much talk that these two countries may take all Turkey then drive into Syria and Lebanon, and I have made up my mind I would rather be under Turkish rule than under European rule."

The sultan was pleased to hear these words and asked Shebly Aryain if he would continue to fight for Turkey. Shebly Aryain said he would be happy to support Turkey if they would give him arms and ammunition and let him fight in his own way.

The sultan said okay to this, then placed his hands upon the shoulders of Shebly Aryain. "I promise you, Shebly Aryain, that your hanging is off and that all charges against you will be dropped. You are a brave and valuable man and your life is not to be destroyed. I now give you the official title of Bashir the Great. This is the highest honor I can confer upon any man in my empire."[4]

Shebly Aryain, Bashir the Great, felt much obliged.

The war continued with Serbia and Montenegro for several years, and Turkey continued to lose ground. Finally the sultan decided to put an end to this war and gave Serbia and Montenegro full freedom from Turkish rule. The countries of Serbia and Montenegro of that date are now known as Yugoslavia.[5]

The sultan of Turkey again invited Shebly Aryain, Bashir the Great, to his palace for a great banquet to be given in his honor. All the bigshots of Turkey were invited to attend this feast and pay their respects to such a great man as Shebly Aryain, Bashir the Great. After the banquet the sultan said to Shebly Aryain, Bashir the Great, "Now that you are a free man and may return to Syria and Lebanon, do you plan to start war on us again?"

Shebly Aryain, Bashir the Great, replied, "I have spent many years fighting your army, and I have lost. So to heck with it! I do not intend to engage in any more wars with you."

When the sultan heard this he placed his hands upon the shoulders of Shebly Aryain, Bashir the Great, and said, "Shebly Aryain,

Bashir the Great, I have plans for a great man like you if you will accept my offer." Taking a Koran (Moslem Bible) the sultan asked Shebly Aryain, Bashir the Great, to place his right hand on it and raise his left hand to Allah, or God, and swear that he would always be faithful and respectful to the Turkish government.

When Shebly Aryain, Bashir the Great, had done this, the sultan told him he was to be the governor of Baghdad and his home was to be one of the palaces in Baghdad. Then as a personal gift the sultan presented his personal sword to Shebly Aryain, Bashir the Great. The handle of this sword was made of solid gold and was set with precious stones. Some years ago when my wife and I were in the Middle East, we visited my distant cousin, another man by the name of Shebly Aryain (then the senator from the district of Rashayya), and he personally showed us this sword the sultan gave Shebly Aryain, Bashir the Great.

Shelby Aryain, Bashir the Great, shared the palace at Baghdad with his sister Biriki Aryain. The names of Shebly Aryain, Bashir the Great, and Biriki Aryain became household words. Male children were named Shebly, and female children were named Biriki.

Shebly Aryain, Bashir the Great, was now an old man, and in his last will and testament he made the stipulation that he be buried in Rashayya.[6] So at his death the sultan of Turkey issued orders that men carry on their shoulders the body of Shebly Aryain, Bashir the Great, from Baghdad to Rashayya, a distance of many hundreds of miles. When the funeral procession entered a village, the casket was transferred to the shoulders of waiting men, who carried it to the next village. Huge crowds were always waiting to view the casket of Shebly Aryain, Bashir the Great.

At the burial in Rashayya eloquent speeches were made honoring this brave man, and for years people told of the deeds of Shebly Aryain, Bashir the Great.

Now you know about Shebly Aryain, Bashir the Great. I will

now tell you about the Massacre of the Christians in 1860, so you will know about that.

To my way of thinking, much of the trouble in the Middle East came about because the different religious bodies—be they Moslem, Christian, Jewish, or Druze—thought their religion to be the one and only true religion. Hard feelings came about when one man made slight remarks about the other man's religion.

As I have said, Druze and Christian people lived peacefully together in villages throughout Syria and Lebanon. At times there would be fistfights between the men, and when this happened the Druze came to the help of their Druze brothers and the Christians did the same for their Christian brothers.

The leaders of both sides called a meeting and decided among themselves that these fights and misunderstandings between Druze and Christians must come to an end. It was decided that any time there was trouble and commotion, the matter would be settled in the presence of the leaders of both sides. This understanding between neighbors and friends helped keep the trouble down, and an orderly way of living continued for years and years. Druze families attended the funerals and weddings of their Christian friends, and the Christians returned the compliment. Druze and Christian women helped in each other's homes when there was sickness.

But then the Turkish government became alarmed at the good relationship of these people, for they feared that the Christians and Druze might organize and start a revolution to free themselves from Turkish rule. So to start trouble between Christians and Druze, the Turkish government sent their men into the villages at night to waylay and kill people. The first killing came about when three Druze men were found shot to death inside a Christian district. When the bodies were found, the Druze immediately accused the Christians of these killings.

A few days later two Christian men who had been plowing in their field failed to return to their homes at suppertime. When the people went to search for these men they found them shot to death; both bodies were beside the plow. Now the Christians blamed the Druze. These back and forth killings happened in several different towns in Syria and Lebanon. The Christians blamed the Druze, and the Druze blamed the Christians. Both sides began to arm themselves, for one way or another these killings had to stop.

In Rashayya one morning at five o'clock a Turkish soldier secretly ran into the street and fired several shots into the air. Then he ran secretly back into the house, and no one knew who had fired the shots. The very same thing happened at the same time in Hasbayya.

Now the Druze and the Christians thought the war was about to start in a big way, and every man ran for his gun and began shooting.

When the battles were over in Rashayya and Hasbayya and surrounding villages, many Christian men had been killed.[7]

The Turkish army made no effort to stop the shootings. In fact, this was the way Turkey wanted it—trouble between the Druze and Christians. But then the Druze came upon the idea of freeing the area of the rich Shabibi family, a wealthy Moslem family in the town of Rashayya and Hasbayya. They massacred every man of that family they could locate, thus ending the rule of rich Moslem overlords. As far as I know these were the only Moslems who got massacred in the Massacre of the Christians in 1860.

The Druze then marched toward Zalah, the third largest city in Lebanon, where they met a large group of Christians and another battle was fought.[8] Many Christians were killed, and others just barely escaped with their lives. The Druze had won all the battles so far. Then the Druze marched on the Christian town of Dayr-Al-Qamar and won another battle.[9]

But in a few months the commotion began to simmer down, and the Turks began arresting both Christians and Druze and sentencing them from two to twenty years in the pen[itentiary].

Now the Christians and Druze talked among themselves and began to suspect that Turkey had caused all the trouble from the beginning, even as far back as when the three Druze men had been found dead in the Christian district and when the Christian men had been shot while plowing their fields.

This terrible slaughtering of the Christian people happened over one hundred years ago, but still the Christians have hard feelings about it. Since I have been in the United States, especially while I was traveling on the road as a peddler, many times when I came into a town where merchants from Syria and Lebanon were located I would go into their places of business and make their acquaintance, and then to my sorrow find them to be Christians. At first these people seemed glad to meet me, but when they learned I was Druze their attitude changed at once. When my name Aryain was mentioned, they seemed to associate me with the Druze who had killed so many Christians in 1860.

In my early days when I lived in Drumright [Oklahoma], my four best friends were young Christian Syrian men who were single, as I was. Often we invited each other to have dinner together, and we went to movies and to the pool hall to play pool. We would be enjoying each other's friendship when out of a clear blue sky one of the Christian boys would make a cutting remark about the trouble in 1860. Some of these boys had been born in this country, but just from hearing the story from their parents they had inherited this hatred of the Druze people. Once after some very curt remarks had been made by these young men, I said, "Why can't we all forget the past? That happened long ago, and I am not responsible for what my grandfathers did. Look what happened here in the United States between the North and South when many more lives were lost than in the Middle East in 1860. Yet the American people have forgotten all that commotion in their country and think nothing of being friends with a person be he from the North or South. They think of themselves as being American and let it go at that."[10]

But the Druze also had trouble with the Moslems. Both Moslems and Druze raised sheep, goats, cattle, horses, and a few camels. Then the Moslems began moving their stock onto Druze grazing land, and skirmishes flared up. These skirmishes soon developed into a pitched battle, and the Druze pushed the invading Moslems back to their own villages, killing a great number of them.

Immediately two thousand telegrams from the Moslem villages were sent to the sultan of Turkey telling him the Druze people were killing them, burning their homes, driving off their livestock, and causing havoc and commotion.

The sultan said, "We have had several wars with the Druze, and they have always won, but this is one time we are going to bring them to their knees if it takes twenty years." The sultan then put his vast army under the command of General Sami Bashir-Al-Ilfrkoa and told him to whip the heck out of the Druze.[11]

When the Druze heard of this they began making their plans to meet the Turks. They had plenty of guns and ammunition to fight with, and in one battle the Druze rushed the Turks and fought them hand to hand. After three or four hours of fighting, the Turks had lost seven thousand men, so they said to heck with it and surrendered.

In the long months of fighting which followed, the Druze won all the battles. But General Sami Bashir-Al-Ilfrkoa ordered the Druze to surrender. "For no matter how long this war continues," he said, "we will win the last battle."

But the Druze ignored his warning and continued fighting.

Then the Turkish General gave orders that his heavy artillery be turned on Druze towns and villages. In a few days thirty to thirty-five Druze towns and villages had been destroyed.

The Druze leaders called a meeting among themselves and said, "We have been winning all the battles so far, but if the Turks continue destroying our Druze towns and villages we will have none left." Then they decided to surrender to the Turks.

The Druze gave up all their arms and ammunition. I well remember the very sad day when the Turkish army came to Henna to confiscate all guns. My father had recently given me a new shotgun of which I was very proud. When the Turkish officer asked if we had any guns on the place, my father told me to give my new gun to the officer. This I did. But from that day to this my hatred of the rule of Turks has increased.

When General Sami Bashir-Al-Ilfrkoa had issued his warning to the Druze, he had promised justice for all and peace over the land. He had also said that although a few of the Druze leaders would be arrested, they would get a fair court trial. But when the Druze surrendered to Turkey, twenty of the leaders were taken to Damascus and given a hanging without a trial.

Then instead of the Turkish government giving the bodies of the hanged men to their families for a decent burial, they were put up in public places for people to view just as a reminder of what the Turkish army did to trouble makers. People came from all over the country to see these bodies, and it is said that many Moslems passing the bodies spat on them.

This happened in 1909 when I was twelve years old.

I do not mean to give you the impression that there were always hard feelings between Druze and Moslems. I well remember when I was a youngster; I sometimes went with my father on trips into Damascus to buy the needed goods for the family, and we always traded with one particular Moslem man who owned a general line store.

On these buying trips my father would buy what we needed—piece goods, buttons, shoes, overcoats, and a few staple groceries—and when the total was run my father always tried his best to get the Moslem merchant to cut down some on the bill. Then after much argument and commotion the owner of the store would give my father a better price.

But once we went into this general line store and found that the

Moslem man had done his duty to Allah, or God, by making a holy pilgrimage to Mecca. The man was now considered a Hadj. Since a Hadj is known for his honesty and honor, and since his word is considered as good as his note, he informed my father that he now conducted his business in a different manner. He said he now put a fair price on his merchandise, and it was sold at that price. There was to be no more haggling and bargaining, and he said he did not want to hear any commotion.

My father took him at his word and continued doing business with this Hadj. I thought this was very interesting.

It was on this particular trip to Damascus that I saw a movie house for the first time. I had heard of these places of entertainment, and I pleaded with my father to let me see a movie. But he told me in no uncertain words that these places were indecent and that no young person should go inside. So that was as far as it went.

3

Leaving Syria for America

. . .

IT WAS MY GOOD FORTUNE THAT SINCE MY FATHER WAS A landowner, he had a good horse stabled at the house. Each morning in the spring and summer it was my chore to ride the horse into the fields so he could graze on the fresh grass while I gathered firewood for my mother to cook with and then fresh vegetables from our fields for our table use.

My father always kept a milk cow, and when my mother churned the butter we children were especially fond of the fresh buttermilk. My mother also made delicious tangy cheese from the milk given by our herd of goats, and she was especially proud of her large flock of chickens, which provided poultry and eggs for her family. There were always plenty of extra eggs, which my mother traded for groceries and clothing at the village store.

Really, I did not do much work in my young days, for my father leased his plots of land for one-third of the crops they produced. But this small income did not begin to cover the expenses of his family and pay the high taxes to the sultan of Turkey, so my father began selling off a tract of land each year. My mother was very disturbed over the selling of our land. I did not approve either, for it was plain to see that soon all the land would be sold and we would be without land or income.

One time when my father was closing the deal to sell some of our land, my grief-stricken mother sat in the adjoining room crying. So far I had witnessed the deal without saying a word, for after all young people are not supposed to interfere with the dealings of their parents. But when the man began counting out the cash to my father (all deals were on a cash basis, for there was not a bank in Henna), my anger flared, and I spoke out in a loud voice, "Mister, I wish you would take your money and leave our house. You are not paying enough for the land! I feel you are stealing the land because you know my father is hard up for money! Someday when I am a grown man, Allah, or God, only knows what I will do to you! For somehow, some way I will even the score of this injustice you have done to my father this day!"

At my outburst of angry words my father grabbed me by the shoulders and punished me severely. It is needless to say that he paid no attention to my words, and more of our land was sold.

But to my way of thinking, our land was some of the best land in Syria, and I did not want to see it sold to a stranger.

Knowing my father would continue selling off our land worried me night and day, and my desire and determination to come to the United States grew greater all the time.

My father, Hussian Aryain, had attended short sessions of school, and in his mind he could record figures and dates and transactions. Once they were in his mind he never forgot them.

It was my father's greatest desire that I should learn to keep accounts and records in writing, for the family whose son attended school and learned to read, write, and figure was well respected. So each morning when my friends and playmates went into the mountains to herd the sheep and goats, I had to trudge off to the school established by the czar of Russia.

My best grades came in reading, writing, and history, and I was always an A, no. 1 student in these subjects. But figures were my downfall. For some reason I could not master arithmetic. Once when I failed to bring up my figure lesson the teacher yelled at me, "Mohammed, I cannot for the life of me see how you can be such a good student in reading, writing, and history and fail so completely in numbers. Sometimes I think you are stupid!" The teacher kept a *mstri*, or paddle, and he used it on my behind several times when I failed to bring up my figure lessons.

But in time these numbers began to make sense to me, and if I do say so myself I am now quick and accurate in figuring numbers.

Three times a year a school examiner from Russia came to inspect our school. These men spoke Arabic, and they came to Henna in a special buggy drawn by a fine span of horses. They spoke kindly to the children and praised their good grades. The small children received a gentle pat on the head. I remember once when we were expecting the examiner from Russia, my father came to visit the school. The examiner from Russia said to him, "You people have better schools here in Henna than we have in Russia. Our government should be spending more money on Russian education rather than here in Syria." My father came to the conclusion that this man was not too crazy about the Russian czar's government.

In school I heard many of my Christian playmates make the remark that the Druze worshipped the calf. I knew this was not true, for my parents had never spoken about worshipping the calf. This bothered me greatly, and in time I asked my father about this matter, but he said he did not know how in the world such a rumor could have gotten started. I asked several other older members of the Druze religion the same question, but they said [they] did not know how this calf business got started either. I could find no answer to my question.

In the town of Rashayya I had three distant cousins I called
Uncle Ollie, Uncle Tafak, and Uncle Mohmood. These men held
high offices under the Turkish government. My parents then came
upon the idea that since Rashayya had a better school than Henna,
I should go to live with Uncle Mohmood and attend school there
for one term. Uncle Mohmood said okay, then gave me a job after
school brushing and feeding his fine Arabian horses.

Later Uncle Mohmood gave me a second job—walking two
miles each day to the home of a Christian friend of his to buy him
a quart of liquor. Each evening without fail I walked up the steep
mountain trail to the Christian's house, bought the liquor, then
walked back down the mountain to Uncle Mohmood's house. I
found these daily trips very interesting.

Uncle Mohmood was a very nice man, but he was a Druze in
name only. He knew nothing of the laws and requirements of this
secret religion, and he never attended the worship services. But he
said being known as a Druze was good for business.

The school teacher in Rashayya was a young Christian man
who had been educated in the American University of Beirut, and
I decided that surely this man of higher learning could clear up for
me this calf worshipping business which had bothered me for so
long. So one day I asked the teacher, "Do you believe that we
Druze worship the calf?"

The teacher laughed and said he should be asking me that, for
I was Druze and he was Christian. Then he asked me several questions about the Druze religion. I told him that we gathered at the
house of worship every Friday night just at sunset and sang and
prayed and worshipped Allah, or God. He then asked me if the
Druze believed in Christ. I told him we definitely believe in Christ,
but we do not believe that Christ was the Son of God. Druze people believe that Christ was the son of earthly parents, Joseph and
Mary, and that God sent this child to teach and lead the people in
the ways of righteousness. When the conversation ended, I felt
that I had answered more questions for the teacher than he had

answered for me, and I was still in the dark about this worshipping the calf business.

While living in Rashayya, I became curious as to how much money Uncle Ollie, Uncle Tafak, and Uncle Mohmood made working for the Turkish government. But I knew that if I asked they would tell me it was none of my business and not to mention it again. So one afternoon I went to visit another distant cousin, a lady I called Aunt Ndi, who lived only a mile from Uncle Mohmood. Aunt Ndi was a wonderful old woman who had raised a big family and worked hard all her life. I loved visiting her home, for she always treated me as if I were her own son.

During this particular visit I told Aunt Ndi that I had been wondering how much salary Uncle Ollie, Uncle Tafak, and Uncle Mohmood made. Aunt Ndi laughed and said that their monthly salary from the Turkish government was not so hot. But then she winked and added, "Do not worry about their salaries, little one, for the bribes and payoffs amount to far more money than their monthly wages amount to."

This confirmed what I had suspected—my relatives took bribes and payoffs.

I know it is not proper or good manners to tell a story like this about one's own people, but I want you, my readers, to know and understand how things were under the sultan.

When I returned to Henna, I was still troubled about this calf worshipping business, and I decided to go to the oldest man in the village and ask him about it. This man was sick. To my mind he seemed about one hundred years old, but he was a very religious man and had lived all his life following the teachings of the Druze religion. This is the story the old man told me:

"In the early history of our Druze religion our Moslem and Christian brothers came upon the idea that beef was not fit to eat after the animal was five months old, so they began slaughtering the calves for meat for their tables. The Druze did not like this idea of killing young calves, for soon the Middle East would be without cattle. But all the reasoning and arguments of the Druze would not stop the Christians and Moslems from killing the young calves. Finally the Druze threatened to go to war over this matter. So rather than fight a war with the Druze the Moslems and Christians stopped killing the calves. Then this talk about the Druze worshipping the calf in secret began."

I do not know if this story is true or not, but I thought it was very interesting, and it was the most satisfactory answer I ever got to the question which had plagued me for so long.[1]

When I was a teenager, my best friends were two Christian boys, one about my age, the other I will say four years my senior. Both boys rolled and smoked cigarettes, and the older boy drank *arak*, or liquor, and at their invitation I began to smoke and drink with them.

I tried to keep my sinful ways a secret from my parents and other members of the Druze religion. But then out of a clear blue sky I was notified that my wrong doings were well known, and that I was no longer a member of the Druze body. Who informed on me I will never know.

When my father and mother heard of this, they just about had a fit. Of all things for a member of their family to smoke or take a drink or use profanity! They said they were disgraced for life and that it was more than they could stand.

The high sheik, or head man of the house of worship in Henna (we thought of him as a preacher and a real big shot) and my parents talked to me about my sinful ways and insisted that I pray over this business for days and days then make a public confession at the Friday night meeting and ask for forgiveness.

This last I could not do, so I was dismissed from the Druze meetings.

There is no question in my mind that the Druze religion is a heavenly order teaching purity of mind and body just like other religions, but their requirements were just a little too strong and strict for me.

Besides, I wanted to come to the United States.

I knew that if I stayed in Henna I would one day inherit my father's land (if there was any left) as he had inherited it from his father and that I would marry a village woman and work hard and raise a family and live as my forefathers had lived. But this did not seem enough for me. I wanted a life that offered more opportunity, a new life in a new country, and I knew America was the answer for me.

As I said before, I had in mind that I would stay in the United States for only ten years, work hard, and save my money, then come back with the wonderful watch and chain and with enough money to improve our land and buy more land as I had seen other Syrian men do who had been to America. But I decided for sure that when I returned to Syria, I would not lease our land for one-third of the crops as my father had done. I knew that if other men could make money on our land, I could, for I was young and strong and would then have the cash to make improvements.

But when I talked to my parents about going to America, they laughed at me and tried to discourage me. Once my father asked, "What will you do in the New World, unable to speak the language, with no money and no friends? What will happen to you if you should become ill? Who will help you?"

I replied, "Allah, or God, will look after me."

Then representatives from a steamship company came to Henna enlisting men to go the United States. I became even more determined, so I went to my parents again.

Again my father said he did not like the idea, for I was just barely fifteen years old and too young to go to a strange land where I did not speak the language. Again I assured him that Allah, or God, would look after me.

Throughout this discussion my mother sat with her head lowered in silent prayer, occasionally wiping the tears from her eyes with the end of the white linen veil, which all Druze women wear over their faces. "My mother, I am sorry to cause you this grief," I said, "but I must make a life of my own. I promise you that with the first extra money I earn when I am in America I will send you yards and yards of silk for a beautiful black dress. Think how beautiful you will be wearing such a dress when you attend the weddings and funerals of our village friends."

Finally my father relented and agreed to lend me the $120 needed for the ticket to America, and I promised to repay the money just as soon as I could.

To come to America, an immigrant had to have the name of a relative or friend to go to. I did not have a friend, but it was arranged that I would use the name of a Mr. Tewell in Rochester, Pennsylvania. I did not actually know this Mr. Tewell, but he had agreed to sponsor me and had promised to give me a job as a peddler selling fancy merchandise for his business.

Since there was no more money for transportation to Beirut, the seaport from which I would sail, I would have to walk the 120 miles to the city. But I did not mind.

On the morning of my departure I bade a sad farewell to my weeping mother, my father, and my sisters. I kissed them all and promised to soon return a very rich man. Then I wiped the tears from my eyes and set off over the mountains, the first stage of my long journey to the New World. But for a very long way I could hear my mother crying out to me, "Please, Mohammed, come back to us. Please, my son, do not leave us with this sorrow." I was tempted to turn back and give up my dream. But then I steeled myself and walked on over the mountain.

Even now, sixty years later, my mother's cries that day still ring in my ears.

. . .

When I reached Beirut, I met other young men who were waiting to go to America, and I quickly made friends. But the men from the steamship line warned us not to form groups and always to walk no more than two abreast, for Turkey did not like the idea of so many young people leaving the country.

Finally the great day of boarding the ship arrived, and we set sail. I was very excited. After sailing all night, we arrived in Haifa, Palestine. Then twenty-four hours later we were in Yafo, Palestine. We made a short stop in Port Said, then in Alexandria, Egypt, but for the next six days we saw nothing but the sea and the sky.

Our next stop was Marseille, France, where we had an eight-day layover. While there, a rash of boils and pimples broke out on my face and neck. These boils and pimples were very ugly and very painful, and I was embarrassed by them.

While waiting out the eight days, I became acquainted with people from different parts of Syria and Lebanon who were also on their way to America. One man approached me from a village [not far] from Henna, and his first remark was, "I am homesick. I am not going to continue the trip to America. I am going back to my home and my wife and children." Then he asked me if I had enough money. When I told him I had very little and would have even less by the time I reached New York, he offered to loan me some. I asked him how he could make a loan to a total stranger, and he said he knew some of my people and was familiar with the Aryain name. He told me he had five English pounds to loan. At that time the English pound was worth about five American dollars. When I asked him the rate of interest he said he wanted 100 percent—for every pound he loaned me I would have to pay back two pounds.

I thought this was a very high interest rate and told him I could not do business with him, and we parted for the day. But after thinking about landing in New York with not much money in my pocket and then having to go to Rochester, Pennsylvania, I located the man and told him I would take the money on his terms. So now I had twenty-five dollars in my pocket and a fifty-dollar debt before even reaching the Atlantic.

On the morning of the eighth day in Marseille we were told to take our belongings and board the train, which would take us across France to La Havre, the seaport city from which we would sail for New York. This was a fourteen-hour train trip, and I found it very interesting. When the train reached La Havre, we passengers were taken directly to the ship by streetcar. I had never seen a streetcar before, and I found it very interesting. It had now been over two weeks since I had said goodbye to my grief-stricken family, and finally I was ready to begin the final stage of my journey to the New World.

On boarding the ship, each person was assigned a bunk bed, which would be his sleeping quarters for the entire trip. My bunk was the second from the floor with strange men sleeping below me, above me, and on all sides of me. At mealtime we went into the large dining room, where food was served family style. I remember one day we were served pork for our dinner. There were three or four Jewish men traveling in our group, and on this day these men were seated at a table to themselves and served a different dinner, as Jewish people do not eat pork in any way.

About the second day we were on the ship, many people became deathly seasick. Vomiting became a common sight. People tried to get to the ship railing before the disgorgement came, but many were so sick that they vomited wherever they were, be it on the deck of the ship, in their bunk beds, or in the dining room.

I was feeling real proud of myself, for we had been on the high seas for four days and I had escaped this sickness.

Then one morning I went up on the deck of the ship when lo and behold here came back all the food I had eaten for days! It was two days before my stomach settled down to normal.

We had been told we would be eight or nine days making the

crossing, and daily we scanned the horizon hoping this would be the day [we would see land]. But we saw only sea and sky.

Then one morning after the long waiting someone called out in a loud voice, "Look, everyone! I can see New York in the distance!" We passengers all rushed to the top deck of the ship to have our first glimpse of America.

We soon could see the outline of tall buildings, and the Statue of Liberty stood out clear and plain as we drew nearer land. Then as our ship came into New York Harbor, the stone lips of the Statue of Liberty seemed to say to me, "Welcome to America, Mohammed Aryain."

I took off my red fez and threw it into the ocean, saying to myself, "I am now a new man in a new world, and I must adjust to the customs of this world."[2]

When our ship came to a stop, all the passengers walked down the gangplank onto Ellis Island. After years of dreaming and after twenty-one days of traveling by foot, by ship, by train, and then again by ship, I finally stepped onto American soil in June of 1913. I was thrilled beyond belief.

But my excitement faded when some of the passengers were permitted to enter a door to the right, and others had a large X chalked on their clothes and were ordered into a room on the left.

I had heard that some people were turned back from America when they were examined on Ellis Island and found to have physical defects. When my coat was marked with an X and I was ordered through the door on the left, I thought I was to be denied entry because of the terrible boils and pimples on my face and neck. To make matters worse, the men I had made friends with in Beirut and on the ship were all permitted to go through the door on the right, so I felt completely alone in the world.

I was frightened and confused when I entered the vast building. The place was packed with people who seemed as frightened and confused as I was. The place was terribly noisy, for children were crying and so were many grown people, especially women. This made me feel even more certain that those of us who had been sent into this building were to be refused admittance into America.

Men and women were carrying or leading children and holding on tightly to bundles which contained all the possessions they had in the world, and no one seemed to know what to do or what was happening to them. I kept going up to people and asking them what was happening, but no one understood Arabic, and they only shook their heads and seemed as bewildered as I was.

My first night in America was sleepless from fear that I would be shipped back to Syria. And I must admit that when I thought no one was awake to hear me that night, I cried.

The next morning I decided to see again if I could find someone who spoke my language. I saw a woman who looked Syrian, and I went up and spoke to her. She replied in Arabic, but what she said made me feel even worse, for she said she thought all the people in this building with the X on their clothes were being sent back. She began crying and told me that she herself had been refused admission into America because she had brought with her a small orphan boy from her village because she had thought he would have a better life in America. But the little boy was underage and was no relative of hers, so they were being turned back. She went on crying as she told me that if she had listed the child on her visa as her own son they would have been admitted. She then tearfully told me that she had sold her home in her village in Syria, and now she had no place to return to. I felt very sorry for this poor frightened woman and the little child and have wondered many times over the years what happened to them.

Several days later I still had not been sent back to Syria, but neither had I been permitted to leave Ellis Island. And I still had not been able to learn why those of us with the X on our clothes were being detained. To increase my worry and fear, the small amount of money I had was dwindling every day.

One day while walking to a café on Ellis Island for a meal I happened to meet a young man from Damascus. It was good to find someone I could talk to, and we decided to have our dinner together. As we walked along we visited in Arabic. Then we realized that a group of men were following us and yelling angrily and calling us "Turks." This made my newfound friend and me very angry. One word led to another, and soon a fistfight broke out. The fight quickly became serious, and I was knocked to the ground. The terrible thought went through my mind that after finally getting this far I was to be killed before I got off Ellis Island.

Then the police intervened and stopped the fighting, and we learned that this commotion had started because the other men were Armenian and they had mistaken my friend and me for Turks. At that time feelings ran high between Armenians and Turks because of the Turkish massacre of the Armenian people.[3]

After ten days on Ellis Island all the people with an X on their clothes were called to a doctor's office for a final examination. This, I knew, would be the time when I would learn finally if I was to be permitted to enter the United States or be sent back to Syria. My heart was pounding, and I was weak from fear as I waited in the long line to approach the doctor.

The boils and pimples on my face and neck had now healed but had left deep scars. After a brief examination the doctor handed me a printed paper and motioned me toward the main entrance of the building. Although I could not read English, I sensed this paper was my permit to remain in the United States.

My hands were trembling from excitement as I hurriedly brushed the chalked X from my coat and gathered up my belongings. Then I passed from the office through a large door, which I was sure was the opening to the world which would give me the freedom and the new life I had dreamed of.

When I was halfway across the large room, a strange man

approached and handed me a large paper sack containing a loaf of bread and links of baloney sausages. The man did not speak Arabic, and I never did figure out why he was there, but I guess he was sent by Mr. Tewell. I had never seen a baloney sausage before, nor had I ever seen bread baked in a loaf. I had no idea how in the world this food was to be eaten, but I was grateful for the food the man had given me. Although I could not tell him so, I knew he understood how I felt.

He took me to Grand Central Station in New York and had me open my purse to show the ticket agent there my ticket for Rochester, Pennsylvania. Then the man smiled and waved a farewell and went away. I was indeed alone in the New World, and once again I felt terribly frightened and confused.

The ticket agent tried to tell me the departure time of my train, but I could not understand him, for he spoke in English. He then tried to show me by the clock when the train would leave, but still I did not understand him. Then the man asked me if I was Syrian. I understood the word "Syrian" and nodded quickly.

The ticket agent motioned for me to be seated. Then he went away.

In a few minutes he returned with a young man who worked in the express office of the depot. It so happened that this young man was from Lebanon, and we could converse in Arabic. After a few minutes of visiting in Arabic, he told me he must return to his job but for me to remain seated until he came back at train time. He would help me get started on my destination.

I will always be grateful to these men who were so kind to me that day now sixty years past.

About an hour later the young man returned and led me to my train and helped me board it. I thanked him many times.

I can truthfully say that the sweetest moment of my life was when that train pulled out of the station. I was fifteen years old, I had only $3.75 in my pocket, I was unable to speak the English language, and I was thousands of miles from my family, but now I knew I would not be returned to Syria. I was a new man in a new world, and I was determined to make my life account for something.

For this I gave thanks to Allah, or God, and asked his guidance through all my life.

4

Peddling in the Midwest

. . .

THE TIME OF TRAVELING TO ROCHESTER, PENNSYLVANIA, TOOK seven or eight hours. Each time the conductor came through the car I gathered up my belongings in preparation of leaving my seat. The kindly man would place his hand on my shoulder and mutter something I could not understand. Then finally I realized he meant for me to remain seated.

Arriving in Rochester, I could not ask anyone about the man I was to go to, so I spent several hours in confused searching. Then over a place of business I saw a sign written in both Arabic and English: "Tewell Brothers Wholesale Dry Goods Co."

Feeling greatly relieved, I entered the store, introduced myself to Mr. Tewell, and began looking over the merchandise.

Mr. Tewell was friendly, and I soon felt comfortable with him. In the following days he explained to me the art of selling the fancy merchandise, which consisted of linens, tapestries, notions, scarves, drawnwork, rugs, bedspreads, and laces. He showed me how to group the merchandise to make the largest sale and taught me how to bargain. He helped me to get located in a rooming house and took me with him for meals. He spoke what I thought must be very good English, and I soon learned to pronounce a few words after him. The easiest word for me to remember was "hamburger." One of the waitresses at the café was kind and considerate and helped me select my food when I went alone to eat. One day the cook came out of the kitchen and showed me by the clock that if I would come in during his less busy hours he too would help me. Small considerations like these meant so much to a boy who was hungry and could not read the menu.

One day I decided to eat alone, and Mr. Tewell repeated several times before I left his store to say "steak and French fries." All the way to the café I repeated to myself "steak and French fries, steak and French fries." But when I was seated at the table my wits left me, and I completely forgot "steak and French fries."

Then I noticed that the customer sitting next to me was having steak and French fries, and I reached over to his plate and he got the idea I was trying to steal his food when all I wanted was to show the waitress I wanted steak and French fries. This little episode in the café caused me great embarrassment. People laughed at me and kept watching me as I ate my steak and French fries.

Then the time came when I had to get to work. Mr. Tewell told me he would give me one hundred dollars in merchandise to sell around Beatrice, Nebraska.[1] Then when I had paid my invoice he would furnish me with more goods. This merchandise he packed in two suitcases, which I was to carry over my shoulders. The remainder of the merchandise he shipped in a large wooden box to Beatrice, Nebraska, so I would have more merchandise when the suitcases were empty.

But before I left for Nebraska, he said to me, "Mohammed, I think you should have some new clothes before going on the road. I like for my salesmen to look their very best."

"Mr. Tewell, I do not have money to spend on clothes," I said.

"We can arrange that, Mohammed," he said. Then during the

morning he took me to a men's clothing store and outfitted me
with a complete change of clothes—underwear, socks, shoes,
shirts, and a dress suit. In those days one could buy a good looking
dress suit for fifteen dollars. The clothes were to be added to the
invoice of merchandise I owed Mr. Tewell.

The next day, feeling very proud of the finest clothes I had ever
worn or even dreamed of, I got on the train with my two suitcases
of merchandise and set off for Nebraska. On the train I was again
helped by kind people. I kept staring out the window of the train,
hardly daring to blink for fear I would miss seeing something.
Everything was so interesting.

I arrived in Beatrice, Nebraska, on the first day of July and was
met at the depot by a group of Syrian men who also worked for Mr.
Tewell. One of these men was the brother of Mr. Tewell. They
told me that they had gathered together to celebrate the Fourth of
July. This puzzled me until they explained what the holiday was,
then I enjoyed it very much.

That evening while I was with these men and after we had
become fairly well acquainted, one of them suggested I should
take for myself a new American name, as the name Mohammed
would seem odd to the American people.

"What are the most common American names?" I asked, and
they began suggesting "George," "Mack," "Joe," and "John."
Then one of them said "Ed," and I liked this immediately, for it
was short and sounded like the last part of my real name, so right
then and there I decided I was Ed Aryain.

The next day Charlie Amer, one of the younger of the group of
Syrian men, said to me, "Ed (or Mohammed), your hair is long and
shaggy, and you should have a haircut before you go to work on the
road." I looked into the mirror and saw that he was right, for
although my mother had trimmed my hair before I had left
Henna, it had now grown over my ears and down my back. Believe
it or not, in my youth I had a fine heavy head of hair!

Charlie Amer then took me to a barber shop where a haircut cost thirty-five cents and a shave cost fifteen cents. I had the haircut, and sure enough I looked much better. I was still too young to need a shave.

Later that night Charlie Amer took me to see a movie, but at the door I hesitated, remembering that my father had told me in Damascus that movies were indecent. But then I thought to heck with it and went inside feeling very daring. It so happened that the movie showing was about an Indian and American war, and I noticed how the Americans used their guns against the Indians and how the Indians made direct hits on the Americans with their bows and arrows. This puzzled me until later when Charlie Amer explained that the Indians had owned this land until the Americans pushed them off of it and moved in themselves. I found the history part very interesting, but my sympathy lay with the Indians. As far back as I could remember I had heard how my own people had been pushed from their homes and land by the powerful Turks.

The next day all the Syrian men went for a picnic near the lake, and late in the afternoon we decided to go for a swim. I had learned to swim in the little mountain stream in Henna and thought I was pretty good. But I guess I went out too far into the lake, for soon I found that I could not get back. I began to struggle. Then Charlie Amer saw my plight and swam out to save me. Just as I was going down for the third time and was thinking how awful my mother would feel when she learned I had died before I had been in America for a month, Charlie Amer reached me, and I grabbed hold of his arms as hard as I could.

"Do not hold me so tightly!" he yelled as he struggled to keep us both afloat. "We will both drown unless you let go of my arms!" Then I released my grip, and he began getting me to safety.

It was a long swim, and he was exhausted when we finally reached the shore. Then when Charlie had regained his breath, he turned on me angrily. "You crazy idiot! Why did you go out so far if you are not a good swimmer?"

His tone angered me and I yelled back and we were just about to have a fistfight when I suddenly realized I was fighting the man who had just saved my life. I felt very ashamed and quickly apologized for being such a smart aleck and a show off.

This was not the only disagreement Charlie Amer and I had over the years, but he was always right and I was always wrong. He was only trying to help me find my way in this new world, and he proved to be a true friend and one of the finest men I have ever known.

Then the box of merchandise arrived from Rochester, and I was eager to go on the road and learn to be a peddler. Mr. Tewell and I parted from the other Syrian men, and I traveled with him for a week. Each day we walked from one farmhouse to another carrying the heavy suitcases over our shoulders, and each time we stopped I observed how he sold the fancy merchandise.

He taught me how to say "good morning," "thank you," and "may I spend the night in your house?" in English. He also taught me that after knocking at a door I should step back a few steps so the person who answered would not feel crowded.

At the end of a week traveling with Mr. Tewell he taught me a few more words I would need to know. Then we parted, and I was on my own. I soon found that I had less trouble selling the fancy merchandise, which the farm ladies wanted, than in counting money and making change. However this did not last long. I soon learned that ten dimes made the same amount as a dollar bill, as did four quarters or two fifty-cent pieces, and then that five one-dollar bills equaled a five-dollar bill. A new man in a new country has plenty to learn and must remember each and every detail.

At the end of the second week I rejoined the Syrian men in Beatrice. Some of them had had fair business peddling, and others had not done so hot. They were all surprised that I had sold over forty dollars. After the weekend five of the older men decided to go to eastern Kansas, and they asked me to go with them. But we did not do much business there, so we moved into eastern Oklahoma. This we realized was going from bad to worse, for there was not much demand for our merchandise, so we kept moving. I was fascinated with everything I saw in this vast new land. My sons say that I still am.

In September we arrived in Fort Worth, Texas, where the cotton crop was good and the harvest just beginning.[2] Every Monday each man took a different train out of Fort Worth and worked the surrounding communities. We worked hard all week, and business was good. For the first time I felt I was doing all right. By the third week in the Fort Worth area my suitcases were empty, and I had to reorder merchandise. I was well pleased with my work and with the way I was learning more English.

One day as I was walking along the highway from Fort Worth to Waxahachie two men driving a wagon stopped and asked me if I would like to ride into Waxahachie with them.[3] Some of the words I understood, but when they used the word "license" I had no idea what they meant, for I had never heard the word before. Arriving in Waxahachie, they drove to the justice of the peace, where an officer wearing a badge did all the talking. He showed me a license card, but still I did not know the meaning. When I told him this, he fined me fifteen dollars and issued me a license to peddle for a year in the state of Texas.[4] I was learning fast but learning the hard way.

Back in Fort Worth I found a letter from my father. He informed me that the man I had borrowed the money from in Marseille, France, had notified him the money was due. The man had explained to my father the terms of the loan (for the twenty-five dollars I borrowed I was to pay fifty dollars), and my father thought I had gone crazy to borrow money at such fantastic rates and asked if I had repaid the man the money.

I answered that I was now able to pay the man and that I was also sending my father the $120 he had given me for passage to America. The following morning I went to the bank and bought a draft for $170 to cover the indebtedness to my father and the other man. I also wrote my father that soon I would send him another $100, for I was making money on the road. That was a very proud day for me.

After two more weeks in Fort Worth, we traveled to Waco, Texas. There too business was good. Then we went to Austin, where I was able to send my father a bank draft for one hundred dollars as I had promised, and I still had money for myself. I was so proud of the way I was doing. I was still traveling with the six older Syrian men, and in January 1914 we moved to San Antonio, then on to Temple, Texas.

Working out of Temple, I came upon a settlement of hard-working German people who had prospered in their new home.[5] Each family had a comfortable house and good barns. It was a thickly settled area, and I did not have to walk far from one house to another. The women admired my merchandise and had the money to buy it. By the end of the week I had done so well that my suitcases were almost empty, so I decided to return early to Temple to replenish my stock. Late Friday afternoon I arrived in Temple, repacked my suitcases, and made arrangements to stay in the rooming house where the other six Syrian men would be arriving the next day.

Throughout the weekend I kept silent about how much business I had done in the German settlement for fear some of the other men would travel to this area and call upon some of my customers.

Then on Monday morning after the others had boarded trains for other communities, I returned on foot to the German settlement, where I did another week's good business. Not only was my business good there but the German people were very accommodating to let me sleep in their homes at night. I always paid for my food then gave the housewife an extra piece of handwork as a thank-you for giving me shelter during the night.

There were many nights, however, when I was not so lucky in finding a place to sleep. Sometimes I would walk for miles and be turned down at dozens of houses before finally being told I could sleep in the barn if I did not smoke. But being homeless I was grateful for whatever I could find.

I remember one night I had been refused shelter everywhere I went. Finally quite late I stopped at a farmhouse where the woman told me very sharply that she did not have room. Then she slammed the door in my face angrily.

It was now too late to go on, and as I left the porch I felt so tired and hungry and so thoroughly depressed that I walked behind the hog house, put my suitcases down upon the ground, and then lay down on top of them. I was so exhausted that I managed to sleep fairly well despite my hunger and the noise of the hogs.

The next morning I was awakened by a young man who had come out to feed the hogs. He was surprised to find me there, and I think he was also frightened. "What is going on here?" he demanded as he backed away from me. "Why are you sleeping next to our hog house?"

"I am a peddler working on road selling fancy merchandise," I replied in my broken English. "I could not find any other place to sleep, and I was tired. I asked the woman in the house, but she slammed the door in my face."

"You must have talked to my mother," the young man said, then he left me and went back into the house.

Soon he returned and told me I could come into the house and eat breakfast with the family. When I had eaten, I paid the woman of the house twenty-five cents for the breakfast, but I did not even open my suitcase to show her my merchandise.

But there were many times which were far worse. Sometimes as I approached a house someone would step out on the porch and shake his fist at me angrily. "Go away!" he would shout. "Go away! We don't want your kind on our place!"

Incidents like these hurt very much at the time, and even now they stand out as vividly in my memory as if they had happened only yesterday and make me feel uneasy.

But other times people were kind and generous, and they offered me food and a room to sleep in and let me pay with merchandise, which the women seemed to appreciate more than money.

We then moved to Corsicana, Texas, where business continued to be good.[6] Each week I paid my wholesale account, and the money I had left over I put into bank drafts. Soon I had four hundred dollars in bank drafts, and I was very proud of myself.

I had not lost track of my dream of buying a gold watch and chain when I came to America, and each time I passed a jewelry store I stopped to window shop and thought of the Syrian men I had known who had returned to Henna from America. When I had paid my debts, sent extra money to my family, and had four hundred dollars in bank drafts, I decided I could well afford to purchase the gold watch and chain of my dreams.

When we reached Dallas, I saw a store where many beautiful watches were displayed in the window.[7] I went inside the store and looked over the beautiful stock of gold watches. The buying of this watch and chain was very important to me, and I took my time looking for just the right one.

Finally, I decided on a watch with a fancy carved flip front and a heavy close-linked gold chain. My, how proud I was as I walked out of the store that day wearing my new watch and chain. Another of my dreams had been realized.[8]

From Dallas we moved to Sherman, Texas, where we worked for several weeks.[9] Then when the weather grew too hot we decided to travel north toward St. Joseph, Missouri,[10] where Mr. Tewell had recently moved his wholesale house from Rochester, Pennsylvania.

It was customary for the peddlers to meet together for the Fourth of July celebration, and when we arrived in St. Joseph, over 150 men were gathered there.

I was especially delighted to see Charlie Amer, the young Syrian man who had saved my life the previous year. He was a very handsome young man with a pleasant disposition. He spoke good English, and he always looked clean and neat, whereas some of the older men I had been traveling with were not too careful about their appearance. In fact I was sometimes embarrassed by their clothes and unkempt ways when we went into boarding houses, for at sixteen I thought myself quite a dandy. So on Sunday morning I asked Charlie Amer to take a walk downtown with me, for I had something on my mind I wanted to talk over with him. When we were away from the rooming house, I told him I had the idea that we would do better if he and I traveled together and left the older men to themselves. He told me that he had been thinking the same thing. Then we decided we would say nothing about our plan until after the Fourth of July.

We spent a week in St. Joseph then told the other men what we were going to do. When they heard that we were striking out together, they laughed and said that because we were young men we wanted to go out to meet young women. Then Charlie Amer and I packed our suitcases and shipped out boxes to Topeka, Kansas, and parted company with the older men.[11]

We spent a week in Topeka, but business was not so hot, so we went to Salina, Kansas.[12] Then we moved to Colby.[13] We began doing well in this part of Kansas, for it was newly settled. Most of the farmers were homesteaders who lived in dugouts covered with sod blocks, but the women wanted our pretty merchandise for their families, so we did good business. This part of the country was also good for peddlers because it sometimes took a family two days to make the wagon trip into town for supplies, so they did not go very often. No matter how crowded these dugouts were, the people were hospitable and kind. They always offered me food and a bed for the night, and the housewives were always delighted, and I think surprised, when I gave them pieces of pretty lace as a thank-you.

Charlie Amer and I spent three months in this territory, but then he became dissatisfied with the amount of money he was making (I always sold more). So because I was lonely and did not feel I yet spoke English well enough to work entirely by myself, I agreed to move on. We went into eastern Colorado, making Akron and Limon our headquarters, and we found more homesteaders living in dugouts.[14] That was a good year for corn and wheat, and we did good business, especially in the German and Bohemian settlements we found.

Because of my constant moving from place to place, I never had a forwarding address for my mail. Sometimes months passed without hearing from my family. I was doing well on the road and saving my money, but deep down in my heart I yearned to have news of my loved ones. At times in strange towns the loneliness and homesickness was so overpowering that I would go into an alley and sit down behind the trash cans and cry and cry. I was deeply ashamed to let anyone see me, a grown man of sixteen, shed tears, but at these times I felt my heart was breaking.

But then my pain would be eased, and I would go on.

I had now been in the United States over a year. I had worked hard traveling on foot and carrying the two heavy suitcases of goods on my back (even today I have deep scars across my shoulders where the heavy load cut into my flesh). But I had saved my money, and I felt I should now move up in the world by buying myself a horse and buggy. When I suggested this to Charlie Amer, he disagreed, but when in Wray, Colorado, I came upon a wagon yard where people were selling horses and buggies, I decided to look around.[15] I found I could buy a good horse and buggy for $150. So after some haggling I closed the deal, and we really began traveling in style.

We worked in that area for several weeks, but when the winter came on suddenly we moved to a warmer climate. We came south to Dodge City, Kansas,[16] which was a very prosperous town with railroad shops and Harvey Houses.[17] Now that I had a horse and buggy, we could make better time and cover more territory. Our business was good, but again Charlie Amer was unhappy.

We had heard that Drumright, Oklahoma, was an oil boomtown, and Charlie wanted to go there. But this time I told him I was well satisfied in Dodge City and would stay there longer. He left, and I stayed working this area for another month or so. Business was good, and I found that since I now had my horse and buggy, I was not as lonely as I had feared. Sometimes at night, though, I still wept from homesickness for my family in Syria.

The business of selling and trading horses was then a big thing, and many people made a good living in this exchange. Since I had worked with horses in the Old Country and thought I knew a great deal about them, I decided to try my luck at horse trading. For the next several weeks I peddled in the country around Dodge City during the week, then spent the weekends trading horses. Each trade brought me a few dollars to add to my savings. To me this sideline of trading horses was great sport.

One day a man came along with two nice horses about four years old. He said he would sell me these horses for $275. I offered him $175, and he refused and walked away. But in an hour or so he returned and said he would sell me the horses for $200. I agreed, and after the deal was closed he said, "Boy, what nationality are you?" When I told him I was Syrian, he nodded and said, "I thought so. You know, son, when the Jew came to this country he beat the devil doing business, but when the Syrian came to this country he beat them both."

The next weekend I sold this team of horses for $230, making a nice little profit.

But a few days later when I was out on the road peddling I was caught in a bad snow and ice storm. I knew I could not work much longer in this climate, so I moved south toward Oklahoma. I had decided that my horse was too heavy for buggy driving and had been considering trading for a lighter horse. One morning I met a farmer who said he had a lighter horse which would be better for my buggy. We went out to the barn, and he showed me a beautiful young mare which was too light for farm work. The man said he would trade me even for my heavier horse.

The mare coughed a few times, and the man said this was because she had been eating dry alfalfa and had dust in her throat. The young mare was very beautiful, and she held her head so high and walked so lightly that she reminded me of the fine Arabian horses I had known as a boy. But I told the man he would have to give me twenty-five dollars and the mare for my heavier horse. To my surprise he agreed at once.

He gave me the twenty-five dollars, took my heavy horse, helped me hitch my new young beauty to my buggy, and waved good-bye. As I started on my way I was very proud of the good deal I had made.

But we had only traveled a few miles when the horse began to cough with every breath, and out of a clear blue sky I realized she had the "heaves," a disease of the lungs.[18] This was something new to me, and I realized I had gotten the bad end of this horse trade after all.

I drove on through Kansas but did not do much business. I was worried and mad about this horse business. I reached Shawnee, Oklahoma, and worked there for a few days.[19] Then I decided to go to the wagon yard and look for another horse. Although we had traveled many miles, and my horse had coughed constantly, she still looked beautiful. The way she carried herself would make anyone get the mistaken idea that she was a healthy young animal.

While I was in the Shawnee wagon yard, a man came up and asked about buying my horse.

"No," I quickly said, "This horse is not for sale, for I need a horse for my work peddling fancy merchandise on the road." But then I casually added that if he had a horse which was buggy broken I *might* consider a trade.

The man replied that he had several fine horses which were buggy broken and that he would like to have my mare for breeding purposes. Seeing the prospect of trading my horse with the heaves for a healthy one, I agreed to go out to the man's farm and look at his horses.

The man's horses were fine looking animals. When I asked if they were buggy broken, he offered to let me try one of them. I hitched a fine strong horse to my buggy, and he pulled it at a steady even pace. I could tell he was a gentle horse.

In the meantime my mare had a hard coughing spell. When the man asked about this, I gave him the same story the farmer I had bought the horse from had given me—that she had eaten some dry alfalfa and gotten dust in her throat.

I then told the man that he was getting the best end of the deal. His stock of horses would increase when my beautiful young mare was among his stallions, and he should pay me twenty-five dollars in addition to the trade.

The man refused to give me any cash, so we traded even. I said a quick good-bye and drove away.

I was afraid that the man would follow me and demand his horse back, so I traveled all day and far into the night without stopping, getting as far away from that farmer and the coughing horse as possible. It was only when I reached Chickasha, Oklahoma, three days later that I finally began stopping to sell merchandise.[20]

But business was not so hot in that part of the country, so after ten days I decided to go back to Texas, where I had really made my start peddling merchandise. The closer I got to Texas, the better my business became. When I crossed the Texas state line, I felt the state held better prospects for me than any other place I had been in America.

It was now 1915, and I was seventeen years old.

I had had new merchandise shipped to Waco, Texas.[21] When I picked it up at the railway depot, I saw a building with a sign which said, "Rooming House."

Learning to read even this much English had been very difficult, for all the letters had at first looked alike to me. But each time I went to a rooming house, hotel, boarding house, or restaurant, I studied the signs very carefully, trying to remember the letters which stood out just a shade different from the others. I can well remember that the words "Rooming House" were the first I could identify on a sign without much trouble, and this was the beginning of the long slow process of my learning to read the English language. Then I began buying newspapers. With much pondering over the headlines, I soon began to read the print and halfway make out the details.

Believe you me, this was not an easy matter, but it was something I knew I had to do. To this very day I cannot read or write handwriting, but I can read printing as good as anybody. I have to recite this book to my wife, and she [handwrites it and then] types it out on the typewriter.

Since I planned to spend some time in Waco, I went on to a house with a sign which said, "Boarding House." I had learned that the meals in boarding houses were better than in cafes, and I could select the foods I liked best. I was still having trouble making out menus. Many were the times when I would point to something on the menu because the length of the name made me think it would be steak and French fries. Then when the order was placed before me it was toast, bacon, and eggs. To this day I have a dislike of eggs because of this.

I knocked at the door of the boarding house. It was answered by a middle-aged woman who was pleasant and understanding when I asked about meals and a room in my still broken English. She told me the rates were fifty cents a night and meals were twenty-five cents each, so I moved in.

When I went down for the evening meal, I found twenty people eating at a long table covered with clean, white oil cloth. On the table were set out high platters of fried chicken, ham, roast beef, and pork chops. There were bowls of beans, corn, peas, potatoes, and turnips and side dishes of pickles, sliced onions, fresh tomatoes, and many relishes. For dessert there was a wide variety of pies and cakes.

Most of the boarders were men who worked in the railroad shops, and after the meal everyone gathered in the adjoining room and sang songs both old and new. To the accompaniment of guitars, the railroad workers sang, "I wish I had a share of the railroad business." I remember that song to this very day.[22]

After several weeks in Waco, I decided to go farther south to Temple, then on to the Texas coast to spend the winter working that area. But when I reached San Antonio I found that money was short and that people frequently would not even let me into their homes to show them my merchandise. I went back to Waco, where my business was better. I had several weeks of good business in this area, then realized it was time to move on.

I worked back into Oklahoma, though I had never done much business in that part of the country. In Chickasha I was overjoyed to find six other peddlers from my homeland. One of the men, Charlie Cabool, had been born and reared in the village neighboring Henna, and it was a great pleasure to talk to someone from my part of the world. The friendship that began that day has been a lasting one, for Charlie and Mary Cabool now live in Lubbock, Texas, and we visit in their home very often.[23]

These six men had been in the United States much longer than

I had, but they were still traveling on foot, carrying their suitcases over their shoulders. When I told them I was driving a horse and buggy, they asked me to help them buy a horse as I had had more experience in buying and selling horses than they had. (I did not tell them of my experience with the horse that had the heaves.)

We spent several days visiting. Then after I had helped them buy a horse and buggy, we parted company, and I began moving toward Kansas. As soon as I crossed the Oklahoma state line into Kansas my business picked up. About this time the Tewell Brothers Wholesale Company became only a retail store, so I began buying from Joseph Izzam of Hannibal, Missouri, and from Hameed Brothers of Fort Smith, Arkansas.[24]

One day I received a letter from Mr. Kassam Hameed of Hameed Brothers telling me his brother was going to be in the area and wanted to get acquainted with me. At the same time I had a very sad letter from my father telling me that there had been no rain in Syria and that the crops had failed. He said he needed money to provide for the family until the next crop was made and asked me to please send him some. I was happy to send my father money, but I had to wait until I reached a large town so I could send a bank draft to the old country.

When I reached the little town where I was to meet Mr. Hameed of Hameed Brothers, I asked him why he wanted to meet me. He explained that he wanted to personally meet their customers on the road and perhaps sell us more merchandise through this personal relationship. He also wanted to borrow some money.

He said he would pay me the same interest he would pay a bank, but I showed him the sad letter from my father and told him I could not lend him money. I also told him that the town we were in did not have a bank, so I would have to wait a few days before sending my father two hundred dollars.

Mr. Hameed of Hameed Brothers told me he would be returning to Fort Smith the next day. Since there was a bank there, he would be happy to forward the money for me. I gave Mr. Hameed of Hameed Brothers the two hundred dollars and my father's address in Syria.

Weeks passed, and I did not hear from my father. Months passed, and still I did not know if my father had received the money. Finally a letter came from my father saying he was very hurt and disappointed that I had failed to send him the much needed money.

I wrote a letter to Mr. Hameed of Hameed Brothers, but he did not answer. I suspected then that the money had never been sent and that I had been cheated of my hard-earned two hundred dollars.

In desperation I called him by long distance telephone, and he said he had sent the money. When I asked him if he had a receipt from the bank, he said he had just forgotten to pick it up. This confirmed my thinking that Mr. Hameed of Hameed Brothers had stolen my money. My anger flared. I told him he was a crook and a cheat, and I gave him a good cursing out. He threatened to report me to the telephone company for using curse words over the telephone. I had been taken for a sucker, and I vowed to be more careful who I trusted in the future.

Months later I learned that Mr. Hameed of Hameed Brothers was shot and killed for having another Syrian man's wife in his apartment. The husband was cleared of killing Mr. Hameed of Hameed Brothers.

Mr. Joseph Izzam of Hannibal, Missouri, was a very different sort of man. He had come to this country many years earlier and had begun working on the road as a peddler. He had been highly successful and was well respected. In all my dealing with him he was fair and honest. He was also an inspiration for me, for I wanted to be like this man who had started out as a peddler like myself and now had a wholesale house. Once when Mr. Izzam got tight for cash and asked me to loan him eight hundred dollars, I gladly did so, and he paid me interest on it.

I was now sending money to my family regularly, had money in the bank, and had money loaned on interest. But the thing I was most proud of was that I now knew enough English to make all my own business transactions. I was also proud that when I visited people I had sold merchandise to on my previous trips, they seemed pleased to see me again. They bought my merchandise and invited me to spend the night in their homes.

I moved into Wray, Colorado, then to Akron, where many Swedes, Bohemians, and Germans had homesteaded. Again my luck held, for these people were eager to buy my merchandise and to give me food, shelter, and feed for my horse for an extra piece of fancy work, tapestry, or a bedspread.

I then decided to spend a weekend in Colorado Springs, a place I had heard much about.[25] I left my horse and buggy in Limon and took a train to Colorado Springs, which I found to be a nice new town. New businesses were opening up. New land was being both homesteaded and sold, and ranching was opening up in a big way. I found a room in a nice rooming house. Then after cleaning up I went out to see the town.

I was surprised to see trucks and automobiles in great numbers. I saw Essexes, Hupmobiles, Fords, Chevrolets, and especially Hudsons. Hudsons were the most popular cars, and just for fun I went into an agency and priced a Hudson car. It sold for $1,700. Fords then sold for $365. This was the beginning of a new era for America.

I then saw a hotel which seemed the most beautiful building I had ever seen. It was trimmed in marble and was surrounded by acres of flower gardens, and I stood for a long time across the street admiring this beautiful scene.[26]

Later I had my dinner in a café and returned to my rooming house and sat out on the porch to rest. The lady who owned the rooming house came out and sat down beside me and talked in a very friendly manner. She told me that the beautiful hotel had

been opened about ten years earlier and was filled with rich people from all over the country who wanted to spend the summer
months in Colorado Springs. She then suggested that I go to the
hotel for a cup of coffee, and I decided to do so.

I sat for an hour over this cup of coffee just admiring the beauty
of the place and watching the people in their fine clothes enter and
leave the lobby and dining room.

It was very interesting, but I knew that this place of elegance
was no place for an immigrant peddler of merchandise like me but
for the very rich people of America. It had been a nice weekend in
Colorado Springs, but the next morning I was eager to take the
train back to Limon to my own horse and buggy and to get back
to work on the road again.

5

Visiting Uncle Ollie

. . .

I TRAVELED THROUGH A RICH IRRIGATED VALLEY WHERE SUGAR beets were being harvested. These were the finest farms I had yet seen in the United States. Each one had a grand house, barns, and storehouses and seemed like a small town. These farmers were so rich they had railroad tracks running directly into their fields so they could load their sugar beets onto the big box cars.

It was very interesting to see this beautiful valley, but I did not even stop to do business. I had learned that people on rich farms did not care for the sort of merchandise carried by a peddler like myself and did not like me on their place.

I drove through the valley and did not stop until I reached Brush, Colorado, where I did fair business. Then I moved on to Fort Morgan, where business was good. I traveled into Nebraska, where I found the country too thinly populated for my kind of business, so I went back to Fort Morgan, where business was good.[1]

Then I heard about Cheyenne, the capital of Wyoming, so I decided to try working in that area.[2] But Wyoming, like Nebraska, was too thinly populated for my kind of business. Ranches were few and far between, and cattle grazed on the open range. On this trip of over a hundred miles I only stopped at six or seven houses. There was not much demand for my merchandise on these ranches, but the people were nice and always offered me food and a place to sleep. Some days I stopped and accepted their hospitality early in the afternoon, for I was afraid I might not find another ranch house by nightfall.

Many times on this lonely journey in Wyoming I was afraid that my horse and I would both be killed by the wild cattle which roamed the open range. These enormous animals had long, sharp horns and shaggy, matted fur, and they would come dangerously close to my buggy and then bellow and snort and stomp the ground until the air was so thick with dust that I could scarcely see what I was doing. My greatest fear was that one of these animals would hook his long horn into the wheels of my buggy, for I knew that if he did he could easily turn it over.

When these cattle came too close, my horse would become frightened and leap forward. Then he would rear up on his hind legs and try to fight them with his front hooves. At these times I could control him only by holding the reins tightly.

After these alarming experiences on the prairie, I was greatly relieved to reach Cheyenne, a nice clean town with a population of perhaps twelve thousand people. Engaging a room in a nice boarding house, I decided to give my horse and myself a few days' rest. We had driven hard through rough country and needed some time off the road. The people I met in cafes and on the streets were very friendly, but at the end of a week I made plans to travel again. I had heard of the town of Laramie, Wyoming, and I decided I had better go there.[3]

Again as I drove over the prairie my horse and I were threatened by wild cattle. But there were railroads which ran parallel to the buggy tracks. Trains went by frequently, and the noise terrified my horse. So now I had noisy trains *and* wild cattle to contend with.

As I rode along I was puzzled by high wooden and wire fences which had been built on both sides of the railroad and buggy tracks. I could not figure out what in the world these fences were for.

In Laramie I made arrangements for my horse to be taken care of. Then after finding a room for myself I went out to look over the town. To my delight I saw a sign with a Middle Eastern name: "Abraham Tumis Dry Goods Co."

I went inside and introduced myself to the owner of the store in Arabic. Mr. Tumis was greatly surprised at hearing his native tongue, and he said it had been five years since he had seen anyone from Syria or Lebanon. We went for coffee, and he told me that when he first came to this country he had lived for several years in New York City before coming west. He had settled in Laramie seven years earlier and established his dry goods store. He said he liked the country and the people. He had made some money and was well satisfied and was very happy to be away from the crowds and noise of the big city.

Then I told Mr. Tumis about the strange fences I had seen on each side of the railroad tracks and asked him about them. He told me that these fences had been built to keep the snow from drifting too deeply over the tracks so the trains could run.

I thought this was very interesting, but I knew at once that my horse and I could not peddle in this country in the wintertime.

I spent a pleasant weekend visiting with this countryman, but on Monday morning I began the long hard journey back to Fort Morgan. As I rode along the prairie I thought of Mr. Abraham Tumis who had begun as an immigrant like me but now had a fine dry goods store. I was determined to someday be just as successful and lead a settled life.

I had spent twenty days in this part of the country and sold very little merchandise, but it had been a very interesting experience, and when I got back into the dry farming area I worked very hard and did a good business.

.   .   .

Since coming to the United States I had known I had a cousin I called Uncle Ollie Aryain living in South Dakota. About this time I wrote to his sister who lived in Lebanon, and she replied that her brother lived on a homestead outside Morristown, South Dakota.[4] I went into a drug store and bought a map to locate Morristown. I found the information I needed and was very pleased with myself for being able to do so. But then I decided to delay going to see Uncle Ollie for the time [being].

I continued working hard, then decided to see Denver, Colorado, while I was in this part of the country.[5] In Fort Morgan I found a place to keep my horse, then took a train to Denver. There I engaged a room in a nice clean, three-story hotel, then went out for my dinner.

When I returned to the hotel lobby, I was delighted to find five men I recognized as being from the Middle East. I introduced myself to them and learned that they were from Palestine and were peddlers like myself. Then one of the men suggested we go to his room where we could talk freely in our Arabic language and not draw the attention of other people in the lobby.

Five of us went to the man's room, and a few minutes later the sixth man joined us with a gallon container of ice cream, paper cups, and small wooden spoons. Then we sat and visited in Arabic and ate ice cream into the late hours of the night.

We each began telling the others about the hard times we had experienced since arriving in the United States, how difficult it had been to learn enough English to communicate with people, and how embarrassed we were at times when we used the wrong word. One man told of his experience when they had been living in an apartment so that they could cook Middle Eastern food, which they missed and were hungry for. One particular day this man went to a grocery store and found meat, vegetables, canned goods, bread, and fruit. But he could not find the eggs, and when he tried to tell the manager what he wanted, he found that he had

forgotten the word. He simply could not make the manager understand that he wanted eggs.

Finally he put his hands down low on the back of his hips as if
they were wings, half doubled over and cackled like a hen.

The other customers in the store screamed with laughter at this
poor man who could not find the eggs he wanted for his breakfast.
But the manager understood what he wanted and showed him
eggs in cartons, which the man had not seen before.

Each of us told of the loneliness and homesickness we had
endured. In fact it was an evening of each man sharing his hardships with others and then feeling better.

The following morning my friends from Palestine said good-
bye and went back to work on the road, and I decided to spend the
day sightseeing in Denver. I enjoyed very much wandering about
the streets and looking at the tall buildings, then going through
hotel lobbies and department stores. Everything was so interesting.
Then I passed a school. As I watched the children playing I was
suddenly overcome with loneliness, and I wished that I had gone
to such a fine school and learned English properly. I decided right
then and there to visit my cousin in South Dakota.

I took the first train I could get back to Fort Morgan to see my
horse and make further arrangements for him to be cared for in
my absence. I went to my boarding house, packed my suitcases,
paid my bill, and then went back to the depot where I boarded
another train—destination Morristown, South Dakota.

At North Platte, Nebraska, I changed trains.[6] Then as we passed
through an Indian Reservation, I saw teepees pitched close to the
tracks. Little Indian children were playing near these teepees, and
Indian women were cooking over open fires. I saw Indian men riding ponies over the prairie. I had heard of the American Indians
even when I was in Syria, and I had seen them in movies, but this
was the first time I had actually seen them.

At Pierre, South Dakota, I changed trains again.[7] Then after

crossing the wide Missouri River we reached Morristown, a small
town consisting of boarding houses, a depot, a wagon yard, and a
few stores, which carried dry goods, groceries, and supplies for the
homesteaders.

I went to a boarding house and had my noon meal. Then when
I paid for my dinner, I asked the lady at the cash register if she
knew a Mr. Ollie Aryain who lived on a homestead. She told me
that she knew four nice Syrian men who lived on homesteads and
who always came to the boarding house for their noon meals when
they came into town to buy supplies. But she did not know in
which direction these men lived or how far it was to their homestead. Then she offered to call her husband who was working in
the kitchen so I could talk to him.

When the man came to the cash register, I explained to him
that I was Mr. Ollie Aryain's cousin. In a very friendly way he told
me of four Syrian men who lived eighteen miles south of
Morristown. He said there were no telephones or taxis or even a
jitney [a small bus] to take me there, for the town could not afford
them. But he suggested that I stay in this boarding house until he
saw someone from that homesteading area in town for supplies.
Then he would talk to them about transportation for me.

I ate and slept in this house for two days. Then on the morning
of the third day the owner came to my room and told me a farmer
who lived near Mr. Ollie Aryain was in town and would be glad to
take me out to the homestead in his wagon.

I located this farmer on the front walk, and he told me we
would be leaving as soon as his supplies were loaded on the wagon.
I paid my bill, thanked the owners of the boarding house for their
kindness, and gave the landlady a piece of tapestry as an extra
thank-you. Then I put my suitcases on the wagon, and we headed
for the country. As we traveled, the farmer told me that when he
came to town in his buggy or in a Ford, he made the trip in one
day easily. When he came in his wagon for supplies, though, he

spent the night in town because the thirty-six mile round trip was too hard on his team of horses.

After four hours of driving, the man pointed to a house where he lived. Then he went two miles further to where Uncle Ollie lived. We stopped at the small house, and I knocked at the door, but there was no answer. Then I looked towards the fields and saw a man working there, and the farmer told me he was sure it was my Uncle Ollie. I asked the farmer how much I owed him for the ride. He said there was no charge because the law of the land said each man always did his best to accommodate his friend and neighbor, but that if I wanted to I could give him a dollar. I gave the man two dollars because he had been so nice and accommodating to me. Then we said good-bye, and I walked out to the field where my Uncle Ollie was gathering corn and loading it into his wagon.

I walked close to him and said hello in Arabic. Of course, he did not know me. When I told him that I was his nephew Mohammed Aryain from Syria, he ran to me, hugged me with all his strength, then gave me an Old Country kissing—first on the right cheek, then on the left cheek, then on the right cheek again. He was so excited and happy that one of his own kin was with him.

We drove the loaded wagon to the house and unhitched the horses, and all the time he talked very fast, trying to tell me many things and asking questions about our people in Syria. He told me how he remembered me as a small boy in the village of Henna when he had left to come to the United States. He could hardly believe that I was now a young man who had been in this country for some time.

We went into the small house, and he apologized for not having more food for supper. He said it had been quite some time since he had been able to go into Morristown for supplies. He said if I would peel some potatoes, he would kill and cook a chicken, and we would have mashed potatoes and boiled chicken stuffed with rice and butter in the Old Country way of cooking chicken. While supper cooked, Uncle Ollie got on his horse and rode to the homes of the other Syrian men to tell them of his good fortune in having his relative in his house and to invite them to visit.

On his return we had our supper and visited some more. Just before nightfall the three Syrian men came to the house. We quickly became acquainted and talked long into the night of things and people in our homeland and of our trials and hardships since we had been in the United States. The visitors left for their homes and the next day's work, telling us they would come again soon.

The next morning after we had our breakfast of eggs, pancakes, and coffee, Uncle Ollie harnessed his horses and prepared to go to work in the fields. I volunteered to go to the fields and help with the work, but he said the work was too hard. He was afraid I would get sick. He said if I felt like it I could clean the house. He showed me where he kept the broom, mop, and rags, and when he left I really got busy on the house. When Uncle Ollie came home, he was pleased with my housecleaning. He remarked that he had not been able to see through the dirty windows for months, but now they shone like a mirror. That evening we enjoyed our supper and then spent the entire evening visiting.

The next day I noticed that Uncle Ollie kept a gun rack on one wall with a double barrel shotgun and a six shooter. When he came in at noon I mentioned that these guns needed cleaning. He got me some rags and oil, and after we had eaten our lunch of rice and hummus and burghol, he went back to the fields, and I began cleaning the guns.[8] First I cleaned the double barrel shotgun, and when I finished, it looked shiny and new. Then I started to work on the six shooter. I gave the six shooter an extra good cleaning and oiling until it too looked shiny and new.

Then while admiring my work, out of a clear sky came a deafening noise from the gun, and I realized I had shot myself. Evidently I had touched the trigger, and the gun was loaded.

Uncle Ollie ran into the house and screamed, "Are you hurt?"

Blood was running from my hand to my elbow, and my entire arm was jerking so badly that I thought the bullet had passed through the palm of my hand. When we cleaned the wound, we found that the bullet had passed through the first finger of my left hand and out below the joint of the second finger, making a very large hole. Uncle Ollie said, "It is only a wound, when it could have been a fatal blow!" Then he bathed my hand in cold water and wrapped it in a clean cloth, but the blood continued to gush forth from my finger onto the floor.

Uncle Ollie decided that instead of taking me into Morristown, which would take many hours, we would go to the neighboring farm, which was owned by a retired doctor. He drove the horses very hard, and soon we were at the neighbor's farm.

The retired doctor answered our knock and was genuinely pleased to see Uncle Ollie, but when he saw all the blood, he knew we were in trouble. He put his arm about my shoulder and asked me what the trouble was. Both the doctor and his wife were very gentle and understanding. The doctor cleaned the wound, then powdered it with medicine and wrapped it again. He said he wanted us to wait thirty minutes. Then he would examine the wound again to see if it had stopped bleeding.

During this time the doctor's wife made coffee and put out muffins on the table. I was glad, for I was weak from having lost so much blood. When thirty minutes had passed, the doctor examined the wound again. He told us that we might go but for me not to use the hand for a few weeks. Then he told me to return and let him examine the wound again in two days.

As we rode home, Uncle Ollie told me that his doctor friend had had a thriving practice in a city, but he had decided he wanted to live on a farm. Some of his land he had homesteaded and part of it he had bought outright. His main interest was in breeding thoroughbred horses. His life was not as hard as that of the other farmers, for he had money to make repairs, to have a nice house, barns, and fences, and to buy good stock. He even had hired help on the place and enjoyed his life of retirement.

Uncle Ollie also told me that there was an Indian reservation southeast of his own place, but that the Indians lived deep inside the reservation and were seldom seen.[9] He said there was another neighbor who sometimes took his wagon into the Indian reservation to gather firewood, although this was strictly against government regulations, for nothing was to be taken from the Indians. Uncle Ollie said he had tried to warn this neighbor that he was making a mistake and would get into serious trouble if the sheriff found out what he was doing.

But the man took Uncle Ollie's advice lightly and laughed and said there was no way for the sheriff to find out. Time after time the man went into the Indian reservation and filled his wagon with firewood.

But one day it so happened that three young Indians were hunting in that area, and when they saw the man taking their firewood, they caught him and gave him a good beating up. When he returned to Uncle Ollie's house, his eyes were swollen, and he was covered with blood. He was in such severe shock that he could scarcely drive his wagon.

Uncle Ollie went to his neighbor the doctor for help, but he was not home, so Uncle Ollie then drove the poor beaten man back to his own house. Then he stayed with the man while his frightened wife went to a friend who had a Ford. Then they drove the poor man into Morristown to be doctored. She begged everyone not to mention what had happened for fear the sheriff would arrest her husband. They all assured her they would not mention the occurrence. The attending physician in Morristown must have given her the same assurance, for the matter closed without a trial.

I found this story so interesting that it took my mind off of my now badly hurting hand.

I had to walk to the doctor's farm three times a week so he

could look after my hand, but there was not much else I could do. Then I got tired of eating potatoes and chicken and rice and noticed that all through the day droves of jackrabbits came close to the house and ate Uncle Ollie's corn and oats. Papa rabbits, mama rabbits, and baby rabbits, but all nice fat rabbits.

One day I took the gun and waited until a very large rabbit came by, then I shot him. When Uncle Ollie came in, I had the rabbit dressed and ready to cook. He was so pleased that he invited the three Syrian friends for dinner. We built a fire and barbecued the rabbit until it was tender and brown.

At the end of four weeks the doctor said my hand was all right and I did not have to return. I asked the doctor how much I owed him, and he said, "Nothing at all, young man, for I am glad to be able to repay your Uncle Ollie's kindness to me." I was very surprised, for I had expected to pay a large fee.

When I reported this to Uncle Ollie, he told me that recently the doctor's horses had jumped the fence and done great damage to his corn. Soon the doctor had come to Uncle Ollie's house and told him he was sorry for what had happened, and that he would pay for the damage—seventy-five or one hundred dollars or whatever he thought he should. But Uncle Ollie invited him in for a cup of coffee and told him he would not accept any money. They were neighbors and friends and this was the sort of thing that could happen to anyone.

When this story was finished, I understood why the doctor had not charged me for doctoring my hand. I knew that to survive, the homesteaders had to live in harmony with each other.

One evening Uncle Ollie told me that he was on a deal with the bank to trade his farm for a better one seven miles north of Morristown in North Dakota, a more thickly populated area. This surprised me, for I had thought Uncle Ollie was well satisfied. When I asked him if his land was clear of debt, he told me he had lived on the homestead the necessary length of time and had a clear deed to his place. When I asked if the deal was for an even trade or if he would have to pay out cash, he said that the new farm was more expensive and he was paying the difference with a long term loan from the bank. The bankers had assured him they were his friends and would work with him.

The more I heard of this deal the more convinced I became that Uncle Ollie was making a mistake, and I pointed out to him that here his farm was paid for and that he was close to friends and neighbors who would come to his aid if he was sick or hurt.

But Uncle Ollie told me he would manage, and I knew from the way he spoke to me that he did not intend to listen to the advice of a young man.

I am sorry to tell you that two or three years after Uncle Ollie moved to the new farm in North Dakota, his crops failed. He could not meet the bank payments, and they foreclosed on his mortgage.

Uncle Ollie was by then an old man without land or a home. He moved to Portland, Oregon, where he bought a small confectionery store with some friends. I did not see him again until he visited with me and my family in 1932 in Littlefield, Texas. He was then en route back to the Old Country, to his sister and friends. Four years later he died in his native town of Rashayya, Syria.

I had now spent the month of September with Uncle Ollie. The weather was changing to cold and cloudy. My hand was well (at least as well as it ever got). To this day I cannot move that finger, for the muscle is still hurt from the bullet. It had been a marvelous visit with my kinsman, but I was now ready to get back to work peddling on the road.

When I told Uncle Ollie I would be leaving, he begged me to stay through Christmas, but my mind was made up. He took me into Morristown, where I bought a ticket to a small town on the Missouri River where I had heard one could cross the river on a ferry boat. I wanted to do this and see what riding on a ferry was like.

At the depot I said good-bye to Uncle Ollie, and he gave me an

Old Country kissing—first on the right cheek, then on the left, then on the right again. Then I got on the train.

When the train reached the small town on the Missouri River, I took a room and spent the night there. The next morning I took the ferry across the river.

The fee was fifty cents, and the ferry was packed with cars, wagons, trucks, horses, cows, and people. It took the ferry twenty minutes to cross the river to the other side. I found it very interesting.

6

Oklahoma Oil Towns

. . .

WHEN WE LANDED ON THE EAST BANK OF THE RIVER, I FELT I was in another world, for this was a well-settled area with large, white farm houses, red barns, windmills, hog pens, and chicken houses. I could not resist the temptation to break up my journey and do some peddling, though now I had to do it on foot as I had when I had first come to the United States. Just working out of the suitcases on my shoulders, I did a very good business for two days. Then I bought myself a ticket to Fort Morgan, for I very much wanted my horse and buggy again.

It was very good to see my horse again, and we set out working at once. I did an unusually good business for several weeks as I peddled my way back to Dodge City, but as good as my business was, I kept wishing I owned a nice dry goods store and led a more settled life.

One Sunday afternoon in Dodge City I went to the Harvey House for some coffee, and while I was there three men at the next table were talking about the oil boom in Drumright, Oklahoma.[1] I listened intently as one of the men said that he would like to go into business in Drumright but that he could not get a location there. Another said the oil companies were building camps for their employees and their families. He also said the town was full of sporting women and that day and night the streets of Drumright were filled with people. When people could not find a room, they lived in tents.

As I listened to these men talk, I thought I should go and see for myself this oil boomtown of Drumright, Oklahoma. So the following morning I began peddling my way south toward the Oklahoma line. Everywhere I stopped I heard people talk about the oil boom in Drumright. Newspapers carried stories about the activities there. Once, in a boarding house, the landlady told me that she had heard that there were many killings in Drumright, Oklahoma. She had known several men who had gone there to work but had returned in a short time because they had feared they would be killed there. I knew how these men felt, for I did not want to be killed in Drumright, Oklahoma, either.

But even so, I could not resist the temptation, so I stored my trunks, made arrangements for my horse to be cared for at the wagon yard, then took a train for Drumright, Oklahoma.

When I got off the train and walked around Drumright, I could hardly believe my eyes. The streets were unpaved, and the mud was axle deep on the wagons moving the heavy equipment out to the oil fields. Cars were bumper to bumper, and people were so thick on the sidewalks that one could hardly walk. There was an air of activity and excitement I liked. As I walked about I was surprised to see that, of the twelve dry goods stores in the town, nine were owned by Syrians and that one furniture store and several grocery stores also had Syrian names.[2] One very nice boarding house served only Syrian food. Needless to say I moved into this boarding house.[3]

My good friend Charlie Cabool (now in Lubbock, Texas) and his uncle Casey Cabool (now in Levelland, Texas) had a pool hall in Drumright, and I was very glad to see them. I was also glad to find that my friend Charlie Amer was also living in Drumright, even in the same boarding house I was in.

Charlie Amer told me that he knew of a confectionery store that could be bought for $1,200, and he suggested that we go partners and buy it. We considered this for several days, then bought the store—$600 each. I had to go back to the sad task of selling my horse and buggy, but when I had done this I returned to Drumright. We took over the store, but I soon realized that although we did a fair business, there was not enough money for two men. An ice cream cone sold for five cents, ice cream sundaes, twenty cents, banana splits, fifteen cents. The volume of business was big, but at the end of the days we would check up with perhaps thirty-five dollars, and some days forty-five dollars. Our biggest day was fifty dollars. The hours were long, working from early morning until midnight and often until 1 a.m. So when a man came along with the big idea that any business could make money and offered to buy my half of the store, I agreed. I did not make any money on this deal, but at least I got my money back and was free to do something else.

I loafed around Drumright for the next three weeks. Finally I decided to go to work in the oil fields until I decided what to do next. I got a job on a crew, which cleaned out the big oil tanks, and although it was dirty, nasty work, it was not really hard. But it was hot in the summer and cold in the winter. My first wages were three dollars a day; then I was increased to four dollars. This was a pretty good salary in those days, and I managed to save money.

Like all oil boomtowns, Drumright was rough and rowdy. Drifters from all over the country landed there, and gambling houses and sporting houses were open for business day and night. Murderers and robbers were also doing good business, for there were killings and robberies every day. Of all the killings that took place while I was in Drumright, Oklahoma, the one that stands out in my mind was between Syrian people. Two Syrian men married

Syrian sisters, and family trouble began at once. A shooting affair began between the men. When one of the wives tried to step between them, she was killed by a flying bullet. Poor lady. The case was tried but then went to a higher court, and I never heard the outcome of it.[4]

I continued working in the oil field tanks for several months, but I was not satisfied with this kind of work. It was now 1917. I knew that I wanted to go into the dry goods business for myself. But then I heard of another confectionery store that was in a good location, across the street from a dance hall, and was for sale. I talked to the owner who said he would sell the place for $1,800. I offered him $900, and he laughed at me, so we settled on a price of $1,200.

The morning I opened my business, I put on a clean apron, washed all the windows inside and out, polished the mirrors, tables, and counter, and scalded all the dishes. When the fruit salesman came in to take my order, he was astonished at the nice appearance of the place. Each time I was not waiting on a customer, I would take a cloth and polish the apples until they shone.

I did a nice business, but the sales were all small. No matter how hard I worked I could only run forty to fifty dollars a day. Often when I bought a stalk of bananas and did not sell them quickly, they would spoil, and there went my profit. The same with apples, oranges, and grapes. I soon realized that being in the confectionary store business was not what I wanted, and that I could do better for myself in the dry goods store business.

But I stayed in that line of business for over a year. Then one day I was notified to register at the draft board in Sapulpa, Oklahoma.[5] Thirty days later I was notified that my number would soon be called. Now I knew for sure that I must get out from under my business. A buyer came forward and offered me eight hundred dollars cash for the confectionery store, and I sold it to him. I had not gotten my investment back, but I was so glad to be out of the confectionery store business that I did not much care.

On November 11, 1918, the Armistice was signed. When the news flashed over the telephone poles that Germany had surrendered to the Allies, the people in Drumright, Oklahoma, went wild over the good news. Church bells rang; fire sirens blew. Drivers honked the horns of their cars and tied tin cans behind them. People made dummies of Kaiser [Wilhelm] and dragged them up and down the streets of Drumright, Oklahoma, as they sang, "I'm going to Germany, and I won't be back till I make Kaiser [Wilhelm] pull the jack." Schools were dismissed, and businesses closed for the day. I heard no more from the draft board.[6]

I would like at this point to pay tribute to one of the greatest men the Middle East has ever known, Thomas Edward Lawrence, better known to us as Lawrence of Arabia.

At the beginning of World War I, he was sent by his British government to the state of Hajas in Saudi Arabia to assist Prince Feisal and Prince Abdulla to train the Arabs to revolt against the Turks. In this part of the world there are many wandering desert tribes known as Bedouins.[7] They closely resemble American Indians here in the United States.

These Bedouins live in black tents made of goat hair, and they raise sheep, goats, and camels. They are known for their fierce fighting and for drinking coffee from small cups, so day and night their strong coffee is brewing over their campfires. It is a known fact that none of these wandering people have ever slept under a roof, with the exception of the tents, which protect them from the cold nights and the blinding sandstorms. All through history there has been much trouble between these Bedouin tribes over grazing rights, water holes, and stray animals. They struck at each other without warning.

The camel, which is called the "Ship of the Desert," is due a lot of credit for the survival of these Bedouin people. Later in this writing I will tell you of our day of fun and excitement when my wife and I rode camels from the Pyramids to the Sphinx while we were in Egypt.

T. E. Lawrence lived as these Bedouins lived. He dressed as they dressed, in long flowing robes with a turban wrapped around his head. He soon learned to eat his food with his fingers without the help of forks and spoons, and above all he learned their difficult language. His sympathy was with these Bedouin people, who were oppressed by the Turks.

In a few months Lawrence had talked to all the sheiks of the Bedouin tribes. After giving them gold from the British government and promising them freedom from the sultan of Turkey, he persuaded them to make peace with each other. Each Sheik promised there would be no more bloodshed among themselves. The gold had bought the friendship of the Bedouins for the British.

Several thousand Bedouins rallied to the call of Lawrence of Arabia. They brought their own camels, and they proved to be tough fighters. They understood the changing weather conditions, and they knew the desert like the back of their hands. Lawrence also assigned some of his men to act as spies, so he always knew the weakest spot of the Turkish army. It was there he always struck. Day and night his raids came, always when they were least expected, and always they were successful.

Then the British sent a fleet to Palestine and began pushing the Turks back to Damascus. Faced with the British and Lawrence's Bedouins against them, the Turks said to heck with it and surrendered. Lawrence entered Damascus in triumph.[8]

All during the fierce fighting Lawrence had the funny feeling that something was going on behind his back, but he could not pinpoint what was taking place. He was suspicious that the British government might double-cross the Arabs.

Then after the war, Lawrence found out that his government had agreed to give Syria and Lebanon to France. At this he went into a wild and angry rage, and he shouted, "These people have fought like lions for their freedom, and now they have been betrayed and double-crossed and lied to by the British government!"[9]

But there was not a thing in the world he could do about it, for soon a French army had moved into Damascus. The people had managed to throw off their Turkish rulers only to find the French over them.

T. E. Lawrence was killed in a motorcycle accident in England in 1935. Had he lived until 1946, he would have seen the fulfillment of his dreams when the French army was finally withdrawn, and Syria and Lebanon became independent nations.[10]

To the Arab people Lawrence is "the "Uncrowned King of Arabia."

Now back to my story.

I stayed in Drumright, Oklahoma, until after the Christmas holidays. During this time I looked for a nice horse and buggy, for I intended to get back on the road peddling. It was no problem to buy a buggy, but it was difficult to find a nice buggy-broken horse. Cars and trucks had taken over the job of the horse. Finally I found a horse that fitted my requirements. I purchased him and bought a brand new buggy. I really felt at home with my own nice horse and buggy and a good supply of merchandise to sell again.

In January of 1919 I started peddling toward western Kansas and eastern Colorado, and my business was good. For some reason or other I had always done good business in these states but had never done any good in Oklahoma, either on the road or in business for myself. So I was glad to leave Oklahoma behind me and be back in Kansas and Colorado. After eight months I started south toward Texas, where I spent the winter [of 1919–20] around Temple, Waco, and Austin, where my business was good. Then in the spring I moved back into western Kansas and eastern Colorado.

This became an annual circle for me, and I worked this way for two years.

But in the third year [1921] I began hearing that a new oil field was opening up fifteen miles from Tonkawa, Oklahoma.[11] I decided to go there. When I arrived in Tonkawa, I was sure surprised to see all the activity in the place. Warehouses were going up. Oil companies were building camps for their employees, and stacks of oil field and pipeline equipment stood taller than the buildings. But I had heard that there was even more activity in Three Sands, a town which had sprung up fifteen miles to the south in the very center of the new oil field.[12]

I drove over to Three Sands and was astonished to see blocks of new frame buildings going up. I found that three Syrian men I had known in Drumright had opened up dry goods stores there. Two of these men were married, and I had hardly known them. The third, Moses Swaydan, a single man, I had known much better and liked very much.[13] One Jewish man had opened a dry goods store and moved his family to the new town of Three Sands. Cafes, drug stores, grocery stores, rooming houses, hotels, sporting houses, and bootleggers by the score were open for business.

But a room was not to be had for love nor money, so I had to drive back to Tonkawa to find one in a boarding house.

Each day I drove back and forth between Tonkawa and Three Sands, a distance of thirty miles round trip. I did very good business, but I spent so much time traveling—over four hours each way—that I had little time left to work. Each day when I returned to Tonkawa I was covered with dirt, for the traffic was heavy on the sandy and dusty unpaved road, and my poor horse was given out from this long trip.

Finally I found a room in a hotel in Three Sands, and I thought my problem was solved. But it wasn't. The room was clean enough, but it was not a suitable place for a decent man to live. There were six prostitutes making dates with men at all hours of the day and night, and there was much drinking, fighting, and commotion. It was dangerous to be in such a place, for one might be robbed or killed. All night long men tromped up and down the halls slamming doors and talking loudly, and drunken women sang at the top of their voices. I did not sleep a wink all night, and when early morning came, I left the room and felt lucky I had gotten out alive.

I then came upon the idea of trying to find a room in one of the farmhouses around Three Sands. At the first farmhouse I stopped at an old gentlemen told me that all their rooms were rented to oil field workers. Then he told me that I had better begin looking for another horse, for he said no horse could stand up for long under the hard driving I was doing. He told me that when horses get hot and tired and sweaty, they can suddenly drop dead without the driver even knowing they are sick. Now I had another big worry. I left the farm and went to other farms looking for a room. Always I got the same reply, "We have rooms for rent, but they are all rented."

Feeling very disgusted, I finally went to see my Syrian friend Moses Swaydan, the single man who lived in the back of his dry goods store. In fact most of the merchants in Three Sands lived in the back of their stores, even those with families, for few residences had been built. Also, living in the back of the store gave the merchant a certain protection against fire and robbery. This place was just like all other oil field boomtowns—robberies, killings, and stealings day and night.

Mr. Swaydan saw at once that something was wrong and asked if I was sick. I told him I was not ill but I was worried and disgusted, for I could not find a place to live. I said that driving to and from Tonkawa each day gave me too little time to work and that the farmer had said my horse might drop dead on the road. I also told him about the terrible night I had spent in the hotel and that I was afraid to stay there for fear someone would knock me in the head.

Mr. Swaydan told me that he had an extra three-quarter bed in the back of his store, and that he had thought of asking me to stay there but was afraid I would not want to sleep there. I told him I could not be too choosy where I lived, and he said I could move in any time I liked. I tried to give him some money for rent, but he refused. He did say that if I quit peddling early on Saturday, I could help him in the store if I wanted to. He also told me he stayed open on Sunday, and I could help him on that day too if I wanted to. I quickly agreed and told him it was very nice of him to offer me a place to sleep.

Mr. Swaydan told me that the lot his building stood on was very long and that I was welcome to park my horse and buggy in the back. Then he very politely showed me where he kept his shovel, so I could clean up under my horse each morning.

I moved my merchandise into the room, and on Saturday afternoon and Sunday I worked in Mr. Swaydan's store. I liked working in the store very much, and it strengthened my determination to someday go into the dry goods business for myself. But early each Monday morning I started out peddling.

This was the best arrangement I had ever known, for I did not have to drive far between customers. I worked the farms and the oil field camps and rooming houses. I called on many people each day, and I always sold them merchandise. My business was good, and I was making money again. I can truthfully say that this is the only time I ever made money in Oklahoma.

Toughs, gamblers, bootleggers, sporting women, and just drifters continued to come in droves to the new town of Three Sands. However, people with good reputations located in the town also, and everyone in business seemed to be doing good.

In time the town hired a new policeman by the name of John.[14] He carried two guns on his hips, and soon he was called "Two Gun Johnny." In fact, that was the only name I ever knew him by. Every time he passed down the street, the people would say, "Here comes Two Gun Johnny."

Two Gun Johnny tried to enforce the law. When he saw a man loafing on the street, he would approach the man and ask him his name and where he was working. The reason for this was that Two Gun Johnny seemed to think that all the crime and commotion in Three Sands was caused by people who were not working.

One day as I stood out in front of Mr. Swaydan's store watching the people go by, Two Gun Johnny stopped. "Young man," he said, "what is your name and where are you working?" When I told him I was a peddler of merchandise working on the road, he asked if I had anyone who could vouch for me. I told him that Mr. Swaydan, the owner of the store, would tell him I was telling the truth and that I worked on the road during the week and in the store on Saturday afternoons and Sundays. Then Two Gun Johnny went inside the store, and Mr. Swaydan assured him that I had told him the truth. From then on when I met Two Gun Johnny on the street, we spoke in a very friendly way.

Two Gun Johnny went to extremes in enforcing the law. Most of the time when he arrested a man for drinking or breaking the law in any way, he would beat up on him good, either with his fists or with the heavy nightclub he always carried. Then he would take the man to the justice of the peace.

Finally, the town got too tough for one man to handle alone, so a deputy was hired to work under Two Gun Johnny. Now when Two Gun Johnny arrested a man, the deputy would hold that man while Two Gun Johnny gave him a good beating up. Public sentiment began rising over the way the officers were manhandling the men they arrested. People said they were acting violently before the accused man could plead to the charges against him. Merchants said this cruel treatment of the men was hurting their business.

About this time Two Gun Johnny moved his mother to Three Sands to live. She was an old woman, and when he settled her in one of the rowdy rooming houses, people really began to criticize and talk about him. These places were not decent for a man to live in, to say nothing of an old woman living there.

During this period of unrest the Carter Oil Company sent a crew of fifty men to work in the field around Three Sands.[15] The head boss man of this crew was readily accepted by the merchants of the town. They invited him to their homes for supper, and he was treated with respect by one and all. A man of his reputation and character was an asset to the town and merchants alike.

This new boss man of the Carter Oil Company was walking down the street one morning when he came face to face with Two Gun Johnny. Two Gun Johnny stopped him and accused him of being drunk. The man told the officer that he had not been drinking, but Two Gun Johnny told him in a loud voice that he could smell liquor on his breath.

A heated argument began, and the boss man of the Carter Oil Company told Two Gun Johnny that he was not a bum and that he had fifty men working under him in the oil field around Three Sands. He held out both his hands to Two Gun Johnny and told him to take a good look at the rings he was wearing. On one hand was a ring of a thirty-second-degree Mason, and on the other hand was the ring of a Shriner.[16]

But Two Gun Johnny said he did not give a damn about the rings or the Masonic Lodge which they represented.

I did not witness this incident, but when I returned to town after peddling all day, everyone was talking about the good beating Two Gun Johnny had given the head boss man of the Carter Oil Company before taking him to the justice of the peace. Later in the day I saw this man on the street, and I hardly recognized him. His face was badly beaten. His eyes were blackened and almost swollen shut, and his lips and face were swollen and badly bruised.

For the next two or three weeks the head boss man of the Carter Oil Company walked the streets of Three Sands in a daze. He did not speak to anyone when he met them or passed them. In fact, he did not look like the same man who had come to Three Sands a short time ago. Something was bothering him, and he looked very worried. I could tell he had something very serious on his mind.

One Saturday afternoon when I came in from my work peddling, I unhitched my horse, tied him to the back of the buggy, and gave him food and water. Then I took my merchandise into the back of the store. It had been a busy morning, and I was tired and hungry. I looked into the store, and it was crowded with customers. Instead of stopping to clean myself up, I went into the store and began waiting on customers. About 2:15 p.m. the customers began thinning out in the store, and I told Mr. Swaydan that during this lull I would go eat my lunch. The happenings of that long ago day stand out as clear in my mind as if it were only yesterday.

I went to the back of the store and washed my hands and face and put on a clean shirt. Then I went to a café three doors down from the store. It was a small café but the best Three Sands had to offer. This café had counter stools and five tables. I sat at the fifth table next to the kitchen door. When the waitress came to my table, I ordered steak and French fries. In those days an order of steak and French fries sold for about forty cents.

While I was waiting for my dinner, Two Gun Johnny and his deputy came into the café and sat at the counter stools. They were drinking coffee and talking and laughing.

Then the waitress brought out my dinner. When I had eaten about four bites of the delicious steak, I saw the head boss man of the Carter Oil Company come into the café. He had his hands in his pockets, and the look on his face was horrible. He walked up behind Two Gun Johnny and exchanged a few brief words with him.

Then he pulled out his revolver and began shooting, changing his gun from Two Gun Johnny to the deputy.

When the shooting was over, both men were on the floor just as dead as they could be. Two Gun Johnny's body had fallen four or five feet from my table and was covered with blood. In fact, there was blood all over the place.

In a matter of minutes the café was crowded with people who had heard the shots and had decided to come in and see what in the world all the commotion was about.

Some men picked up the two dead bodies and carried them outside, and soon the crowd of curious dispersed.

I was too terrified to move from my table. Hungry as I was, I could not eat after all this excitement. The waitress came to my table and asked if the steak was not good and why I had not eaten.

I told her I had lost my appetite. Something seemed to have happened to my stomach.

She asked if I was scared.

I told her I was not scared, but I just wasn't as hungry as when I ordered the steak and French fries. This was the first and last time I ever left uneaten steak on my plate, for steak was then and always will be my favorite food.

The head boss man who had done all the shooting walked to the justice of the peace and gave himself up and admitted the killing. The officers then took him to the County Seat at Tonkawa and placed him under a one-hundred-thousand-dollar bond. He put in a long distance telephone call to the main office of the Carter Oil Company in Tulsa, Oklahoma, and explained what he had done. The Carter Oil Company said okay and made his one-hundred-thousand-dollar bail, and the man was released. The next morning he was back on the job in the oil field.

Four or five weeks later the trial came to court in Tonkawa. It was a very short trial. Men testified in court how they had taken good beatings from Two Gun Johnny, and merchants testified how this had been bad for their business and how before the killings they had tried to circulate a petition to get Two Gun Johnny fired.

The jury decided it was a murder but a justified one. The head boss man of the Carter Oil Company was cleared of all charges.[17]

Later we heard that the Carter Oil Company was actually the Humble Oil Company. It had been outlawed in Oklahoma because of a disagreement with the state but was now doing business under that name, which I guess was okay.

Three Sands continued to boom. New people and new businesses located there. Then the people began to talk that the town had too many sporting women settling down there. They said these women were diseased and were going to ruin the health of too many young men. In those days when a man was exposed to this dangerous disease, there was not much cure known for the disease.[18]

Talk and gossip went on for a long time about what could happen to the young men of Three Sands, but no positive steps were taken to prevent these sporting women from settling down in town with their disease.

Do not let me leave the impression that all the women in Three Sands were indecent. Many nice girls worked in the different stores and cafes, and many married women worked shifts while their husbands worked in the oil fields.

Then one day out of a clear blue sky something happened in Three Sands that I had never seen or heard of before. Nor has anyone I have ever talked to heard of anything like this thing that happened.

One day a bus loaded with officers and three doctors came to Three Sands. I am not quite sure where they came from, but we understood they were sent out to Three Sands from the state capital, Oklahoma City. The bus stopped, and the officers scattered out all over the town. First they went to all the rooming houses and hotels and took all the women to the doctors for an examination. Then they rounded up every working girl in town for the same examination. Some of the husbands of these women objected to this invasion of their wives and threatened to sue the State of Oklahoma.

The officers did not pay any attention to the threats and continued rounding up the women until every woman in Three Sands either had a clean bill of health or was placed under medication. No lawsuits were ever filed.

There were only three women in Three Sands who escaped this embarrassing episode. They were the wives of the two Syrian merchants and the wife of the Jewish merchant. These women were not bothered in any way.

For days Oklahoma newspapers carried articles about this raid. It was the most talked about event of the year.[19]

7

Storefronts in Texas

· · ·

I STAYED IN AND AROUND THREE SANDS FOR CLOSE TO TWO years [1922–23], but then the oil boom began slowing down. People were leaving the field, and boarding and rooming houses were moving out. There was excitement over a new oil boom in Corsicana, Texas. When many oil companies began moving their men and drilling equipment to that new field, I decided to follow the crowd.

Once again I began peddling my way toward Texas. I had been in Corsicana many times in my travels, and I knew that there was an abundance of dry goods stores there. But if the oil boom ran true to form, other towns would open up in the fields. Usually a farsighted promoter with an eye for making a quick dollar would buy up acreage in open country, mark off streets, stake off business lots, call it a town, give it a name, and trust to luck that he would sell these lots to someone who was looking for a place to locate.

I decided that if I found such a town that looked promising, I would go into the dry goods business for myself and get in on the ground floor of the town. This was what I had always wanted to do, and perhaps this would be the right opportunity.

SALOON, CABIN, AND STEERAGE ALIENS MUST BE COMPLETELY MANIFESTED.

LIST OR MANIFEST OF ALIEN PASSENGERS FOR THE UNITED

Required by the regulations of the Secretary of Commerce and Labor of the United States, under Act of Congress approved February 20, 1907, to be delivered

S. S. "NIAGARA" sailing from HAVRE JUN -7 1913 19

Ed Aryain's great-grandson Jordan Robins visited Ellis Island in July 2005 and obtained this copy of the manifest of his great-grandfather's ship, the Niagara. Mohamed Aryen [sic] is No. 30 at the bottom of the page.

Ed worked in the oil boomtown of Drumright, Oklahoma, in 1917 and 1918. This is a scene of Drumright's main thoroughfare from about 1915 to 1917. Photo courtesy of Eileene Russell Huff Collection, Drumright, Oklahoma.

High school graduation photo of Etta Elizabeth Stone of Marshfield, Missouri.
After attending business school in Missouri and working for a short while, Etta
traveled to Texas and married Ed when she was twenty-two years old.

This photograph probably was taken in Lamesa shortly before Etta and Ed got married. From left to right on the running board are friends Fays Fandy, Etta Stone, Ed Aryain, Luma Hameed, and Sam Hameed.

Interior scene of The Fair Store in Littlefield, Texas, in approximately 1927, with Etta and Ed Aryain behind the counter.

The Fair Store ads from the 1920s: (a) Lamb County Leader, *September 2, 1926;*
(b) Lamb County Leader, *March 17, 1927; (c)* Lamb County Leader, *March 28, 1929.*
Photos courtesy of the Southwest Collection, Texas Tech University, Lubbock, Texas.

Dressed up Jameil and Eddie Aryain (left to right) in Brownfield, Texas, 1937.

Ed Aryain with sons Jameil (left) and Eddie in 1937 in Brownfield, Texas.

Ed Aryain's U.S. naturalization document no. 4482648, dated May 16, 1939.

Scene from town square, Seminole, Texas, in the early 1940s with Aryain's Dry Goods Co. in the center of the block at 110 South Main Street. Photo courtesy of Seminole Chamber of Commerce.

Etta and Ed Aryain (seated) with Eddie and Jameil, about 1948.

Etta and Ed Aryain, 1948.

*Eddie Aryain, Patricia Denton,
Jameil Aryain (standing), and
Ed Aryain, 1949.*

Etta Stone Aryain's family came to Seminole for the occasion of Jameil Aryain's marriage to Pat Denton on October 22, 1950. From left, Willie (Etta's sister) and her husband, Oscar Carter; Burnice (Etta's sister-in-law) and Etta's brother, Ancell Stone. Etta and Ed Aryain are on the far right.

A proud Ed Aryain and his wife, Etta, attended their son Jameil's graduation from Southern Methodist University in Dallas in August 1951.

These three youngsters are the only grandchildren of Ed and Etta Aryain, children of Jameil and Pat Aryain. They are Linda, age four and one-half, and Amy, age two and one-half, from 1955. Dwight "Chip" Aryain, was four years old in his photo from 1968.

DOLLAR DAYS

LADIES' NYLON HOSE—Two beautiful
   Fall colors, all sizes, reg. 89c, DOLLAR DAY 77c
TWO PAIR $1.50

LADIES STRETCH HOSE—A regular $1.29 Value
DOLLAR DAY – PAIR $1.00

EXTRA SPECIAL

LADIES' JEWELED SWEATERS & CREST SWEATERS
   Beautiful Jeweled and Crest Sweaters in Wool
   and Orlon in an assortment of colors
DOLLAR DAY ONLY $5.77

MENS JACKETS AND COATS
   Values to $15.95, broken lots, A real value
DOLLAR DAY $6.98

MEN'S CORDUROY JACKETS
   Knit Collar, cuffs and buttons. A regular $4.98
Value—CLOSE OUT $3.49

CORDUROY
   Ten beautiul colors. Guaranteed Washable
DOLLAR DAY ONLY 98c

LADIES' SWEATERS
   One group of Slip-Over Sweaters in an assortment
   .of colors and patterns. Values to $3.49
DOLLAR DAY $1.98

MEN'S NYLON STRETCH SOX
TWO PAIR FOR $1.00

ARYAIN'S DRY GOODS

"QUALITY ABOVE PRICE"

This is a typical business ad for Aryain's Dry Goods in the local newspaper the Seminole Sentinel, *October 6, 1955. Ed had turned the store over to his son Jameil to manage in 1952. Photo courtesy of the* Seminole (TX) Sentinel.

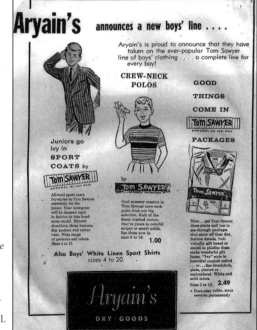

Aryain's announced that it would carry a new boys line of clothing on March 27, 1958. The advertisement appeared in the Seminole Sentinel. *Photo courtesy of the* Seminole (TX) Sentinel.

The day before they left on their four-month-long trip to Syria and the Middle East, March 7, 1961, friends gave Etta and Ed Aryain a going away party, where this snapshot was made.

Ed and Etta saw the Dome of the Rock, also called the Mosque of Omar, when they visited in Jerusalem during their 1961 trip to Ed's homeland. The dome received a gold covering after they saw it. From a postcard by Rex Studio Garbis Smerdjian, Old City, Jerusalem.

Ruins of the interior of the Temple of Bacchus at Baalbek in the valley of Lebanon. From a postcard by Bab Edriss, Souk Seyour, Beirut.

Toward the end of their Middle East trip, Ed and Etta Aryain spent a few days in Egypt and posed on camels in front of the pyramids and Sphinx.

This interior shot of Aryain's Dry Goods at 110 South Main Street in Seminole was made after the store was remodeled in approximately 1970.

I peddled my way south for eight days until I was seventy miles from the Texas state line. Then I stopped at a farmhouse where a man told me he did not need my merchandise but that he would buy my horse and buggy. I told him I needed my horse and buggy for my work, but even as I said this I realized that if I went into the dry goods business for myself I would have to get rid of them anyway. So I agreed.

My heart was saddened at leaving my horse in the barnyard, for he had been my companion for several years.

I took the first train for Corsicana, and when I got there I found a nice room. The next morning I began looking around. Corsicana had plenty of dry goods stores, so I talked to people and heard talk that three new towns were opening up in the oil fields—Tucker Town, Whitney, and Navarro.[1] I took a jitney to Tucker Town and then to Whitney, but I did not much like what I saw there. Then I went to Navarro.

Navarro was eighteen miles from Corsicana and had been only a crossroads town with a post office, one general store, and a few shack houses before the oil drilling began. A real estate man had bought some acreage and begun dividing it into business lots. But now several new buildings were under construction. I talked to some people and heard that the general store was owned by two old bachelor brothers who had operated the store all their lives. I also talked to the real estate man, and he told me that Navarro now had a population of about seven hundred people and was going to develop into a good business town. I was in no hurry to make up my mind.

I returned the next day and went into the general store to see what line of goods they carried. I told the owner I needed a new handkerchief. Then after making this purchase I had an excuse to look around the store. The stock of goods consisted of groceries, hardware, and dry goods. I could tell at once that it was a very old timey store and did not smell very good. The merchandise was not straightened, and it looked as if a month's collection of dust was on the stock.

One thing that caught my attention was a table of ladies' millinery. In those days a woman was not properly dressed if she did not wear a hat when she went out, so all stores carried ladies' hats. Next to the millinery table in this store was a table of salt pork slabs. When I saw this, I laughed to myself, feeling certain that if I went into business here in Navarro, these merchants would be no competition. I had in mind to stock my store with better and very up-to-date merchandise and to display it properly and keep the dust cleaned off of it.

That night I made up my mind, and the next morning I went back to the real estate man and bought the best lot in Navarro for six hundred dollars. It was 25x140 feet in size, and I paid cash rather than make a down payment so I would be clear of debt when I began my building. This was in the late summer of 1923.

By this time buildings were being completed, and new businesses were opening up every day in Navarro. There were two contractors, each with a crew of five or six carpenters, in the town.

I went to one of these contractors, and he took me into a drug store for a Coke. I told him I wanted him to figure me the cost of a frame store building 25x80 feet, complete with nice display front windows, an outside toilet, and a water hydrant at the back door of the store. I also wanted a partition in the back of my building so I could have my living quarters in my store. I also told him that I would have the building figured by the other contractor in Navarro and also by one in Corsicana and that his figure would be a standing bid. He said that was fair enough and that I should certainly look for the best deal. Then he drew me a picture of how he would build me the windows and gave me a figure of $1,400 on a turnkey cost of the building. I thanked him and said I would talk to him again in a few days.

Then I went to the other contractor and told him what I wanted and that the first man had bid $1,400. "Young man," he said, "you better take the other man's bid, for I could not build your building for his price."

I decided not even to talk to the contractor in Corsicana but told the first man in Navarro that he could build my building. He said, "Fine," but it would be a few days before he could start to work on my building. I said, "Fine."

But in the meantime I began to get cold feet. I watched the merchants in Navarro, and they all seemed to be doing a nice business. But there was not a bank in Navarro, and so to get the business of the men who worked in the oil fields, the merchants had to cash payroll checks. This meant that a merchant had to keep a lot of cash on hand and that he had to travel eighteen miles to Corsicana at least twice a week to bank. It was this last part that worried me, because sometimes when it rained several days in succession, the unpaved road would be so bad that the jitney could not get between Navarro and Corsicana. I feared that when I went to the bank I might get stranded in Corsicana and not be able to get back to my business for a day or so. In fact, this had been a particularly rainy season in that part of the country, and cars and trucks were frequently stuck up to their axles in the deep, thick mud on the main street of Navarro.

In fact, one farmer saw his chance of a lifetime to make some quick money, and he brought his team of heavy work horses to the edge of town after every rain. Then when cars and trucks got bogged down right in the middle of the main street, he would pull them out of the mud for a dollar. People began to laugh and say, "If this rainy weather continues, that farmer will make more money here in town than he will in raising a crop."

I was so worried about leaving my business to get to and from the bank in Corsicana that I decided to delay the start of my building until I had thought this critical matter through.

In the meantime a Syrian man and his sister had opened up a

grocery store just about four doors from my lot. One day as I passed by the store the owner was standing in the door.

"Seems I have seen you somewhere," he said.

"Yes, I remember you in Drumright, Oklahoma, but we never became acquainted," I said. "Aren't you the Syrian man whose wife was killed by a flying bullet in Drumright, Oklahoma?" I asked. And he said he was the husband of that poor slain woman. He seemed grieved when I mentioned this. I asked him how the case had come out, and he said the case had been appealed to a higher court.

In those days men wore one-piece, long sleeved, long legged union suits for underwear, and this Syrian merchant was waiting on customers with his pants pulled over his underwear without a dress shirt. The pants and underwear were not very clean. I thought this was an odd way for a man to dress when he was waiting on customers. I had never seen this before.

He invited me to have a cup of coffee in their living quarters in the back of the store, and when I went in he made me acquainted with his sister Mary.

When I saw Mary, I knew I was not going to drink coffee with these people. She was a big, fat, sloppy woman. Her dress was downright dirty, and she was barefooted. I looked into their living quarters and saw that the two beds were not made and that dirty dishes covered the stove and small cabinet. I made up my mind in a hurry I did not want any coffee. Furthermore, I decided I would stay away from these people.

I loafed around Navarro for several days, not able to decide about going ahead with the building and worrying about having paid six hundred dollars for the lot I might not want to use.

One day as I was sitting on the corner sidewalk, an old-looking man sat down beside me. He introduced himself as Hassen Soub from Lebanon. He had a moustache and gray hair, which was well trimmed and combed, and he looked strong and in the best of health. Still, I could tell he was a very old man. He asked me what I was doing in Navarro. I told him I had bought a lot and had the cost of a building figured. I maybe planned to open a dry goods store but had not fully decided to do so.

Mr. Soub asked me where my lot was, and I told him we could walk over and see it. When he saw my lot, he asked me how much I had paid for it. I told him. He said he thought it was a good buy, for it was the best location in town. He was sure I would do good when I opened my store.

Then Mr. Soub told me that he was looking for a location and made the suggestion we go partners. He wanted to make a combination grocery and dry goods store. I told him I did not know anything about the grocery business and did not want to get involved in that business. But he said he knew the grocery business well, and we could build a partition though the building with a door in the middle, and he would operate the grocery side. He said this arrangement would bring both grocery customer and dry goods customer traffic into the store, which was true enough.

I told him dividing the twenty-five-foot-wide store down the middle would make it look too narrow. He said, "What the heck difference does it make? This is a brand new town, and most of the buildings are on a small scale. The other buildings are only fifty feet long, and ours will be eighty feet long. That will be the longest building Navarro has ever seen." Which was true enough.

He offered to give me three hundred dollars in cash for half interest in the lot, and then we agreed on a partnership. He drew from his pocket a big roll of money and counted out three hundred dollars. I asked, "Mr. Soub, why do you carry so much money around on you?" He replied, "I guess it's just a habit."

Later I asked him if he knew the Syrian grocery merchant and his big, fat, sloppy sister Mary. He said he barely knew them, had seen them in different boomtowns, but had never become well acquainted with them.

Some time later, after we had opened the store, I found out from different sources that Mr. Soub had lied to me. I learned that these two men had been in business together in Oklahoma before coming to Texas. I also learned that Mary was Mr. Soub's lady friend. I never could figure out what he saw in her.

I then talked to the contractor and told him I was ready to begin the building. He said, "Fine."

In less than two weeks the store building was completed. Then Mr. Soub and I had counters and shelving made for both the grocery and dry goods sides. Then we went by train to Dallas and Fort Worth to buy goods for the new store. We gave a financial statement and established our credit. Then we bought a complete line of dry goods, shoes for men, women, and children, ladies' ready-to-wear and millinery, men's work clothes, and hats. Then we had a wholesale grocery house in Corsicana stock the grocery side of our store.

Immediately after opening our doors we began doing a good business, for we had well advertised our new store. Also we cashed company checks. Twice a week I went by jitney into Corsicana to deposit the checks and bring back cash.

Each week the business grew, and I was making fast friends and customers with the oil field workers. On pay day, when the men came to buy merchandise, I would cash their checks and then take time off from the store to buy them a cup of coffee. Sometimes I would take eight or ten men to the café for coffee. I really enjoyed this, and I felt I was really doing all right. These men appreciated the favors I did for them, especially cashing their checks. Sometimes I would give them a tie or a handkerchief and would give the boss men of the crews a new hat.

More people came to Navarro and established different businesses. Two new dry goods stores opened up, one by a Syrian man, and the other by a Jewish man. But they did not have much stock and were not much competition, for I still had far and away the best dry goods stock in town.

Two sporting houses opened up across the street, and I did a real good negligee and kimono business with the women in that line of work.

Navarro was like all other oil boomtowns—killings, stealings, and robberies happened often. But the merchants were more worried because Navarro had no fire insurance, for the insurance companies would not write fire policies on frame buildings in oil boomtowns.

Business grew better all the time. Farmers around Navarro were raising good corn crops. Soon many of the farmers learned that they could make more money by converting their corn crops into corn liquor and going into the bootlegging business as a sideline. Corn liquor was easy to come by, as bootleggers worked the town and the oil fields.[2]

Another Syrian man and his American wife, Mr. and Mrs. S. F. Hameed from Springfield, Missouri, opened a nice, clean dry goods store just down the street from me.[3] They did a good business but did not hurt my business. I had not been acquainted with these people previously, but we soon became good friends.

About this time misunderstandings began arising between myself and my partner, Mr. Soub. In the beginning Mary, the big, fat, sloppy woman I mentioned before, began loafing around our store. I told Mr. Soub that I did not want her coming to our store, for she was not helping our business any. She was not clean, and she was ugly and loud-mouthed.

She kept coming regardless of my objections. Mr. Soub began talking to her in a very nasty way, telling her he did not want her to come to the store and calling her names. But it did not seem to bother Mary when Mr. Soub talked to her in this manner. She just laughed as though nothing had happened.

I decided that they were in cahoots together and that he would talk to her disrespectfully in my presence, but he did not mean a word of what he said.

Finally, I told Mr. Soub in no uncertain terms that Mary must stop coming to the store, or we would have to dissolve our partnership.

Mary did stop coming to the store when I was there, but on days when I went to Corsicana to bank, I would look out the back window of the jitney and see her going from her brother's grocery store to my store to see Mr. Soub.

Another trouble between myself and Mr. Soub was that when I was on my side of the store, I would see men going into the grocery section, but when they came out they had not bought any groceries. When I would go into that side of the store, Mr. Soub and these men would be whispering to each other. But when I approached, they ceased their conversation. I asked Mr. Soub several times what they were talking about. He said these men were just his friends and they had just come in for a little visit.

But this reply did not satisfy my curiosity. Something out of order was going on behind my back, and I could not find out what in the world it was.

Navarro did not have any police protection with the exception of one lawman who was sent from Corsicana to stay eight hours each day. When he went home at night, Navarro was without police protection. At night the drunks prowled the streets, and fights and shootings started. This lawman who came out each day was a nice, friendly fellow. Each morning he called at every place of business to inquire if everything was orderly. When he came to our store, he always spoke to me in a friendly way, and sometimes we went out for a cup of coffee. But when he went into the grocery side of the store, he hardly spoke to Mr. Soub and came right out.

One day over a cup of coffee this lawman said to me, "Ed, I know the old man in the store with you is not your father, for you do not have the same name." This took me by surprise, and I told him that Mr. Soub was indeed not my father, only a business partner. Then I told him the story of how we had formed our partnership because I could not operate my business by myself and go back and forth to Corsicana to the bank and that Mr. Soub was a total stranger to me until the day we formed our partnership.

The lawman then said to me, "Ed, I hate to tell you this, but the law has a record as long as my arm on that old man. Everything from bootlegging and gambling to operating a house of prostitution."

He went on to tell me that when he had been in the house of prostitution business some woman was in partnership with him.

I asked who the woman was, but he said he did not know.

"I'll bet it was Mary, the big, fat, sloppy woman in the grocery store with her brother," I said.

Then the officer said again that Mr. Soub had a record of bootlegging, and I told him I had been suspicious about this, for I had seen men go in and not buy groceries. The lawman said that when he came back the next day, he would bring another officer with him and a search warrant. They would make a thorough investigation.

I asked the officer to please not do this, for it would hurt my business. I said that tomorrow I would send Mr. Soub to Corsicana to the bank, and while he was gone, I would search the place.

On the following morning after Mr. Soub left for Corsicana, I went through his trunks and suitcases. I also went through the pockets of his clothes. I looked under the counters and in packing cases, but I found no evidence of corn liquor.

About this time I had heard tell that some bootleggers buried the bottles of corn whiskey close to their outdoor toilet. In fact, I had had some experience in this line, for only a few days before as I sat resting outside my store late in the evening a driller I had known for some time came by and asked me if I would like to take a little ride with him and see some friends who lived two miles from town. "Sure," I said.

When we arrived at a small farmhouse, the man and woman

living there seemed pleased to see the driller. But when he made me acquainted with these people, I could tell they were suspicious of me. After a few minutes of visiting, the driller told the man he needed a quart of his good corn whiskey. The couple looked at me, then at the driller.

"Ed here is a friend of mine," the driller said. "He would not report on you." He also told them I was in business for myself in Navarro. The woman said she recognized me and had traded in my store. I told her I was glad to have her business.

The man took a shovel, and the four of us walked to within four feet of their outdoor toilet. He dug a shallow hole and brought up a bottle of corn whiskey. He washed off the bottle and dried it and handed it to the driller. The driller told me on our way home that he had a credit rating with these people and paid his liquor bill once a month. I thought this was all very interesting.

Remembering this, I went out behind the store to see if maybe Mr. Soub had been burying bootleg whiskey near our outside toilet. But I could see no place where the ground had been dug up.

When I reported to the lawman that I had made a thorough investigation of our living quarters, store, and even out around the outside toilet but had found nothing to indicate that Mr. Soub was in the bootlegging business as a sideline, the inquiry was dropped.

Then my good friend Charlie Cabool came to Navarro looking for a location. He stayed with Mr. Soub and myself in our back of the store living quarters. When I had the chance, I told Charlie that I was having trouble with Mr. Soub and that I had wished a thousand times I had someone else rather than the old man as my partner. Charlie said to me, "I would like to buy his part of the store, for I think you and I would make suitable partners."

This pleased me very much, and soon I told Mr. Soub that we must dissolve the partnership, for I was not satisfied. I told him Charlie Cabool would buy his interest.

When the old man heard this, he flew into a rage and told Charlie, "I thought something like this was about to happen! You have slept in our bed and eaten our food, and now you are trying to put me out of business." The longer he talked, the louder he raved.

I said, "Mr. Soub, there is just no use of all this commotion. You know you and I are not getting along well as partners, and a change must be made."

Immediately, a deal was made. Charlie Cabool paid Mr. Soub the price he asked, and Charlie and I were now partners in an up and going business.

Mr. Soub packed his belongings and moved out. I did not hear of him for several years. Then someone told me had gone to Las Vegas, Nevada, and gone into business. Then he had gotten into some kind of trouble and served time in jail. Still later, I heard the old fellow had gone back to the Old Country and died soon after.

Charlie and I closed out the grocery side of the store and made it into a more complete dry goods store. Our business grew by leaps and bounds. With a partner I liked, I felt that my long dream of being in the dry goods business had finally come true.

Then one day out of a clear blue sky Charlie came up with the idea that we buy a partnership Model T Ford car. I thought this was a good idea, so we went to Corsicana and purchased a brand new car. As well as I remember, we paid $450 for the car. I had never driven a car, and since Charlie had once owned a car, he taught me to drive.

About two months later we heard the sad news that the oil field town of Tucker Town had been destroyed by fire and that the two Syrian merchants there had lost everything they had. They had no insurance, and it is doubtful if they had any extra cash. After this fire in the neighboring town, the merchants of Navarro really became worried and frightened. Such a catastrophe as this could happen to us.

My friend Sam Hameed (now we were such good friends we used given names—Sam, Luma, Charlie, and Ed) mentioned to me that we should go looking for another location away from the oil fields and settle in a more substantial town. We had heard the talk that all West Texas was growing. It was good farming land. The small towns there were growing, and new towns were being established. When I talked to Charlie about this, he agreed we should see about making a move and suggested that I go with Sam and he would stay in the store.

The next morning Sam and I took the bus to San Angelo, Texas, for we had heard of a new oil development in Big Lake, which was seventy miles away.[4] Big Lake had been a good ranch town. Now with the oil field starting, it promised to be a good business town. We liked the looks of Big Lake, for all the merchants were busy. But the best thing about it was that all the buildings were of brick or tile. We learned that we could buy fire insurance, for Big Lake had a volunteer fire department. But we could not find a building to rent. Since lots were selling for five thousand dollars, we knew we could not afford to build.

Sam suggested that we go to Lamesa, Texas, out in far West Texas.[5] But then we heard of a new town called Best, which was just getting started.[6] I told Sam we should go see this place while we were so close. Sam wasn't too crazy about this trip, but we finally decided to take a jitney and go there for one day.

When we arrived in Best, all we could see was a real estate office. The promoter had bought three hundred acres of land and was dividing it into lots. He was selling the business lots for three hundred dollars each, and he began talking big about what an ideal place this was for a town and how Best was going to grow. I suggested to Sam that we buy a lot together, but he flatly refused, saying he was not looking for an oil field location, for that was what he was trying to get away from.

I decided, however, that I would make a twenty-five dollar down payment on a lot with the understanding that if the town grew, I would pay the balance. I thought this might be a good investment. I had lost money before, and this twenty-five dollars would not break me.

Leaving Best, we went to Lamesa, Texas, which we found to be a well-established little town. I liked the looks and the feel of this part of West Texas. The plains were as flat as the palm of your hand, and the wind was always blowing, but it was good farming land. Lamesa was the county seat of Dawson County. New farmers were buying land, and all lines of businesses were locating in the town. Sam was lucky in finding a newly completed brick building, which he leased for two years. But I could not find a location. On the way back Sam teased me by saying that I did not really want to leave Navarro, for when he and Luma moved their store, Charlie and I would have all the business in the town.

Back in Navarro Sam started a close-out sale, and in a few days he and Luma were ready to pack the remaining merchandise and move to Lamesa. This was the spring of 1924.

For several months I talked to people who had been in Best, where I had made the twenty-five-dollar down payment on a lot. They always told me that the town did not develop. Thus me and another twenty-five dollars parted company.

Often I heard from Sam and Luma, who were doing a good business in Lamesa. Traveling salesmen gave me the story that cotton crops were extra good in West Texas in the fall of 1924.

But our business in Navarro was still good. In fact, it had grown better since Sam and Luma moved out. But in the back of my mind I still had the idea that after the Christmas business, I would make another trip to West Texas to look for a location.

In the early part of January 1925, Charlie Cabool made a trip to Shreveport, Louisiana, by train to try to collect some money which a man had been owing him for several years. I was left alone in the store.

After closing the store for the day, I went to our living quarters in the back and ate my evening meal. Then I sat and rested and read the paper until about eleven o'clock. Then I went to bed.

About midnight someone pounded on my door and yelled out, "Ed, get up! The town is on fire!"

I ran to the door and saw that, sure enough, flames were leaping from a building seven or eight doors up the street. I rushed back to the living quarters and put on my shoes and pants and gathered up all my other clothes and carried them out to the middle of the street. I then made another trip through the store and got Charlie's clothes. By this time our building was on fire, and I could feel the heat from the roof.

I made a third trip into the store, thinking maybe I would have time to save some of the merchandise. I went to the west side of the store to the men's department, but the heat was already too intense. I turned and rushed to the east side and grabbed up about a dozen ladies' dresses off the rack. But by this time flames were breaking through the west wall, and I knew I must get out before the roof caved in.

When morning came, I was in the middle of the street with my clothes and Charlie's and the dozen ladies' dresses, and I am not ashamed to say I cried like a baby. Everything I had worked for since coming to America had been consumed by fire in only a few minutes. I had even forgotten to try to save the new Ford, which had been parked behind the building, until after the car had caught fire and the horn began blowing.

Anyone who has not had this experience can never know the sickening sensation and the horror of a fire. When you see everything you have worked hard for years to acquire go up in smoke in minutes, it is enough to kill a man. As I looked about at the ashes of Navarro, I wished I had been inside the store when it burned. Then my troubles and struggles would have been over, and I would not have to worry about making a new start. But make a new beginning I would, so help me God.

A friend who had delivered freight and express to the merchants came to me and said, "Ed, my wife and I would like very much for you to move into our home for a few days until you know what you want to do."

I thanked him but told him sleep was impossible, so I would stay around town through the day and then move into the hotel in Corsicana.

Later when Charlie Cabool returned to Navarro, he found me still in the middle of the street. He put his arms around my shaking shoulders and tried to console me. I felt embarrassed to tell him I had even forgotten about the car and could only show him the pile of our clothes and the ladies' dresses I had brought out.

At night I lay awake and wondered where I would go and what I would do. But I knew one thing for sure: I was not going to peddle merchandise on the road again. I would make a new start in the dry goods business. Luckily the store had few outstanding debts, and the bank account was $1,500. So my part would be $750.

Sam and Luma Hameed were making a trip to Dallas to buy merchandise and to meet Luma's niece, Miss Etta E. Stone from Marshfield, Missouri, who was going to work for them in the store in Lamesa. But while they were in Dallas they heard that Navarro had burned, and they decided that after picking up Miss Etta E. Stone they would drive that night to Navarro to see Charlie and me.

Marriage had never entered my mind, but this was one time in my life when I did not have to think things over very carefully. The minute I saw this pretty young girl with brown hair, fair skin, and big brown eyes, I knew I wanted to marry Miss Etta E. Stone of Marshfield, Missouri.

8

Marriage to Etta

. . .

THE HAMEEDS AND MISS ETTA E. STONE LEFT FOR LAMESA
the following day. The next week I went to West Texas by bus,
making Lamesa my headquarters and going each week to see the
new towns, which I heard were growing.

I heard talk about the towns of Amherst, Littlefield, and Sudan,
and I took a bus to see these towns, which were in the new farming and ranching country.[1] Of these three towns I liked Littlefield
the best, for it was larger and was more centrally located and
because it had some paved streets. New buildings were going up in
Littlefield, and several real estate offices had opened up.[2]

The Yellow House Ranch, which had changed their name to
Yellow House Land Company, had put up their land for sale for
farming.[3] The company was sending buses to Oklahoma and East
and South Texas to bring farmers, on the expense of the Yellow
House Land Company, to Littlefield to buy this new land.

I was astonished to hear that the raw prairie land around
Littlefield was selling for forty dollars an acre. I thought this was
an awfully high price for unbroken raw land. How wrong I was
again. I have wished a million times since those early days that I
had bought some land at that price.

Going back to Littlefield the second time, I found a brick building for rent in the middle of the block on Main Street and, feeling
that I could get in on the ground floor and grow with the new
town, I leased it. Then I hurried back to Lamesa.

Now that I had leased a building in Littlefield and was about to
go back into business for myself, I asked Miss Etta E. Stone of
Marshfield, Missouri, to be my wife.

Two weeks later, on May 14, 1925, we were married in the
apartment of Mr. and Mrs. Sam Hameed in Lamesa, Texas.
Immediately after the ceremony, we left for the Dallas and Fort
Worth markets to buy merchandise for the new store.

Arriving in Fort Worth, we went to the Monnig Dry Goods
Wholesale Company, where Mr. [William] Monnig, the elderly
owner of this very successful firm, was known to be very under-
standing about the problems of Syrian merchants in Oklahoma,
Texas, and Louisiana. In fact, he was often called the "Daddy of
Syrian Merchants."[4]

When I introduced my bride to Mr. Monnig, he said, "Ed, I am
glad you are married, and I wish you a long happy life together."

Then we got down to business. I told him I had rented a building in Littlefield and that I had very little money after the fire in
Navarro. I wanted to go back into business for myself, and I asked
him to extend me a line of credit for $1,600. He said he could not
sell me that much on credit but that he would extend me a line of
credit for $800. I said, "Fine."

Mr. Monnig then gave me his honest advice on how we would
have to be very careful to cut our overhead in every way possible,
since we would be working on a small capital. I assured him we
would be extra careful about our expenses, for we were to have living quarters in the back of the store and do all our own work.

My bride and I spent most of the day buying the general line
of goods for the new store. Then we went back to the office to
thank Mr. Monnig for the line of credit. While we were in his
office, he said, "Ed, I am so proud to see you going back into busi-

ness after your hard luck in Navarro. You are an ambitious young man, and you will go far." I told him we were now going to Dallas to buy ladies' ready-to-wear and millinery, men's hats and work clothes, and a line of shoes and that if any of the wholesale houses called him about me, would he give me a good reference. He said, "Fine."

Arriving in Dallas, we went to the Willard Hat Company, where I knew and liked Mr. Rube [Reuben] Tobolowsky, the credit manager there.[5] When I told him I was going to locate in Littlefield, he gave me a line of credit and some more advice about watching overhead. The Graham-Brown Shoe Company gave me eight hundred dollars in credit for shoes because I had done business with them in Navarro and paid my bills.[6] Some of the ladies' ready-to-wear and millinery houses made me pay a third down on what I bought. Others gave me a line of credit.

When we reached Littlefield, I had a partition 12x25 feet built across the back of the store for our living quarters. After my wife finished furnishing it with the barest necessities, I was very proud to have a home for the first time in my life.

I had shelving built in the store, and a few days later the new merchandise began arriving. My wife and I worked together to unpack it and put it on the shelves. We found we had bought four thousand dollars in merchandise, which was a pretty good stock of goods in those days. On opening our doors, we began doing some business, nothing big but steady. I well remember the first sale I made—a pair of pants to a man for ninety-eight cents.

It did not take us long to realize that some of the citizens in Littlefield had no use for foreign-born merchants and would never set foot inside our store, even though my wife's people had been in the Civil War.

This feeling of prejudice was not directed just at me. One merchant in Littlefield named Mr. Replin, a very nice old Jewish gentleman with a fine growing family, had some remodeling done in his store. The carpenters worked three or four hours. When they were finished, Mr. Replin thought they had overcharged him and told them so.

The carpenters became very angry and began fighting the old man and beating him across the face and head. Customers in the store stood by and laughed and made no effort to break up the fight. Many of them shouted, "That old Jew is getting just what he had coming to him. He should be run out of town."[7]

It so happened that there was a Greek man, also a very old man, who had a small café in the same block. His café was known as the Hamburger King Café.[8] When this old Greek gentleman heard of the trouble in Mr. Replin's store, he ran to the dry goods store to help the poor old Jewish man out. The carpenters then turned upon the old Greek man and gave him an even more severe beating than they had given Mr. Replin. For days the poor old Greek man's face was swollen, and he was so badly beaten that he could not open his café.

For days every time I stepped out on the sidewalk, someone would say, "That damn Jew and Greek should be run out of town." And I knew they meant I should be run out of town also.

One morning when I went out for coffee, a farmer who had been a good customer and was nice and friendly to me came over and sat down beside me. Over our coffee he brought up this fight. He seemed to be deeply hurt over this ugly affair. He told me that at the time of the fight he was in his car across the street. Next to his car was a police officer sitting in another parked car. The farmer then told me, and I believe this to be true, that he asked the policeman if he was not going to stop the fight in Mr. Replin's store. The policeman told the farmer, "No. Let the carpenters beat up on them and run them out of town. Littlefield can get along just fine without any Jews and Greeks."

I knew people were saying the same things about Syrians.

For several days and nights I thought about this sad state of affairs. Why so much hate in the United States against foreign-born people? Why in America, the greatest and richest country in the world, the most civilized and the cleanest place on earth to live, with the best schools in the world and the most opportunities for men to do good for themselves? Also the religions of America puzzled me. Every town had fine churches, which is fine and good, but from the people who went to these churches there was hatred and envy of foreigners. I took notice that some foreigners were more despised than others. The people most disliked in America were Jews, Greeks, Italians, Syrians, Poles, Chinese, Japanese, and Turks. But the German, French, Belgian, Swedish, and Bohemian people did not seem to suffer as much as other foreigners did in America. Why should a great country like America hold so much hate for these immigrant people who were only asking to be allowed to make an honest living?[9]

In the early fall of 1925 cotton crops looked good, but they were late. Everyone expected a big fall business, and my store was heavily stocked in preparation.

But on October 7, 1925, a blue norther blew into the plains, and the white, almost ready-to-pick bolls of cotton were frozen stiff. Stalks fell to the ground. Everyone was ruined on that cold, windy night.

I have never seen so many heartsick people—farmers and merchants alike—for they knew there would be no income that fall. Many farmers who had used their life savings to make a down payment on this new land lost everything they had. They had gone deeply into debt and Mother Nature had played her hand against them. I personally knew men who left Littlefield flat broke, without even enough for bus fare back to their old homes.

But in spite of these conditions, my wife and I were surprised that we did a fair business. Christmas shopping helped some, but it was nothing like what we had hoped for.

In the spring of 1926, a larger building came up for rent on our block, and I quickly leased it. To avoid losing a day's business, I decided to move the stock of goods on Sunday. I hired a truck and a crew of helpers.

But just as the helpers began loading the counters and shelves, a police officer came into the store yelling, "You know this is Sunday, and I will not allow this moving today!" He began hitting me across my face and shoving me around. "You and your Syrian people are all a gang of thieves, and your father in Lubbock is the ringleader!"

I tried to tell him that my father had never been in Lubbock, or even in the United States, and that he had died in 1916.

He told me to shut my goddamned mouth and hit me across the face again. Then he put his hand on his gun, and I really believe he wanted to kill me. Every time I looked at him, he put his hand on his gun. I told him to go ahead and shoot me, for that was what he had come into the store to do.

Again he told me to shut my goddamned mouth. Then he yelled that he was taking me and my wife to the justice of the peace, and he pushed us both roughly out of the store.

He kept cursing my wife and me as he pushed us down the sidewalk the length of the town to the justice of the peace, and he kept making threatening moves toward his gun.

I paid the justice of the peace our fines. Then my wife and I went back to the store humiliated beyond words.

Now my fears were confirmed. We were not to be accepted by the people of Littlefield.

Here we were—two young people starting a business from scratch, trying to do right by our customers, living right, going to church, and cutting every possible expense to make a go of our business. Now everyone in Littlefield had heard this ugly story and was talking about us.

As many ups and downs as I had had in my life, nothing, not even the fire in Navarro, hurt me as badly as this terrible incident

because my wife was so deeply hurt and so bewildered by it. I felt
so sorry for her and so helpless to do anything about it. I felt it was
my fault she was suffering so badly and that she should never have
married me. I seemed to be a misfit, and bad luck followed closely
on my heels. I even wondered if I should have stayed in Syria and
lived the life of my forefathers.

But as hurt and embarrassed as my wife and I were, we knew
that there was nothing we could do to stop this ugly talk which was
on every tongue. So we went ahead working and tending to our
affairs.

The next week we made the move to the larger building and
tried to go on living. We bought more merchandise, and our business increased, nothing big, but we were grateful for what we did
have. During the summer cotton crops looked good. It stood knee
high and was loaded with bolls. Everyone said this was going to be
an excellent year for farmers and merchants. The cotton began to
open in late September, and the fields were soon snow white with
open bolls. I made a late trip to Dallas to buy heavy goods in expec-
tation of a big fall business.

I felt so hopeful about the good crops that I even went out and
spent five hundred dollars on a new Model T Ford. My wife and I
were both so proud of our new car.

Then on Thanksgiving Day 1926 the worst sandstorm ever to
hit West Texas swept into the plains.[10] It blew for two days and two
nights without ceasing. West Texas had always been known for its
dreadful sandstorms, but that one went down in history! One could
not see across the street. The air was so filled with sand that it sift-
ed into every house and business. Sand lay so thick across the front
of my store that I had to get a shovel and push the sand away so I
could open the door. The air was so filled with electricity that grass
fires broke out, and one of the new gins in Littlefield burned down
during the storm.

When the storm was finally over, the farmers sadly went into their fields and found that 80 percent of the cotton bolls had been blown off the stalks. What little remained was so damaged and brown and filled with sand that it was hardly worth picking and sending to market.

So here we were again—after two years of crop failures, we were no better off than when we started. In fact, we were worse off, for when crops had looked so good we had extended a line of credit to a lot of farmer customers who were to pay when their crops were harvested. But now with their crops destroyed, they could not pay their debts. We lost just about every dime we had put out on credit.

All we could do was to continue to fight it out. At Christmas we did a little business but nothing like what we needed or had expected before the terrible sandstorm.

Then in the beginning of 1927, our business began growing. We were surprised that after such a hard fall and winter that new farmers were buying land around Littlefield.[11]

We then moved into a small, four-room, rented frame house which looked like a mansion to us. My wife and I were indeed proud to be living in a house instead of in the back of the store. Also we needed more room, for we were expecting a new arrival in our family in the late summer.

On July 31, 1927, our son Edward Eugene Aryain was born.

Now I was indeed a proud man. I had my business, owned a Ford, had a home, and, most important, a wife and a baby son.

In the fall of 1927 crops again looked splendid, and the farmers who had managed to raise the money to buy seed for cotton were ready to harvest a big crop. And that year they did. Mexican, Negro, and white cotton pickers came to West Texas in droves, and they made good money and wanted to spend it on heavy dry goods.

Most of our business came on Saturdays and on rainy days when the workers could not work in the fields. Some Saturdays we hired as many as eight clerks to work the floor. Also we hired

English speaking Mexicans to help with the Mexican trade who could not speak any English. Business continued to be good all through the fall and winter months. That year at Christmas time our store was crowded with shoppers. By the end of 1927 we felt for the first time that we were making progress. The store was clear of debt, and we had built up such a good credit rating that the wholesale houses that had refused to give me a line of credit when I first opened my store were now eager to sell to me.

Business continued to be good at the beginning of 1928. I made many buying trips to Dallas, which had now passed St. Louis as a manufacturing center and was second only to New York. Many of the manufacturing concerns in Dallas were owned and operated by Jewish men.[12] I learned to bargain with them, and many of them were good friends of mine throughout their lives, especially Mr. Rube Tobolowsky, who was one of the finest men I ever knew.

In the late summer of 1928 I went to Dallas and ran into a Jewish manufacturer of ladies' hats I had done business with before. He asked me how business was, and I said, "Fine." Then he told me he had overstocked his spring and summer line of hats and that he had 150 ladies' hats he would close-out to me cheap, since he needed the room for his fall line. I went into his display room and saw the hats he was closing out. They were indeed beautiful hats, all colors, shapes, and styles.

The manufacturer's prices were $2.25 (retail price $4.00) and $4.00 (retail price $6.95). He asked me if I could use these beautiful hats, and I said, "Maybe, if they're a real bargain."

He offered to take a dollar off the original price of each hat. I said, "No, thank you. That is still too much for so late in the season." Then he said, "Ed, to show you I am a good sport, I will let you have these beautiful hats at half price."

"No, thank you," I said again. "But I will give you fifty cents for each hat and buy the whole bunch."

When he declined my offer, I left the show room and went up Commerce Street to do more buying. Each time I entered or left a show room, I would look back toward this man's display room and find him standing in the door watching me. In the late afternoon when I had finished my buying, I passed this millinery room again on my way to my hotel. "Ed," he called out, "Make me a better offer on these beautiful hats."

I then told him I would give him seventy-five cents for each hat and for him to either take the offer or leave it, for I was not going to argue with him. He replied, "Ed, I really hate to sell these beautiful hats at that price, for I feel like I am giving them away. But to show you I am a good sport, I will accept your offer."

He gave me an invoice for 150 hats at seventy-five cents each and immediately began packing them.[13]

In a few days when the hats arrived at the store, four or five big cardboard boxes, not heavy but bulky, my wife thought I had lost my mind and told me so.

The next day I filled the show windows full of ladies' hats and ran an ad in the weekly newspaper: —"Factory Close Out on Ladies' Hats—$6.95 Hats to Close Out at $2.98—$4.00 Hats to Close Out at $1.98."

In less than two weeks we had sold every hat I had bought and made money on them. This was just the beginning of such deals.

Talk was beginning that chain stores were taking over the country and that soon there would be no more independent merchants. This talk made me think of myself as a merchant with more than one store. The more I thought on this idea, the better it pleased me.

In the summer of 1928 I made a trip to Sudan, Texas, a little town eighteen miles west of Littlefield. I located a brick building for rent and leased it for two years. I then made arrangements for a lady who had been working for us in Littlefield to manage the store in Sudan. Then I went to Dallas to buy stock for the new store. Most of the wholesale people I talked to wished me luck and said I was doing the right thing.

But when I went to see Mr. Monnig in Fort Worth, he said, "Ed, I will sell you merchandise, but I am sorry to see you opening this second store. Your business is now in good financial condition, but with two stores you will need more merchandise, more help, and your expenses will be greater. At times when you are needed in one store, you will be in the other one. It is very important in running a business that the owner be available at all times."

But I told Mr. Monnig I had signed the lease and had to open.

And open the store in Sudan I did in the early fall of 1928. Immediately we began doing a booming business. Crops were the best they had ever been on the plains, and cotton was selling at a good price. Both of my stores were doing well. At the end of 1928 and into 1929 our business was wonderful, and we showed a nice profit in both stores. And business continued to do well through the spring and summer of 1929.

To add to our joy we were expecting another baby in the coming winter.

In the fall of 1929 business was the best it had ever been. On Saturdays we now had ten or twelve clerks in each store, and we hired floorwalkers to watch for shoplifters. At times the stores would be so crowded that I would be forced to close and lock the doors until the customers in the stores had been waited on. Then I would let them out and open the doors for the people who were waiting outside. The amount of business we did in those two small stores was almost unbelievable.

On Friday, December 13, 1929, our second son, Jameil Aryain, was born. He was the picture of health with dark brown hair and big brown eyes like his mother's. Edward's eyes are blue like mine. Many Druze Arabs have blue eyes.

Now my world seemed complete. I had two sons and two stores. What more could a man ask?

At the end of 1929 the statement I gave Dunn and Bradstreet showed I was worth seventy-two thousand dollars, which was a lot more money than it is today. I was thirty-two years old and had been in America sixteen years.

I made a trip to Dallas after the inventory just to buy fill-ins. Everywhere I went wholesalers and manufacturers wanted my business. They complimented me on how well I had done for myself in such a few years. They bought me cigars, took me to dinner, and begged me to give them more business. I was really Mr. Ed Aryain.

Mr. Rube Tobolowsky, the credit manager of Davis and Willard Hat Company, was greatly pleased with my financial statement. "Ed, I am very proud of you," he said. "Not many young men have done so well for themselves in such a short time. But I am not going to give you all the credit, for to my way of thinking a great deal of this success goes to your wife who had worked hard and been such a great help to you in the business."

He was right.

9

Difficult Depression Years

. . .

EARLY IN 1930 MY BUSINESS BEGAN FALLING OFF. EACH
month my volume was lower than the month before. I could not
understand the how or why of this situation, for in the previous
year I could hardly get enough merchandise to take care of my
trade. Now my business suddenly dropped to half of what it had
been.

In the previous fall I had read newspaper reports of an unstable stock market. And I had read of Black Tuesday—October 29,
1929—and of how angry and frightened crowds on the Stock
Exchange floor had fought to unload their holdings before the
day's business had closed. I had also read in the newspapers that
suicides were at an all time high. But I never dreamed that these
activities in far away New York could affect a bigshot Texas merchant like myself.

Then I suddenly realized that it affected me deeply.

All across the country businesses were failing. Factories were
closing. Savings accounts were wiped out, and local governments
went bankrupt. Small towns and cities alike were suddenly unable
to pay their teachers in money, so they gave them vouchers instead.

It was just a matter of time until banks refused to honor these vouchers. All over the country banks were foreclosing mortgages on both schools and houses.

Banks began closing their doors, and depositors lost heavily. The highways were crowded with hungry men going from town to town trying to find work. Many times I saw a man pushing a small cart, or perhaps a child's play wagon, along the highway with his wife and children walking behind him. Crops rotted in the field because there was no market for wheat, corn, or cotton.

All through these trying months President [Herbert] Hoover told the hungry people, "Prosperity is just around the corner." Soon each garage will house two cars and there will be "a chicken in every pot." But this did not fill the stomachs of hungry men, women, and children.

Everyone was talking about the Depression. "Depression" was a word I had never heard before, but it did not take me long to find out the hard way what the word really meant.

The thing that opened my eyes was when another merchant in Littlefield began selling overalls for 98¢ a pair. I went to this man's store one morning and asked him how in the world he could sell overalls for only 98¢ when the ones in my store had cost me $1.50 a pair. "Ed, have you been asleep these last few months?" he asked. "Haven't you been keeping up with market prices?" Then he showed me his new invoices, where he had bought overalls at $8.50 a dozen, or 71¢ apiece. Therefore he could sell his overalls for 98¢, and I had a storeful of them which had cost me $1.50. This was particularly bad because overalls were good leaders for specials.

Merchants all over the country began having stock reducing sales, cutting prices to the bone. Big stores and little stores were all in the same boat. They were loaded with high priced merchandise, and wholesale prices were falling every day.

In July 1930 I started a summer clearance sale. I cut the price of merchandise to below what it had cost me, but I did not turn much merchandise. We had hopes that things would be better in the fall, for crops looked good. But by the time the cotton was ready to be picked, the price had dropped to eight cents a pound or less. We did no business. People needed my merchandise, but they simply did not have the money to buy it. Farmers and merchants were in the same shape.

In the middle of 1930 I went to the Dallas market again. I was stunned to find that the people who six months earlier had begged for my business, bought me cigars, and taken me to dinner now acted like I was a total stranger. They did not seem in the least concerned to sell me merchandise.

Finally in desperation I talked to the credit manager of a ladies' ready-to-wear house. "What in the world is the matter with the people here in Dallas?" I asked. "Six months ago when I was here everyone wanted to sell me merchandise, but now people are not even friendly."

"Ed, it is easy to see what the trouble is," he replied. "Six months ago the stock in your two stores was worth one hundred cents on the dollar. Now it is worth thirty cents on the dollar, so you are broke like the rest of the merchants."

I went back to Littlefield a very depressed man. Immediately I started another price cutting sale, trying desperately to get some of my money out of all my high priced merchandise. But every merchant in the country was doing the same thing, so it did little good. Sales, sales, and more sales.

Before the Depression I had a big stock of Manhattan shirts, which I sold for $2.95 and $3.95. Then before I knew what was happening, other merchants were selling these same shirts at 98¢ and $1.50. I immediately cut my prices to be in line with the other merchants, losing money on every shirt I sold. But the bad thing was that even at these prices I sold very few. It was the same story with Florsheim shoes, which I carried in both stores.

We started 1931 on a sour note. Business was at a standstill.

Instead of things getting better as Hoover had said they would, they got worse. Sale or no sale, people had no money to buy goods. I remember one day in the Sudan store when we only sold a pair of canvas gloves for nineteen cents. That was the *total* for the entire day. Another day in the Littlefield store we only sold a thirty-nine-cent towel.

It was impossible to raise money to pay my bills. Creditors began pushing me for their money. They wrote threatening letters, called me long distance, wired me, and even sent out collectors to my store. But all I could do was worry and fret in the daytime and walk the floor at night.

Merchants all over the country began filing bankruptcy and trying to get out with a small amount of money. I could have done the same and gotten out from under the load, but all my life I had hated the word "bankruptcy." I felt that to file bankruptcy would be a black mark against my name, which would follow me all the rest of my life. I had not come to America and worked so hard to get ahead just to let that happen. My idea was to keep fighting this thing and maybe pull through and have my name and my store.

In the early part of 1932, I went to Dallas to talk to the creditors and ask them to be patient with me, for I was trying my level best to pay them. If they gave me some time, I could maybe work things out. Some of the creditors promised to work with me, but in the long run most of their promises were lies.

I went back and closed the Sudan store, thinking maybe I could cut some of the expenses and at least have all the merchandise under one roof. I operated like this for a couple of months, but it was impossible to sell merchandise. Things were going from bad to worse. The creditors who had made the biggest promises were now pushing me the hardest.

I made a trip to Fort Worth to talk to Mr. Monnig. "Ed," he said, "I do not think you can possibly pull through this, for your creditors are now threatening to throw you into bankruptcy. But if you will make an assignment to us, we will take the store over, sell what we can out of it, and divide the cash among the creditors. No creditor will get the full amount owed him, but each will get a small amount. In making this arrangement I do not think the creditors will throw you into bankruptcy. You will get clear of indebtedness, and they will not bother you any further, for I will tell them you did your level best."

He then drew up the assignment papers, and I signed them.

Never, never was there a longer road than the one from Fort Worth to Littlefield when I returned home the following day. Here I was at the end of my road again. I had lost everything I had worked for. A job could not be had for love nor money. I was worse off than after the fire in Navarro, for I now had only four hundred dollars in cash, and I had a wife and two babies to feed and care for.

In a few days a sales promoter from the Monnig Dry Goods Company came to Littlefield and asked for the keys to my store. He took over full control of the business and started a close-out sale. He sold what he could, then shipped the balance to retail stores in Waco and Fort Worth.

Before he locked the doors of my store for the last time, I told him that the shelves were still in the Sudan store building and that I would like to make some arrangement for them, since I must somehow get back in business. He said that the shelves were of no use to them, since they could not sell them, so I could keep them.

Then the man looked at me and said, "Ed, how much money do you have?" I told him I had four hundred dollars. "Ed, how in the world can you manage to get back in business on that small amount?"

I told him that I had to make a living for my family at something and that the dry goods business was all I knew. Somehow or other I must manage to get back in business.

He wished me luck and left me standing there.

For me the following days were horrible, and the nights were pure hell. Many were the nights I did not close my eyes.

I loafed around Littlefield for two or three weeks feeling miserable and helpless. Each time I walked downtown and passed the empty building where my store had been, my heart turned to stone. But I knew I must have an income for my family. Since there was no possibility of finding a job, I definitely decided to try to open another store in Sudan. The shelves were already there, and I knew I could rent the building cheap.

I managed to borrow a few dollars from some Syrian friends. Then with this added to my measly four hundred dollars, I went again to Fort Worth to tell Mr. Monnig that I must get back into business, since no jobs were available, especially for a man like me without any education or training.

Mr. Monnig nodded. "How well I know there are no jobs. All over the country people are out of work." Then he said, "Ed, I will give you another line of credit of eight hundred dollars as I did when you opened in Littlefield." I thanked him from the bottom of my heart, then went to buy the most essential merchandise.

In Dallas my friend Mr. Rube Tobolowsky at the Willard and Davis Hat Company gave me four hundred dollars' credit for men's hats. I will always be grateful to this kind and warm man. But some of the credit managers who had been so friendly to me when I had been doing well made me beg and plead and then turned me down flat. This was very humiliating.

I went back to Littlefield and moved my little family to Sudan. Since we could not spend money to rent a house, I again had a partition built in the back of the store for our living quarters. It had an outside toilet and only a water hydrant outside, but in 1932 who dared complain? I at least had a roof over my family's head, and many men were not this fortunate.

When the new merchandise came in, my wife and I only had to put it on the shelves. Then we opened our doors for business. This was in late August. Crops looked good, and I thought we might have some fall business. But I was in for a big disappointment. The farmers got so little money for their crops they could only pay the cotton picker fifty cents for a hundred pounds. The workers just barely had enough money to buy food for their families and simply did without dry goods, even shoes in the cold weather. The farmers were no better off.

Early in 1933 business came to a complete halt. Through January, February, and March, we hardly did enough business to pay the rent and buy groceries. We did not actually go to bed hungry as many people did, but we got awfully tired of beans, potatoes, and baloney. We bought day-old bread at the bakery and made it last. Round steak was twenty-five cents a pound, but who had a quarter during those hard times?

In desperation I decided to try peddling on the road while my wife ran the store. But I could not sell enough on the road even to pay for gasoline, so I hurried back to Sudan, where I could at least be with my family. I had found that having a family made being on the road unbearably lonely now.

My creditors were pushing me, and I knew that I must make another move. I made a trip into New Mexico and considered moving to Clovis, Portales, Fort Sumner, or Las Vegas, but these towns all seemed to have an abundance of stores.

Finally in Brownfield, Texas, I found a building a block from the courthouse square and rented it.[1] I also rented a little four-room frame house, for living in the back of the store with two small boys was not very satisfactory. Also I wanted them to have some place to play rather than in a back alley or front sidewalk of the store.

I had the idea things would better in Brownfield, but I soon realized I had moved from bad to worse. Brownfield had two big department stores and several smaller stores I had to compete with. I never saw another town that had so many interrelated families, and most of them were related in one way or another to the merchants who owned the other stores. It was simply impossible for a foreign-born merchant to break through in such a clannish town. At least it was for me.

About this time Franklin Delano Roosevelt became president of the United States, and he began furnishing food to needy families and giving part-time jobs to men working on bridges and highways.[2] This helped some but not enough. The Depression was still on, and money was scarce.

The only way I could survive in Brownfield was to run sales and cut prices, but even this did not help much.[3] I remember so well that when I had an especially good buy on merchandise, the wife of the owner of one of the automobile agencies would drive up and send her colored maid in to bring merchandise out to the car for her inspection. The woman liked to take advantage of my low prices, but she did not want to be seen in my store. This hurt my wife and me very much. We always felt that the poor colored maid was embarrassed to have to do this to us.

Sometimes I would go for a week at a time without seeing my little boys awake, for I was trying so hard to earn some money for us that I left for the store before they were awake in the morning and did not return home until after they had gone to bed.

When our son Eddie was six years old, he started to school, and soon after he started helping in the store. He was so small that he could hardly see the customers over the stacks of overalls and work pants, but he liked to do it, and I liked for him to be there with me. Customers teased him and said they could hardly see him behind the counters, which was true enough.

One particular woman would come into the store and ask for "the little one" to wait on her. She was generally about half drunk, and she invariably wanted to kiss Eddie. He liked waiting on customers, but he did not want any of that kissing business. One day she came in drunker than usual and began giggling loudly and chasing him around the store. I finally had to step in and quiet things down.

When our son Jameil was old enough to go to school, my wife spent even more time at the store. But as many long hard hours as she spent at the store, she always managed to somehow run our home. We only took a dollar a day out of the cash register to pay for groceries, and on Saturday afternoons we gave the boys each a dime so they could see a movie.

But no matter how hard we worked, we could not get a volume of business, and the years of failure and despair and worry dragged by.

In 1937 there was drilling for oil in neighboring Yoakum County. We hoped desperately that this drilling would come closer to Brownfield and that business would improve. We held on to this hope into 1938, but nothing much happened. We had to continue struggling for every dime we could get our hands on.

It was during this period that I was startled to realize that I had lived in the United States over twenty years but still had not made application for citizenship. I felt ashamed of this, for despite all the hard times I had known in this country I knew that I always wanted America to be my home. As the children grew older, I knew it was even more important that I become a citizen.

Since business was so slow, I decided to close the store for two days and go to visit our good friends Mr. and Mrs. Charlie Shebly in El Paso, Texas, who were personally acquainted with a man in the Immigration Office who would help get the papers started.[4] This was the only vacation we had ever had, and the boys were wild with excitement when the Sheblys took them over the border into Juarez, Mexico.

Charlie took me to the Immigration Office and made me acquainted with the man who would help me. The man asked me for my entry permit, and I told him it had burned up in the fire in Navarro, Texas. He then asked me the name of the ship I had come over on, and I told him I did not remember. I also told him I did not remember the exact date of my arrival. All I could tell him was my real name, Mohammed Aryain, that I was from Henna, Syria, and that I had arrived in New York in June of 1913.

"My friend," the man said, "that is not much to go on, but I will see what I can do. If you don't mind spending four or five dollars for a long distance telephone call, I can get the information from New York and we can get started sooner."

Four or five dollars sounded like a fortune to me then, but I told him I would be happy if he would make the call.

When we went back the next day, the man smiled and said he had been informed that I had entered the country legally. He gave me some papers to fill out and sign. Then he gave me a book to study, so I would know all the answers about democracy at the court hearing.

Later I was notified to appear at the Naturalization Office of the District Court in Lubbock, Texas. I had studied the book very hard, and Eddie and Jameil had helped me very much. But I was very worried that I might not be able to answer all the questions on United States history.

But the judge was very kind and lenient, and I answered all the questions accurately.

About forty or fifty people had their hearings that day— Germans, Mexicans, Frenchmen, Italians, and other Syrians. Every person answered his questions correctly except for one old German gentleman who had trouble understanding. Trying to make the old gentleman relax and feel less afraid, the nice judge asked him if he had a family.

The old German gentleman replied, "Your Honor, I have a wife and seven children, and I own and operate a seven-hundred-acre farm."

The nice judge smiled and said, "Any man who has seven children and owns and operates a seven-hundred-acre farm deserves to be an American citizen."

It was a solemn but joyful occasion for me when I stood with the other foreign-born people and we took our oath of allegiance and were declared citizens of the United States of America.[5]

10

Fresh Start in Seminole

. . .

I FOUND THAT MY GROWING BOYS ATE JUST AS MUCH NOW that I was an American citizen as they had before. I realized that I had to move away from Brownfield and find a town where I had a chance of making a living.

About that time there began to be some oil drilling in Gaines County, and I thought I might do better there. I went to Seagraves, a little town twenty-eight miles from Brownfield, which appeared about to boom, and looked for a location for the store.[1] But there was not one. So I went seventeen miles further south to Seminole, an even smaller town but the county seat of Gaines County.[2]

At that time Seminole was just a little cattle town with the very beginning of some oil production. There was the court house, a post office, three small grocery stores, one dry goods store and funeral home combined, a little movie theater, two small cafes, a barber shop, a drug store, and several filling stations and churches. There was not a bank in Seminole, but there was a very fine school system.

I found a nice brick building for rent just across the street from the court house and, realizing that any move I made would be an improvement over Brownfield, I rented it.

Once again there was no money to rent a house, so I had a partition built in the back of the store so we would have living quarters. But this time at least there was an inside toilet and a sink, and, wonder of wonders in West Texas, there were three trees in the back for the kids to play under.

I immediately moved the store fixtures and merchandise to Seminole, and my wife stayed in Brownfield a few days longer until school was out. This was June of 1939.

When the fixtures were in the store and the merchandise on the shelves, I paid the movers. Then feeling hungry, I decided to go have a hamburger. But when I looked into my pocket, I found I only had eight cents. Since hamburgers were ten cents, I decided to be hungry until my wife got there, since I did not want to start off in Seminole asking for two cents' credit in the café next door.

Thank heavens my wife arrived the next day with the boys, our shabby furniture, and three dollars.

When we opened the store, we began doing some business at once. Living in Seminole was like living in a different world, for people were friendly and nice to us. Old time ranchers who had lived here before Gaines County was even organized came into the store to introduce themselves and told us they were glad we were settling in Seminole. Oil field workers and their wives came in and wished us luck. And they in turn seemed to appreciate it when we invited them into the back of the store for pie and coffee and sometimes at night to play Chinese checkers.

We appreciated their business, but we appreciated even more their friendliness. We decided that if God would let us make a living in Seminole, Texas, we were there to stay.

Running the store was really a family affair. Our boys were still youngsters. Eddie was in the seventh grade, and Jameil in the fourth, but they pitched right in with the work that needed to be done. They did the janitor work in the store, washing the display windows and sweeping out every morning. Eddie could now wait on customers as well as any adult, and Jameil shined shoes in the

barbershop next door. With the money Jameil earned from shining shoes, he bought himself a bicycle and began delivering the
Lubbock Avalanche-Journal newspaper, which came to Seminole
on the bus each day. Later when he was older, Jameil began working weekends as a roughneck in the oil fields, making very good
money for a boy in his early teens.

May I say to you now, my sons, that we thank you for the help
you gave us when we were struggling to get our little store started.

My wife bought ladies' ready-to-wear, was saleslady and alter-
ation woman, and did the bookkeeping. When these tasks were
done, she was cook, wife, and mother for our family.

I can truthfully say that for the first time in our life my wife
had some social life. She was being invited to parties and enter-
tainments by other ladies, where in the other towns we had lived
in she had never been invited anywhere.

Our stock in the store was small but complete, and with better
business I could keep new merchandise coming in all the time. We
did a nice business through 1939 and into 1940.

People knew that we lived in the back of the store and that we
would open up and sell them anything they needed on Sunday or
even in the middle of the night if they got a long distance telephone call about sickness or a death in the family and had to leave
immediately. They seemed to appreciate this, and we were glad to
do it. Since there was no bank in Seminole, we had to drive eighteen miles to Seagraves two or three times a week to make deposits
and get change, so we could cash the payroll checks.

In the spring of 1940 the Seminole Chamber of Commerce
decided to sponsor a rodeo and to invite people from all over West
Texas and New Mexico to attend. They asked that everybody wear
cowboy clothes through the week. I had a good stock of western
hats and boots in the store, for these were good staple items for me,
but I did not have the fancy, brightly colored cowboy shirts people
wanted to wear for the rodeo. Since it was too late to order these

shirts from Dallas or St. Louis, the boys and I got in the car and went to Hobbs, New Mexico, then to Odessa, Texas, and other neighboring towns, where we went to every store and managed to buy at wholesale or less the cowboy shirts the merchants were stuck with. I managed to get, I will say, twenty dozen of these brightly colored cowboy shirts, which I took back to Seminole. I put them on display and promptly sold every one. The money I made off these shirts helped pay off some creditors and took some of the financial pressure off of me. But more important, my family and I had fun at the rodeo, barbecue, and western street dance, and for the first time we felt we were a part of the community in which we lived and not just that foreign family.

Later that summer my wife took the boys by bus to visit her parents in Missouri. Two Sundays later I went into the drug store to get my morning paper when a blackness came over me, and I fell to the floor. Some of the men took my store keys and carried me back to our living quarters and put me to bed.

When I regained consciousness, the doctor was watching me closely and told me I had better call my wife to come home.

I asked the doctor what my trouble was, and he said it might have been a heart attack. He told me to stay in bed for a day or two, but I told him I had to open the store, for I needed the business. He said, "Okay," but not to do any lifting.

In two days my wife came home and took me to the hospital, where the doctor put me to bed for rest and examination. Then I was sent home and told to take medicine and to stay in bed for a few weeks.

Never have I seen anything like the way people in Seminole rallied around us during this illness. Ranchers and business people offered their help and sympathy, and oil field workers who had first been customers and then good friends came and helped my wife in the store and told her to feel free to call upon them and their wives at any time of the day or night we might need assistance. Nothing like this friendliness and concern had ever happened to us before.

Then before I was well enough to work full time in the store, my wife became ill. She had long suffered from a tightness in her throat and pains in her shoulders and arms, and in recent weeks she had found it increasingly hard to breathe. Then one morning she fainted and afterward had so much difficulty breathing that the Seminole doctor insisted that I take her to the hospital in Lubbock for extensive tests.

There it was discovered that she had two large goiters on her thyroid gland, which were pressing against her windpipe and making it increasingly difficult for her to breathe. But she was in such a rundown condition that the doctor did not dare operate immediately, even though she needed it. Instead, he ordered her to bed for thirty days of complete rest, and then when her strength was up he would do surgery.

So here I was, hardly well enough to drag myself across the store, with my wife sick in bed and with two boys to cope with and facing a huge hospital bill.

But once again the people of Seminole came to our aid. Different ladies of the town prepared food and brought it in every day and helped me with the housecleaning. I was very fortunate to have had at that time a marvelous woman working in the store, Mrs. Alva Bingham. I will always be grateful to this lady and her husband, Boss Bingham, for the kindness they showed us. They had a young son with serious heart trouble, but they always found the time and strength to help us.

Fred and Pauline Farrar, who still live five miles east of Seminole on a farm and are still our good friends, were especially kind to us also. On Sundays they would come in and get the boys and then take them to Sunday school and then to their farm for the day. Both the boys loved these days with the Farrars, and I will always be grateful to these good people.

At the end of thirty days of bed rest, I took my wife back to Lubbock, where she had the surgery on her neck, and in ten days she was back home, where the fine people of Seminole saw her through her recuperation. We both now feel that the help and kindness of the people of Seminole helped us both to get well almost as much as the medicine and surgery. When a man has sickness in his family, he never forgets kind deeds.

As the years pass, I think God each day for allowing me to be a part of America and for a town called Seminole, Texas.

In the two years we had lived in Seminole [1939–41], it had almost doubled in size until it had a population of 1,500 people. It had outgrown Seagraves and was building on a firm foundation. Instead of the hastily thrown together frame structures, which went up in most oil towns, Seminole was building brick buildings and nice houses. Business was steady and good.

In the summer of 1941 we decided we were finally in a position to build a home. We wanted to move out of the back of the store, for the children were growing up fast. In fact, as impossible as it seemed, Eddie was in high school.

A new residential area had been opened up on the edge of town, and I went there and bought a choice corner lot for $300. Then I went to the lumber yard in Seminole and told the man there just what we wanted, a nice five-room house complete with bathroom and a garage. When the plans for the house were complete, the contractor made me a building price of $3,200. I had no trouble making the loan with a Lubbock bank for ten years, and the building began.

We were a proud family when we moved into our nice new house that October.

But all too soon we heard the special news broadcast of the Japanese bombing of Pearl Harbor, and the United States was at war.

Young men from Gaines County began going off to war as they did all over the United States. Those were terrible months for all of us as we heard of one Japanese victory after another and read of the terrible losses of American lives and ships. Our boys were much too young to have to go to service at that time, but often at night I worried that if the war lasted as long as everybody said it would, they would go off and be killed.

The United States needed more oil, more cotton, and more cattle now that we were at war, and Gaines County produced all of these things. More people moved to Seminole and found work in the oil fields and on the farms and ranches. But now that people had money to spend in my store, it was almost impossible to get merchandise, especially the things they needed. Khaki work clothes, heavy underwear, and men's shoes were now going to the armed services. A merchant could not buy sheets or pillowcases for love nor money. Salesmen continued to call on us, but they did not have the merchandise we needed.

I decided that the only way to stay in business was to make buying trips to Dallas, Fort Worth, and San Antonio every two or three weeks. I had to make these long trips by bus, for there was no railroad in Seminole, and I certainly could not get enough gasoline to drive my car. I even made several trips to St. Louis, trying to get badly needed merchandise.

Once in St. Louis I found a small wholesale house, which had men's shirts, nylon hose, work clothes, sheets and pillowcases, and for a minute I thought I was in heaven. But then the manager said that to get these badly needed things, I would have to buy seven hundred dollars' worth in other goods. Then when he showed me the stuff I would have to buy to get the good merchandise, it was puredee junk. And I do mean junk! I said, "No, thank you! I would rather go without merchandise than offer my customers in Seminole puredee junk like that!"

Another time in Dallas I was given the address of a wholesale house where I was told I could buy sheets and pillowcases. I went to the address and found that the door was locked and the windows covered. I knocked at the door, and after a very long wait a man answered. I told him I had heard I could buy sheets and pillowcases here, and he looked around, then let me in. I will say forty or fifty women were working at sewing machines making sheets. But when he showed me his sheets and pillowcases, I can honestly say that they were the thinnest and flimsiest material I ever saw. But then the man told me that the sheets would cost me $27 a dozen, or $2.25 each.

Always before I had sold good, well-advertised sheets for less than I would be paying for these. I was ashamed to offer my customers in Seminole such bad merchandise at such a high price, but I was so desperate for goods that I told the man I would buy forty dozen of each. But he said I could only have fifteen dozen of each, so I said, "Okay."

He then asked me to make him a check for the full amount.

"Why do you want a check?" I asked. "I have a good credit rating." But he said they did not do any credit business, so I said, "Okay," and gave him a check for the full amount. But I thought this was a very funny way to do business.

The man then began packing up the order himself, which also struck me as a funny way to do business. Then he said, "Bring your car around to the back, and I will load it up."

I told him that I did not have my car but had come to Dallas on the bus and that the merchandise would have to be shipped.

"Then we cannot do business," he said as he tore up my check. "We do not ship our merchandise."

I knew then that this man was selling on the black market, and he was afraid to ship his merchandise. I took a taxi back to the regular wholesale district, bought what little I could find, and that night I took the bus back to Seminole without the badly needed sheets and pillowcases.

But most wholesale houses and manufacturers tried to be fair, and customers understood and bought what I could get for them.

Our business held up so well that only two years after we moved into the house I had the money to pay off the loan. I went to the bank in Lubbock where the man in the loan department did his level best to talk me out of paying off the house, saying that I should put my money into another investment. But I told him I had made up my mind to pay off the loan and have my family's home clear of debt. I was a proud man when I picked up the mortgage paper on the house, for now I felt I really owned a piece of the United States of America.

Gasoline was limited and sold only with ration coupons. Grocery stores were having their troubles for sugar, coffee, and most canned foods were rationed. In my store shoes were rationed. Cigarettes and many other things were almost impossible to get. But these were mere inconveniences. All over the world people were suffering and starving and dying.

One of the things that bothered me most during the war was the fact that it was impossible to get any word from my family in the Middle East. France still ruled Syria and Lebanon, even after Paris, France, had fallen to the Germans. I was constantly afraid that the fighting and killing would break out in the Middle East, especially when the English and Germans fought over North Africa almost to the walls of Cairo. One of my greatest fears was that Turkey would again join sides with Germany in a war against Russia, as she had in the First World War, and try to take back Syria and Lebanon from France. Not that I was so crazy about French rule—I just wanted my homeland to be free.

Since coming to the United States, I had carefully read all newspaper accounts about happenings in the Middle East, and I had been especially interested in what happened in Turkey after Mustafa Kemal took over the country in 1922. Mustafa Kemal was an entirely new and different type of ruler for Turkey, which had been under the rule of thirty-six sultans between 1300 and 1922. His first official act was to do away completely with the title of sultan and bestow upon himself the title of President Mustafa Kemal. Then he started from scratch to build Turkey into a whole new country.[3]

He started building roads, schools, hospitals, railroads, government buildings, and a modern air force. President Mustafa Kemal passed a law that the veil Turkish women had worn over their faces for centuries was to be cast off. He advocated the freedom of women, and if a woman was well educated, she could electioneer and hold the office of her choice. It was hard luck for Greece when President Mustafa Kemal came to power, for just a few months earlier they had invaded Turkey. He held them at a standstill. All through history, Turkey and Greece had been bitter enemies.

President and Mrs. Mustafa Kemal did not have children of their own, but once when they were on official business traveling through the country, they saw a beautiful little girl standing in the crowd which had gathered to greet them. For some unknown reason, both the president and his wife were immediately drawn to this little girl. I will say she was seven years old at the time. They talked to the child in a friendly manner and asked where her father and mother lived. The child pointed out the little rundown shack where she lived and offered to introduce them to her parents. When they arrived at the little shack, President Kemal knew immediately that these people could not afford to give the little girl a good education. There were several other children playing around the house, and the father's means of caring for his family was limited.

When they went inside the house and the president of Turkey introduced himself and his wife as President and Mrs. Mustafa Kemal, the parents were pretty surprised and highly honored.

President Kemal told the couple that both he and his wife had fallen in love with their little daughter at first sight and would like to take her to live with them and give her the best education possible, for she showed great talent. He explained, "I am not forcing you to give me the child in any way. You will always be welcome to visit her in my castle at any time, and should she desire to visit you here in your home, she will be well guarded."

The parents agreed with the president that this was a wonderful opportunity for their daughter to have a better way of life than they could provide.

This beautiful little girl was an A, no. 1 student in grade school, high school, and college. President and Mrs. Kemal loved the child as if she were their own and gave her every advantage they could think of. I never heard what happened to her real parents.

The girl's greatest ambition was to be a pilot in her father's air force. So President Kemal said, "Okay," and placed her in a training school for pilots, and soon she had won her wings. She handled the plane as well as any man in the air force.[4]

In Turkey there lived a class of people called the Kurds (I told you about them earlier). Their ancestors had moved from Russia to the Middle East because they were Moslems, and they wanted to live in the Moslem world. They had their own language, but they also spoke Arabic and Turkish.

These Kurdish people then came upon the idea that they wanted a country to call their own, so they asked President Kemal to give them a parcel of Turkey.

Naturally he refused.

So then the Kurds started a revolution to take by force what they wanted. President Kemal sent his officers to talk to these Kurdish people, telling them that they were all Moslem brothers and Turkey belonged to them both. But the Kurds did not see it this way. They refused to listen, and soon guerilla warfare broke out in a big way!

President Kemal then came upon the idea that he should send his air force to end all this revolution and commotion. But when his daughter, now a young woman, heard tell of the plans to attack, she begged her father to let her fly her own plane and drop the bombs. He said, "Okay," and soon the young lady was on her way in a plane with plenty of gasoline and a good stock of bombs. When she was over the Kurdish villages, she dropped the bombs.

It became known that this plane was being flown by President Mustafa Kemal's daughter, and she was dropping all the bombs.

The Kurdish people had a meeting among themselves and said, "If one woman flying one plane can drop so many bombs, think what will happen if President Mustafa Kemal sends his entire air force! We will be wiped out!"

So the Kurdish leaders made peace and promised not to make any more commotion. I thought this was very interesting.

When President Mustafa Kemal gave his people their personal freedom, they really took him at his word. They began living as we Westerners do, and Turkey was a different world. I remember reading in a newspaper about a reporter who had gone to Istanbul and was astonished to see thousands of Turkish men and women at the beach in—of all things—bathing suits!

He went on to say in the article that he would not have thought he would see such a thing in a thousand years, for only a short time before, Turkish women had worn veils over their faces and been covered from head to foot by long dresses.

Later President Mustafa Kemal changed his name to Ataturk and took to drinking.

Anyway, I am happy to tell you that Turkey did not make the mistake of getting into the Second World War on the side of Germany against Russia as she had in the First World War.

Now, back to my story.

Since moving to Seminole, I had been paying one hundred dollars a month rent on the store building. Then in 1944 I heard that my landlord, Judge A. J. Roach, was selling his home and moving to South Texas. Since for the first time I had some cash which was not needed for merchandise, I decided to try to buy the building. I thought it would probably cost a great deal of money. When I asked Judge Roach what he would sell the building for, and he said seven thousand dollars, I immediately closed the deal for the building at 110 South Main Street, which still houses Aryain's Dry Goods.

Now I owned *two* pieces of the United States of America.

It was a proud day when on May 19, 1944, our son Edward graduated from Seminole High School. He enrolled in Texas Tech College in September. He was not eighteen until after Japan had surrendered, and then he went into the United States Air Force and was stationed in San Antonio before receiving a medical discharge. He then moved to Los Angeles, California. He likes it out there, but I don't see how he stands all that traffic.

Ever since coming to the United States, I had wanted to be a member of the Masonic Lodge. I had applied for membership in Littlefield, but of course, the vote had gone against me in that town. But I knew that people in Seminole did not resent foreigners so much, so I decided to try again. I asked for the application blanks, filled them out, and in less than two weeks' time a vote was taken on me, and I was accepted. This made me feel so good.

There are a great many things to learn in secret in this organization. I am particularly indebted to Mr. Ollie Haywood, an elderly man who owned the barbershop next door to my store, for helping me so much. For weeks Mr. Haywood worked with me every night, teaching me the secret work. Learning the work was hard for me to remember, but Mr. Haywood was always patient and ready to help me again. Once he said, "Ed, not only do I have to teach you the Masonic work, but I also have to teach you better English." Which was true enough. But I finally passed the work and felt honored to be a thirty-second-degree Mason.

Soon after this my wife was voted into the Order of the Eastern Star, and to this day being a member of this organization is very important to her.[5]

It was our own adult decision when we united with the First United Methodist Church. The warmth of this church and the association with the members in Seminole has meant a great deal to us and made going to church on Sunday morning a regular part of the week. The Methodists do not fuss and fight among themselves as much as some churches in Seminole do.

Now that the war was over, merchandise was again easy to get, and business was good. But more important, I could again hear from my family in the Old Country. I was relieved to learn that they were still alive, but conditions were not so hot.

You will remember that I told you that France got Syria and Lebanon after World War I. At first some of the people were pleased to hear this, especially the Christian Arabs in Lebanon, who were sick and tired of being under the Turks, who were Moslem. But I'm sorry to tell you that they soon found that being under the French was no better than being under the Turks. There was always trouble and killing and commotion.

Guerilla warfare against the French continued in Syria and Lebanon. The French used their artillery to destroy the Druze villages just as cruelly as the Turks had.

Then the French came upon the idea that the headquarters for the guerilla rebels was in a certain part of Damascus. One morning they turned their heavy artillery on that part of the city, and a great amount of damage was done.

News travels fast. President Harry S Truman, now the president of the United States, immediately called Paris, France, by long distance telephone and asked to talk to the high government officials. He insisted that they stop their artillery from destroying Damascus, Syria, saying, "Damascus is the oldest city in the world, and from the earliest Bible times the city has played an important part in history. This city should be preserved and respected for all generations."

President Harry S Truman urged and insisted that the French

come to some agreement with Syria and end the long war. By this time the French were sick and tired of the long war, and their supply of men and money was exhausted, so in a short while they said to heck with it and began pulling out their army. Lo and Behold! Syria and Lebanon were finally free at last![6]

With the French out of Syria and Lebanon, both countries were free to hold free elections. In both countries a president and a vice president were elected by popular vote.

On May 16, 1947, our youngest son, Jameil, graduated from Seminole High School. In the fall he enrolled in Southern Methodist University (SMU) in Dallas, Texas. Again I was proud as a peacock. I had been able to give my sons the foundation for a good education, which I had been denied.

During his last two years in high school Jameil had courted a beautiful blond girl by the name of Patricia Lee Denton, daughter of Reverend and Mrs. T. L. Denton of Seminole, Texas. She enrolled at TSCW [Texas State College for Women, now Texas Woman's University] in Denton, Texas.

At the end of their third year in college, the Korean War began, and Jameil was just the right age to be drafted. With the shadow of war hanging over all young people, Jameil and Patricia were married October 22, 1950.

Jameil was given a deferment by the draft board to finish his last year of college. Then when he had graduated, he was inducted into the army and stationed for a year at Fort Ord, California. Patricia lived in Monterey, California, which is right by Fort Ord.

In the fall—October 9, 1952—our first grandchild was born, Linda Lisa Aryain, beautiful daughter of Mr. and Mrs. Jameil Aryain. When the baby was two weeks old, her father left for overseas. He was stationed for a year in Japan.

At the end of the year Jameil returned to his little family in Seminole. Since his degree from SMU had been in business administration, he immediately took over our business. We thought this was a good arrangement, for it is the way of life that older people must step aside and turn their affairs over to the younger generation. Jameil was young and strong and had the training to operate the business, and both my wife and I were tired and ready to get away from the business world. As much as we had enjoyed being with the people of Seminole—and for us each and every customer was a special person—it was time for us to retire.

Now we had the time and money to travel and see this beautiful America and to enjoy our grandchildren. Another beautiful blond baby girl was born to Jameil and Patricia on October 13, 1954, Amy Susan Aryain. Dwight Allen (Chip) Aryain joined our family circle November 24, 1964, and what a wonderful boy he is.

Jameil did a marvelous job managing the store, and he will never know how much we appreciate his hard work and accomplishments. With this energetic young man at the controls, the face of the entire store was changed—new display windows, the floor covered with carpet, a twenty-five-foot extension added to the back of the store, then a giant remodeling project with all new modern fixtures. Later Jameil added a special men's section in the store building next door where Mr. Ollie Haywood had once had his barbershop.[7]

11

Middle Eastern Welcome

. . .

SEMINOLE WAS BUILDING FOR THE FUTURE. NEW BUSINESS buildings were going up, and older buildings were being remodeled. We had a prosperous bank, automobile agencies, and a new hospital. Many beautiful new brick homes were being constructed.

Seeing all these beautiful new brick homes upset my wife and made her nervous, and she came upon the idea that we should have a new home. She said we needed a new home with three bedrooms, two baths, a combination den and kitchen with a fireplace, a separate living room, and a double garage. So she argued.

Our children were now grown and had left the nest, and since we were alone again, we did not need a larger house. So I argued.

We should keep up with the Joneses. So she argued.

We spent a lot of time arguing.

Each time my wife brought out the book of house plans, she would ask me, "Do you like this house plan as well as the one I showed you yesterday?"

"Yes," I would reply in a lukewarm manner without much interest. "It is a nice plan. It would be nice to have a new home. Maybe some day we will build a new house." Nothing definite.

So my wife continued to study house plan books and draw up her own plans. Still nothing definite.

But in the back of my mind I had my own ideas, which I had never mentioned to my wife. For all through the years, I had secretly dreamed that one day I would make a trip back to the Old Country to visit my people. My parents had both been dead for many years. My half sister Safaka was now a very old woman and very ill, and my sister Hameedie was living with her husband and two grown sons on a fruit farm eighteen miles from Beirut, Lebanon. But I kept putting the trip off, saying to myself, "Maybe next year I will go."[1]

It had now been forty-eight years since I had left Syria, and one day I made up my mind that if I was ever to make this long dreamed of trip, it would have to be now.

I said to my wife, "You may build the new house of your dreams, or we can make the trip to the Old Country. Make your decision one way or the other, for we cannot afford to do both."

"We will make the trip," she replied immediately, then put away the house plan books and her own drawings for her dream house. (More about this later in the writing.)

We found that there were many things to take care of before making such a trip. First we had to go to Lubbock, Texas, to consult with a travel agent. He informed us we would be required to have smallpox shots with the doctor's signature. Also we must have a birth certificate for my wife and a copy of my naturalization papers. The travel agent said he would arrange for passports and visas for entry into Lebanon, Syria, Jordan, and Egypt. Then he issued the tickets. Our departure date was to be March 7, 1961, on Pan American World Air Ways from Lubbock, Texas, to Beirut, Lebanon. Neither my wife nor I had ever flown on an airplane before.

Excitement now ran high. I made the preparations for the final details. A cablegram was dispatched to my people telling them of our arrival time in Beirut.

On Sunday afternoon before we were to leave Seminole on Monday, our good friends Mr. and Mrs. J. L. Skaggs entertained with a going away party. Many of our friends called there during the day to wish us a pleasant trip and to say good-bye. Thanks a lot, Luke and Mila, for this delightful afternoon.

I cannot recall the color of the dress my wife wore that afternoon, but I do remember she wore a beautiful orchid corsage, which our son Edward had sent from California. And I proudly wore the white boutonniere, which came with the orchid. Thanks a lot, Eddie, for remembering us.

On Monday morning our son Jameil drove us to Lubbock, Texas, and we spent the night with our good friends Charlie and Mary Cabool. Thanks a lot, Jameil and Patricia, for all the help you gave us in preparing for the trip.

We were now on our way. The past weeks had been exciting and at times sad. Leaving one's country, home, children, grandchildren, and friends is not so easy when the time comes to leave.

We boarded the plane on Tuesday morning at six o'clock. I will never forget the thrill as the plane took off and we began the first leg of the journey. With a short layover in Dallas, Texas, we landed in New York City in the late afternoon of the same day.

There we boarded a huge plane which would fly us over to London, England. But before our arrival in London, England, the next morning, the Captain of the airplane advised us passengers that because of the heavy fog, our landing would be postponed until the skies cleared. He circled the plane several times over London, England, before coming to a stop.

I must say I was greatly disappointed when I saw the airport in London, England, just a big, shacky-looking building both inside and from the outside. The place was cold and dark and badly in need of repair.

Leaving London, England, our next stop was Vienna, Austria. In Vienna, Austria, we stopped so the Captain could have the airplane filled up with gasoline.

We then flew from Vienna, Austria, to Dusseldorf, Germany, where all the passengers were taken off the plane, and it was put into the airport building. I don't know why it was.

Our next stop was Istanbul, Turkey. Then after a short layover, we began the final leg of the journey to the land and family I had not seen in forty-eight years. No one can imagine what I felt at that time. My wife says I was trembling.

At seven o'clock in the evening our plane landed at the beautiful airport in Beirut, Lebanon. We were now eight thousand miles from Seminole, Texas. Because of the time changes, I did not know how many hours we had been en route. I only knew that I was finally back in my homeland.

As we approached the vast building, we saw a huge neon sign flashing in Arabic, French, and English, "You are welcome to Lebanon." That was the way I felt as my wife and I entered the huge airport lobby, which was filled with people coming and going.

We took our place in the long line of people waiting to go through customs. Then out of a clear blue sky a call came over the loud speaker, "Mr. Ed Aryain of the United States, please come to the head of the line. Your people are waiting for you."

The reason for this was that I have a cousin, Shebly Aryain, who had been the senator from the district of Rashayya for twelve years, and he had called the airport by telephone to tell them we were expected and just not to detain us.[2] Because Senator Shebly Aryain is so well respected in Lebanon, our luggage was not even opened for inspection.

Arriving at the main desk, the first person to make himself acquainted with us was my cousin Mr. Jameil Aryain, who lived in Beirut with his wife and four small sons.[3] This man had been left an orphan at a very early age, and my mother and sister had taken him into their home and provided for him. Since I had corresponded with this man by letter for several years, I felt I knew him very well.

He took us to another part of the airport, where I saw for the first time the family I had left so long ago. I saw my sister, her husband, their two fine sons, and cousins and family friends galore. I will say there were seventy-five or eighty people waiting for us. Everyone was very excited and happy at our arrival in Beirut, Lebanon. Some gave thanks to Allah, and others sang out their joy in a loud voice. My sister Hameedie prayed and cried in the same breath.

My sons said later that the airport officials let us go to the head of the line not because of the influence of my cousin Senator Shebly Aryain, but because they feared a riot might break out. Perhaps they are right.

Immediately after the introductions were made and the Old Country style of kissing, first on the right cheek, then on the left, then on the right again, people began asking questions about the English language and if it was hard to learn. Others asked about conditions in the United States, and did I know their people who lived in America, especially Texas.

Everyone took my wife to their hearts, especially my sister Hameedie, and although neither of them had any idea of what the other was saying (my wife speaks only English and my sister only Arabic) the feeling of closeness was immediate and warm.

Among the crowd at the airport was a newspaper man taking pictures of all the commotion and asking for information. The following day a long article appeared in a daily Arabic newspaper telling how I, Mohammed Aryain, had spent most of my life— forty-eight years—in the United States and had now returned with my American wife for a long visit with my people. He closed the article by saying in Arabic, "Welcome home, Mohammed Aryain, after forty-eight years in the Western World."

We spent the next four days in the home of my cousin Jameil Aryain in Beirut. Company came. Company came. My God, more company came! Day and night people came to see us. It is the custom in that country that each visitor is served Turkish coffee in a small china cup, and we were expected to drink coffee with each and every new arrival. My wife and I had terrible indigestion.

The day after our arrival, my cousin Senator Shebly Aryain and his beautiful young wife came to visit us along with his two brothers and their families and more cousins from his district of Rashayya. All day there was some merry making and feasting.

At the end of four days we moved from Beirut to the home of my sister in the village of Djedie, which is eighteen miles away and high in the mountains of Lebanon. I have never seen more beautiful scenery. The high mountains were covered with snow, and the running water and the cedars against this snow were a beautiful sight.

It is the custom of the Middle East that when a daughter marries, she moves to the home of her husband's family. A son remains on the home place with his parents. The children of Hameedie and Milhem al-Baraki (my sister and brother-in-law) are their daughter Bahawa, who lives away with her husband's family, and Neweff and Fayese. Neweff, the oldest son, was married and lived with his wife and two small children on the second floor of his parents' house. The youngest son Fayese, who was still single at that time, also lived with his parents.

Both of these fine young men are healthy and strong and are very hard workers. They have formed their own business of cutting out the white rock from the mountainside, crushing it into fine white sand, and then delivering it in their trucks and selling it to cement manufacturers. Since Lebanon had been experiencing the greatest building boom in its history, there was a big demand for this sand. My nephews' business had flourished.

The al-Baraki home is made of white stone and has a red tile roof. Because it is built on the side of the mountain, one must always be climbing or descending stairs. But the view is spectacular, and one can see the beautiful country for miles around. Across the front of the house is a combination kitchen and family room, a formal living room, a bedroom (which we occupied), and another complete kitchen so that my sister and her daughter-in-law can cook separately for their families. More bedrooms, a bathroom, and store rooms are on the upper and back part of the house. Across the length of the house there is a cement patio, which is shaded by grapevines, and it was on this beautiful vine-covered patio that we spent so many happy hours.

Calling on neighbors and friends is a very important part of the social life in the villages of the Middle East, and early the morning after our arrival in Djedie, company began arriving to welcome us. A few days later, friends from surrounding villages began calling upon us, so we had more company and more Turkish coffee and more indigestion.

We were very honored when Mr. Kamal Jumblatt, secretary of education in Lebanon, came on Sunday afternoon to pay his respects.[4] Mr. Jumblatt is a very pleasant man who lives in the neighboring village of Mukhtara.[5] He was educated in England and speaks Arabic, French, and English. This was nice for my wife who until this time had had to carry on most of her conversations in sign language, which tired her out. At first Mr. Jumblatt told us of a nice visit he had had with President Eisenhower at the White House in Washington, DC, a few years earlier.

My wife had been very concerned at seeing so many little children on the streets of Beirut, when they should have been in school. Now she asked about this. Mr. Jumblatt told her that several of the past presidents of Lebanon had misused money allocated for education and had used it to build beach attractions, casinos, and sports arenas. He also told us that the country was beginning a three-year program to improve education and that much money was to be spent building schools and training and hiring good teachers.

At the close of the visit, my wife and I felt very honored when the secretary of education for Lebanon invited us to come and visit his nearby castle, and we said, "Sure."

Then a bad snowstorm came to the mountains. Since we had not brought warm clothes from Texas, we were very uncomfortable. My wife decided she needed a warm skirt and heavy sweater, so we returned to Beirut to buy them. In a very nice shop my wife selected a beautiful Italian knit sweater, but when she finally made up her mind on a skirt, we found that the shop was out of her size. The owner of the shop then told us that he carried material in stock, and that if we returned in an hour the skirt would be ready.

We went out for lunch, then returned to the shop. Sure enough the skirt was ready in her size. We purchased the nice warm sweater and the skirt. Then we bought some beautiful little red shoes for Hameedie's grandchildren When we got back to Djedie, you have never seen such excited little children.

In a week or so the weather grew warmer, and my nephew Neweff said to me, "Uncle, it is time we began returning the visits of the people who have called upon you."

"Must we visit *every* person who has come to call upon us?" I asked in surprise.

"Yes, Uncle, we must return each call," he replied.

"That will take a very long time, for many people have come to visit us."

"Uncle, our family will be disgraced if we do not return the visits. That is the custom in this country."

So I agreed, and we began our round of calls. First we started in the village of Djedie. We called on several homes, and in each we were served Turkish coffee, candy, and fruit. Long before the morning was over I was full up to my ears with coffee, for it is the height of bad manners to refuse their treats.

Finally, I said to my nephew, "Enough visiting is enough. My wife is tired, and we are not accustomed to so much walking, especially since there are no sidewalks and we often have to climb steep steps to get to the houses built on the side of this mountain." I had in my mind that this excuse would settle the matter of all this visiting.

But my nephew replied, "We will go home so you and Auntie can rest for a while. Then we will start out visiting again this afternoon."

Heavenly days! What a day!

So that afternoon we did some more visiting. We made a lot of calls, but then my wife and I gave completely out.

On Saturday morning, however, we did go visit Mr. Kamal Jumblatt at his Mukhtara castle. This castle was built of brown sandstone in the eighteenth century. It fronts on a courtyard with a fountain and beautiful flowers. After climbing a flight of stairs, a servant ushered us into a large reception room where we found another fountain and pots of brightly colored flowers.

While we were admiring this room and the beautiful view of the valley, Mr. Jumblatt appeared. "Good morning, my friends from America. I am honored to have you in my home."

Turkish coffee, candy, and fruit were served (of course), and the conversation—in English—was very interesting, for Mr. Jumblatt, who has written three books on the history of Lebanon, told us about life for the Druze people in this community.

Then Mr. Jumblatt asked my wife if she would like to see the heirlooms which had been in his family for generations. Nothing could have pleased her more, for she is a great admirer of antiques. We went down several flights of stairs to a large basement where the fine china, silver, lamps, and furniture were stored. Mr. Jumblatt explained that these treasures had been removed from the rooms above to protect them when first the Turkish and then the French were bombarding this area with their heavy artillery. I thought this was very interesting.

Time passed quickly, and we had to bring our wonderful visit to Mukhtara castle to a close, but we will always remember our nice visit with Mr. Kamal Jumblatt, secretary of education for Lebanon.

We soon found that having a cousin who was a senator opened many doors for us. Frequently Senator Shebly Aryain called for us and drove us about the city showing us the sights. Beirut, Lebanon, is certainly one of the most beautiful cities in the world. It has wide sandy beaches on the Mediterranean Sea and yet is only a short drive from mountainous ski areas. Or one can drive over good highways to see the magnificent Roman ruins at Baalbek or perhaps ancient churches and mosques or visit the famous Cedars of Lebanon. Beirut is justly called the "Playground of the Middle East," and thousands upon thousands of people vacation there every year. To accommodate these tourists many modern hotels have been built, and I do mean *modern*, complete with running elevators, plush red carpets, and porters and maids to attend your every need.

Of particular interest to us was the famous American University of Beirut, which was established in 1866 under the guidance of David Bliss, who was sent to Lebanon by the American Presbyterian Mission Board.[6] I remember reading when the United Nations was being established in San Francisco that more of the delegates had received their education at the American University of Beirut than any other university in the world.

It was our privilege to spend several afternoons walking about the campus of this beautiful university, which is built on the side of a mountain overlooking the blue Mediterranean. As we watched the students from all over the world in their native costumes, the thought came to my mind that when our sons, Edward and Jameil, were small children, my wife and I had talked and hoped that we would be able to educate them at this American University of Beirut. But it is needless to say we never got around to it.

We were particularly pleased when Senator Shebly Aryain invited us to be his guests at a Parliament session and gave us visitors' permits. Guards are stationed at the entrance, and before a man is allowed to enter, he must unbutton his coat and be searched. A lady visitor must open her purse for inspection. The reason for this is that the guards are on the lookout for anyone with a gun. I thought this was very interesting.

When we had been in Lebanon three weeks, Senator and Mrs. Shebly Aryain invited us to spend the weekend at their plantation home in Rashayya. At the appointed hour he called for us at our hotel in his big, black, American-made Cadillac car. The drive of fifty miles was very beautiful. When we arrived at his home, we were welcomed by his family and the employees.

News travels fast. Soon company began coming in to visit the Senator's cousin from America and his American wife. Some of these people I actually remembered, for you will recall I told you about attending school here in Rashayya for one year.

Never will I forget the feast that was prepared in our honor. It is the custom of the Middle East that when a special guest is in the home, a young mutton is cooked whole and served with rice. This was done in our honor, and the dining room table was set with beautiful china, crystal, and silver. Twenty-five people were at the table, and toasts were proposed and speeches made before the serving of the lengthy Syrian dinner. Then more [speeches] were made later over Turkish coffee and fresh oranges.

It was in the home of Senator Shebly Aryain that I saw the sword, which the sultan of Turkey had given Shebly Aryain, Bashir the Great, over a century ago. I told you that story early in this writing. Remember?

The one sadness of this gathering, in fact of the entire trip to the Middle East, was that my mother and father had not lived to witness the return home of their son at long last. My father had died in 1916, and my mother in 1926.

During the feast I noticed one very handsome young man named Assam Aryain, who always politely raised his glass when toasts were made but did not take even one sip of the liquor. Later in the evening I learned that this young man was the grandson of

Uncle Mohmood Aryain, the man I had lived with when I had gone to school in Rashayya and who each day had sent me up the mountain to buy him a quart of liquor from a Christian friend. I had also heard that Uncle Mohmood's son Zeid Aryain (this young man's father) had also been a heavy drinker and that between the two of them had sold most of the family land to buy liquor. In fact, they had drunk so much and sold so much of the land that only a few acres had come down to this poor young man, Assam Aryain.

Noticing that this young man did not drink at all, I said to him, "Son, you are not like your father or grandfather."

He replied, "I do not drink or smoke, for I promised my mother before she died that I would not be like my father or grandfather, and to this day I have not broken my promise by taking a drink." I thought this was very interesting.

The next morning we visited the school, which I had attended in Rashayya. The white rock buildings stand high on a hill and are in remarkably good condition, considering the bombing Rashayya took when Lebanon was fighting to free itself from French rule.

It so happened that a cousin of mine, Adel Aryain, was now a teacher in this school. To me this young man was a person I could be proud of. He had not had money or land, but he had worked hard and managed to educate himself at the American University of Beirut and could now command a good teaching job.

I will say three-fourths of the children in the school were Christian, one-fourth were Druze, and a handful were Moslems. Adel Aryain proudly displayed the work of his pupils, and the children were delighted that they could recite their learning before a visitor from the United States. I must say that we were as happy as the children.

My wife was an added attraction to these bright-eyed little children, and they took in every detail of her dress, purse, gloves, hairstyle, and just general appearance. I am sure that most of these children were seeing an American woman for the first time in their lives. I also have the feeling that our visit to the school was discussed again and again on the school grounds and later in the homes of these children. It was an extremely pleasant morning.

Leaving the school, we walked down the main street of Rashayya and stopped in a small store so I could buy a card of bobby pins my wife needed for her hair. The owner of the store charged me two liras for the bobby pins, which meant I paid about seventy-five cents in American money.

All through the day, the thought kept coming through my head that I had been overcharged by the store owner for the card of bobby pins. And that evening as we all sat quietly around the fire I asked Mrs. Shebly Aryain how much she usually paid for a card of bobby pins for her hair.

"About seven cents in Lebanese money," she replied.

Then I knew for sure that I had been taken in. The store owner had the same idea that so many merchants in the Middle East have—that all American tourists are rich, and now was the time to take them for a ride and get their share of the American dollar.

The weekend in Rashayya was wonderful. We had been wined and dined to no end, but it was nice to get back to the peace and quiet of our hotel room in Beirut.

12

Holy Land Tourists

· · ·

WHEN WE HAD APPLIED FOR OUR VISAS BEFORE LEAVING the United States, we had planned to spend Easter Sunday in Jerusalem, Jordan [Israel], but in all the commotion and visiting during the past three weeks, we had honestly neglected to make advance reservations for this trip, which my wife particularly longed for.

When we realized that Easter Sunday was almost upon us, we went to an airline office, only to be told there were no reservations to be had. Every seat had been sold weeks ago. We tried a second office and were told the same thing—no space available.

At the third airline office, however, we were told that the last two seats on the plane going to Amman, Jordan, the following afternoon were still available. The ticket agent advised me to take this flight to Amman, then go by taxi to Jerusalem, for it would be impossible to get hotel accommodations in Jerusalem (the Holy City) at this late date. So we took these two seats and were glad to get them.

The next day while waiting at the Beirut airport for our flight, we became acquainted with an American tourist, Mrs. Hazel

Hayman of Denver, Colorado, who was going to Amman, Jordan, to visit her family. Her son-in-law, Mr. Paul Arnold, was employed in the American Embassy in Jordan.

Arriving in Amman, Jordan, in the late afternoon, we went through customs, and then Mrs. Hayman introduced us to her family who were there to meet her. Mr. Paul Arnold insisted that we drive into the city with them and said he would help us find a place to stay, for all hotels were filled to overflowing.

At first we declined this offer, not wanting to be a bother to him, but he told us it was part of his job to help American tourists in Jordan. So we accepted his kind invitation and have always been grateful for his help. After trying two hotels without success, Mr. Paul Arnold found us a room at the Amman Hotel for one night. We were told, though, we would have to move out of the room the next day, since it was reserved from that time on. We thanked Mr. Paul Arnold and went to our room.

The room was quiet and comfortable, and we had a good night's rest. Then the next morning our first chore was to locate a hotel room for the coming night, since we must vacate our present pleasant quarters. After asking for rooms in other nice hotels without success, I found a small out-of-the-way hotel which had a vacancy. But when we saw the room, my wife flatly refused to move in. I cannot say I blamed her, for it was nothing but a rat hole. We then tried the Continental, where we were relieved to find that they had a room, and we promptly moved in. The beds were clean, and there were no drunks wandering about the place.

I then hired a taxi to drive us to Jerusalem, a distance, I will say, of fifty miles. We arrived there about 10 a.m.

Easter Sunday in all its glory was reflected in the crowd of thousands upon thousands of people moving through the narrow street toward the gates of the Old City of Jerusalem down to the Tomb and the Dome of the Rock. Christian people from all over the world in their native costumes had come to celebrate Easter

Sunday in the Holy City of Jerusalem, and once you were in this crowd, there was no turning back. You simply had to move along with it.

Arriving at the entrance gate of the Old City, we entered into another narrow street. On each side of this street were small shops and stalls selling everything under the sun—fish, crosses, souvenirs, bread, baskets, embroidery work, beautiful copper pots, fruit, candy, and more crosses. Each man was hawking his goods and inviting the crowd into his shop. By our dress, they recognized us as Americans and called out to my wife in English, "Please, American Madam, come into my shop and look around." They didn't seem to be doing much business to me.

We moved with the crowd through a courtyard. Then we began moving slowly down a long, dark stairway. The original walls of solid rock had been reinforced with iron strips for the safety of the crowd. There were other signs that repair work had been done. I thought this was very interesting.

As we moved slowly down the long, narrow stairway, my wife told me we were about to visit the traditional site of the burial tomb and resurrection of Our Lord (Jesus). At the time I didn't think to ask her how in the world she knew what we were going to see, and now she says she doesn't remember.

At the bottom of the stairs we entered a small room where people were kneeling and praying over the tomb and placing small green leaves on the marble slab. When our turn came, we knelt and placed our hands on the marble slab and offered our prayers of thankfulness for the privilege of visiting this holy place and mixing with these people from all over the world.

On leaving the courtyard, we walked into one of the small shops to look for gifts to take home to our family. For our sons we selected copies of the New Testament with front and back covers made of wood from the famous Cedars of Lebanon. For our youngest granddaughter, Amy, we bought a group of camels carved from olive wood, and for Linda, a dainty filigree silver bracelet. Since our grandson Chip was not to be born for another three years, we did not buy him a present. Sorry, Chip.

Then my wife came upon a beautiful white Bible with a cover of mother-of-pearl and quickly purchased it. Later, I asked her why she had bought this white Bible, and she replied, "I would like very much for our granddaughters to carry this Bible at their wedding ceremonies."[1]

How is that for long-range planning? At that time Linda was eight years old, and Amy was only six years of age. But my wife believes in being prepared for any and all occasions.

Within the walls of Old Jerusalem is located the Dome of the Rock. In the very center of this building is the sacred rock from Mount Mariah where Abraham prepared to sacrifice his son Isaac.[2] This rock is sacred to Moslem people as well as Christians, for they believe that from this rock the Prophet Mohammed ascended into heaven. I thought this was very interesting.

Later our guide, a young Arab man who spoke English, showed us what they believe to be the original key to the stables where King Solomon kept his horses. He was even kind enough to let me hold this ten-inch solid iron key while my wife took pictures on our movie camera.

Late in the afternoon we returned by taxi to Amman, two very tired but happy people. We had planned to visit both Jerusalem and Bethlehem the same day, but we had learned that one could not see in a week—let alone one day—all the sights of Jerusalem, the Holy City.

Bright and early the following morning we were dressed and ready for the trip to Bethlehem. Now that Easter Sunday had passed, it was easy to engage a taxi, though the highway was crowded bumper to bumper with traffic coming the other way as people left the Holy Land in droves.

The main street of Bethlehem is typical of all small towns in the Middle East. The streets are narrow and crowded with shops where merchants are alert and eager to get their share of the American tourist's dollar. The Church of the Nativity, built by King Justinian in the sixth century, is a vast and beautiful building, but it has only one small door, which one must stoop under to get through. Our English-speaking guide told us that this small door was probably the only part of the original inn which remained.

At the time we passed through this church, an Armenian service was being conducted (in Armenian).

On the floor is a silver star showing the actual spot where Jesus was born. There are also slabs of stone where the Wise Men of the East placed their gifts for the Christ child.

From the balcony of the Church of the Nativity one looks across to Shepherd's Field, where the shepherds were watching over their flocks when the great light appeared in the night and where, according to my wife, the Heavenly Hosts sang out their praises of "Glory to God" at the birth of the Savior. Maybe so.

High in the towers of the Church of the Nativity are the famous bells, which we have all heard and seen on television when they ring out on Christmas Eve. I found these bells very interesting.

Leaving Bethlehem, we drove to Jericho, then down to the River Jordan to the very spot where my wife said Jesus was baptized by John the Baptist. It is a very slow flowing river. Our daughter-in-law's father is a Baptist preacher.

Both my wife and I were pleased to see that this spot had not been turned into a commercial attraction. There is only one booth there where one can buy bottles of water from the River Jordan and Cokes.

Looking at the River Jordan one can scarcely believe that so much fighting and killing had raged, and is still raging, over this peaceful body of water.

The sad part of this trip was seeing the makeshift refugee camps where thousands upon thousands of Arabs have had to live in poverty and degradation since they fled their homes in the border war of 1948. Here men and their families just barely exist.

Going back to Amman in the late afternoon, we made reservations to return to Beirut the following day. Our wonderful trip to the Holy Land had ended.

13

Cutting Ties in Henna

. . .

AFTER A DAY OR TWO OF COMPLETE REST IN OUR HOTEL, WE moved lock, stock, and luggage to my sister's home in Djedie. From then on that would be our headquarters. The weather had turned warm, and the snow on the mountains had melted. The sun shone, and the flowers were in full bloom. We had an opportunity to sit on the grapevine-covered porch and visit and become really acquainted with my family. It was pleasant to be in this quiet mountain home away from the hustle and bustle of a city, even if it was the Holy City of Jerusalem. Only occasionally did friends and neighbors come to visit us, Hameedie had more time to sit with us, and we could talk of the long years I had been away.

One evening as the family sat quietly together, my brother-in-law Milham al-Baraki told me that during the First World War the Turkish government sent Jamal Pasha to be commander-in-chief of the Turkish army stationed in Lebanon.[1] This was the same man who had been responsible for the Armenian massacre and was known throughout the Middle East as Saffah the Blood Shedder.

Jamal Pasha ruled by terror. He seized the fine monasteries and turned them into private castles for himself and his officials. He imposed military conscription of all Lebanese men, seized live-stock, and replaced Lebanese currency with inflated Turkish money.

But he was particularly cruel to the Christians of Lebanon, for he thought all Christians were traitors to Turkey and spies for the Allies, especially for France. He went so far as to build a Hanging House, and it was in this building that the hangings of most of the Christian leaders took place. Occasionally Jamal Pasha would also order the hanging of a Moslem so that the public and newspapers would not get the idea that all his hatred was directed just toward the Christians.

Jamal Pasha then ordered all food supplies coming into Lebanon stopped and closed all roads leading into Syria and Palestine and put them under heavy guard. Since Lebanon is a small country and gets its wheat, corn, and barley from Syria and Palestine, famine was soon upon the land. It is a known fact that thousands of Lebanese people died from starvation and disease. Never, never in all history had Lebanon suffered as during the rule of Jamal Pasha, the Blood Shedder.

Milham al-Baraki then told me that the only way people could survive was to escape over the mountain paths into Syria and that soon thousands of Lebanese were in Damascus begging for food and living off bread lines. Or perhaps a man could feed his family by slipping over the mountains into Syria and buying food and then taking a chance on getting it back to his home in Lebanon. Such trips were difficult and dangerous and took a week or ten days, although ordinarily the journey took only two days.

Of course, this was not a new story to me, for I had read close-ly in both American and Arabic newspapers the accounts of dread-ful suffering in Lebanon under the rule of Jamal Pasha, the Blood Shedder.

"When I was a young man," my brother-in-law told me, "my

family was in dire need of wheat, corn, and barley. Since my father was dead and I was the oldest son, it was my responsibility to provide for my mother and the younger children. I therefore had to make the dangerous trip to Syria for food, or the family would starve. Riding one donkey and leading three pack donkeys, I began the trip to Damascus. I traveled the mountain paths only during the night and hid in bushes and behind rocks in the daytime. It took me a long while, and several times I was almost caught by the Turks, but finally I reached Damascus. Then I was told there was no wheat, corn, or barley for sale in the city but that I might be able to buy some in the village of Henna, which was eighteen miles south of Damascus. I then went to Henna and was fortunate enough to find the food my family needed so desperately. It was also on this trip that I met your sister Hameedie Aryain. Later when I could, I went back and married her and brought her back here to Lebanon as my wife."

I thought this was all very interesting. I had often wondered over the years how my sister of Henna, Syria, had met and married a native of Lebanon. Now I knew.

Here in this mountain country my wife and I felt relaxed and good. Our appetites were good, and our sleeping hours were regular. When we wished to go sight-seeing, we could very easily, for three times a day a bus stopped near Hameedie's house, and we could go into Beirut or perhaps to a different village in the mountains. Through our binoculars, we could look across the valley and see the waterfalls near the village of Jezzine, so one day we decided to go there.[2]

The people of Jezzine make their living by carving cutlery sets, salad serving sets, letter openers, and pocket knives from the horns of mountain sheep. They give their goods the shape of birds and decorate them with bright stones. Now, my sons Edward and Jameil, you know where we bought the beautiful letter openers which we brought home to you.

My sister's home sits upon a small parcel of land which has been cut out of the mountain. At the back of the house and on each side, the mountain is covered with ancient, gnarled, twisted olive trees. A narrow path leads down to a sparkling clear mountain spring. The menfolk have built a retaining wall across the stream, thus forming a pool of clear, cold water, which then overflows the wall and flows on down the mountain. This is a very restful and relaxing spot, and many were the times my wife and I would walk through the olive trees and down to the pool for a cool drink of water.

Late one afternoon as we approached the pool, we heard the clatter of voices. This was not too unusual, for the neighbor women frequently came to the pool to fill their water jugs and young boys sometimes drove their goats to the streams to let them drink. We always exchanged a friendly greeting with these people. Then they would be on their way.

But this particular afternoon the voices we heard did not sound like those of the people my wife and I had encountered there before.

We walked to within ten feet of the pool, where we found five or six women filling their water jugs, two washing clothes in the stream, and several children playing in the water. I only had to glance at their clothes to realize that they were Gypsies, and they seemed to realize just as quickly that we were Americans.

I will never know which of us were the most startled—the Gypsy women or my wife and me.

The women quickly filled their jugs, gathered up their laundry, and herded the bewildered looking little children down the mountainside toward the highway.

Later in the evening we heard from a neighbor that a band of Gypsies were camped down by the river a mile or so from the house.

Early the following morning while we were having coffee on

the patio, three of these Gypsy women came to the house. Hameedie was nice and friendly to them, but when they said they wanted to trade her some goat's butter for flour, she gave them a very firm "no." Later Hameedie told us that she would have no part of this trading, for their butter might not be clean, or their goats might be diseased.

I will never forget how during this conversation these Gypsy women kept watching my wife, admiring her dress, shoes, and her fair skin. I had the feeling that these women wanted very much to touch my wife's dress and feel the material. But Hameedie—bless her heart—would not permit them to get close to my wife. She very politely managed always to stand between my wife and the Gypsy women.

As the only son, I was still the owner of the old house and a small parcel of land in Henna, Syria, but I wanted to sell the house and give the money and the land to my sister Hameedie. So bright and early on a Saturday morning a taxi arrived at the door to take my sister, my brother-in-law, my wife, and me to Damascus, Syria.

At the Syrian border a guard looked at our visas and asked, "Are you a relative of Senator Shebly Aryain from the district of Rashayya?" When I told him that I was the senator's cousin, the guard smiled and waved us through without inspecting our luggage. "Welcome to our country. Any kin of Senator Aryain's is a friend of ours."

We arrived in Damascus in time for lunch. Then my wife and I checked into the Cattan Hotel for the night, and the driver took my sister and her husband on out to Henna to stay the night.

Early the following morning our driver returned to our hotel to take us to Henna. As we approached the little village where I had been born, my heart began pounding. When we drew up before the little rock house where I had grown up and which I had not seen for forty-eight years, my eyes filled with tears.

The house was in good repair and was much the same as when I had left it so long ago. The young man from Damascus who was buying it for his parents seemed pleased with the price I had asked.

Within thirty minutes after our arrival, people began coming to visit us, and I spent most of the morning answering questions about America, questions much like those I had asked as a boy of the men who had been to the United States.

Everyone was kind and friendly to me and especially to my wife, but I could not help feeling sad and somehow a stranger. For this was a whole new generation. Most of the people I had known here had either died or gone away. Only one old man I talked to remembered the day I had left this village to come to the New World. Two Christian men, one Druze man, and a Druze woman were the only ones left who remembered my parents.

I asked about the family of the famous outlaw Joseph-Al-Hamid and was told that his youngest son, Joseph, who had been my playmate and close friend, had long been dead. No one even remembered the two sisters. They did tell me, however, that the oldest son, Hamid-Al-Hamid, still lived in Henna but that at this time of the year he stayed in the valley, where the weather was warmer and he could tend to his sheep and goats.

In the afternoon we walked to the top of the mountain where the Druze people are buried. As we climbed the steep trail, I remembered vividly the day I had said good-bye to my parents and sisters and begun the long walk over these mountains to Beirut where I would take a ship to America. It seemed I could still hear my mother crying out to me, "Please, Mohammed, come back to us. Do not leave us with this sorrow."

When we reached the windswept Druze cemetery, I stood for a long time before the graves of my mother and father. My heart was filled with sorrow, and I made no effort to check the tears which ran down my face. After a while I removed my hat and offered a prayer of thanks for the life which these good people had given me, and I asked forgiveness for the sorrow I had caused them.

As sad as I felt, I was thankful that I had been given the privilege of visiting these two graves, for in doing so I felt I had finally kept my promise to my parents to return. I had not returned when I had planned to, and certainly not when I had wanted to, but finally I *had* returned. That seems to be the way life frequently works out, and I felt very peaceful as my wife and I were driven back to Damascus.

The following morning I left my wife to spend the day in the hotel, and I returned alone to Henna to draw up the papers for the sale of the old homeplace and to give my sister the money and to turn over to her the deed for the plot of land.

When this was done, I went for a walk through the little village I had once known so well, but I was saddened because I did not really know anyone here now.

I was told that Hamid-Al-Hamid had heard that I was in Henna and had asked about him, so he had made the trip from the valley to see me the previous night. But of course by the time he reached Henna we had returned to Damascus.

I have always been sorry that I missed seeing him, for I think we could have spent a pleasant time together.

That afternoon my sister, my brother-in-law, and I took the taxi back to Damascus to join my wife. The two days I had spent in Henna, my birthplace, ended forever the ties with the past. Only the memories remain.

14

Gunshots in Lebanon

. . .

DAMASCUS IS A BEAUTIFUL CITY, COMBINING THE MODERN AND
the ancient. There are fine hotels, and yet the streets are decorated with magnificent Roman arches and pillars. A trip to the
"Street Called Straight" is a must for every tourist, for it was here
my wife tells me that Saul was taken to the home of Ananias after
he was blinded while on his way to persecute the early Christians.
After his eyesight was restored Saul changed his name to Paul and
became a teacher and preacher.[1]

Shops line both sides of this street, and in one of them we purchased beautiful copper bowls, trays, and vases and handwork,
mosaic jewelry boxes, and lovely tables of teakwood and mother-
of-pearl which decorate our home today.

We also visited the Omayades [Omayyad] Mosque, which is one
of the most magnificent buildings we have ever seen. The head of
John the Baptist is buried in the mosque.[2]

Sooner or later almost every American tourist suffers a stomach
upset caused by the drastic change in food, irregular hours, or
impure water. My luck ran out in Damascus. Never have I had
such a spell of upset stomach, and for one day and night I was con-

fined to the hotel room. It is no fun to have such a sickness in a strange city. The several days we had planned to spend in Damascus were cut down to three, and we returned to Djedie, which was a pleasant change.

The famous olive trees play an important part in the lives of the people of the Middle East, and my wife was particularly interested in seeing these lovely old gnarled trees with long grayish green leaves growing on the terraced sides of mountains. The trunks of trees are sometimes bent and twisted into strange shapes. In some the wind has worn large holes in their lower branches, but the trees continue to live and produce olives. It is a known fact that some of these trees are hundreds of years old.

Often in conversation one man will ask another, "How was your olive crop this year?" just as an American farmer will ask his neighbor, "How was your wheat, cotton, or corn crop?" And as in all agriculture, the harvest varies greatly. One grove of trees may produce only a few hundred pounds of olive oil, and the next may produce a half a ton. Olive oil is of great importance throughout the Mediterranean world, so of course it is one of Lebanon's most important exports.

About twenty-five years ago I began reading that many Lebanese farmers were pulling up their olive trees and replacing them with apple trees because there was such a large market for apples in Europe. American agricultural experts had been sent there to oversee and advise in this very important changeover. At the time I wondered if this was a wise thing for the Lebanese farmers to do. While I was there, I asked many questions and learned that Lebanon had proved to be an ideal place for growing apples and that the new trees had produced a great quantity of fruit. For a few years the farmers had enjoyed a larger income from their orchards.

But then the apples had been over-produced, and the market had fallen, and so the farmers were worse off than before.

Every farmer I talked to in Lebanon expressed regret that he had sacrificed his faithful olive trees, which always provided a yearly income for his family, for the get-rich-quick plan of growing apples. Always they added, "I wish I had my old olive trees back."

Since our arrival in Lebanon, we had seen posters advertising Baalbek as one of the greatest sights in the world.[3] We had read of the vast amounts of money the country spends trying to restore these ancient Roman ruins. When we were recovered from the trip to Henna, I rented the same taxi and hired the same driver to take us, my sister and her husband, and their son Fayeze to see this sight, which everyone said would be the high point of our trip.

For several hours we drove through the most beautiful mountain country I have ever seen. Then we descended into the Bekaa Valley and traveled through marvelous wheat fields, citrus orchards, and groves of olive trees.[4] It was good for the family to be together in the car. The only sad part was that the driver was so eager to get to the United States that he said that if I could help him, he would gladly be our housekeeper, cook, chauffeur, and gardener. I was very sorry to have to tell this poor man that there was nothing I could do to help him.

We had, of course, seen pictures of Baalbek, but they had not prepared us for the first actual sight of the ruins of the magnificent temples built in the first century A.D. by the Romans in this valley, which provided their armies with wheat and grain.

I particularly liked two enormous stone lions guarding the entry to the Great Temple, which my wife says was built to honor Baal. Of the original fifty-four columns which supported the Temple of Jupiter, only six are still standing, but we could walk around the fallen columns and study and admire the beautifully carved vines, flowers, lions, emperors, and sheaves of wheat. These columns were sixty-two feet high and eight feet in diameter!

The Temple of Bacchus is the best preserved of the original buildings. Its walls rise up 130 feet, and the columns are still standing.[5] As we studied them, we wondered how in the world it had been possible for men to build such structures back in those days, for there has never been unearthed a piece of equipment for moving these enormous slabs of stone from distant quarries and then lifting them into place. Some of these stones weigh *seven hundred tons* and are as large as our bedroom in Seminole. I am not exaggerating!

The Temple of Venus is particularly lovely, for it is built in the shape of a nice horseshoe. Its pillars are of pink marble and decorated with flowers and young children and their mothers.[6]

It is anybody's guess how these temples were constructed. They are beautiful today as ruins, and centuries ago, before they were touched by earthquakes, fires, and war, their beauty must have been beyond description.

A trip to Baalbek is time and money well spent.

Something else every tourist wishes to see are the famous Cedars of the Lord, or as they are commonly known, the Cedars of Lebanon. In ancient times these vast forests provided wood for paneling the palaces of the pharaohs and for King Solomon's temple. The wood was used for the ships which explored and set up trade throughout the Mediterranean world. But during the centuries Turkey ruled Lebanon, the famous trees were cut down without any consideration for the future. Later the French also used the wood wastefully, until now only four hundred of the ancient cedars remain.

The loss of these cedar forests have had a damaging effect upon Lebanon's economy, for tourists who visit the famous groves in the mountains near Bsharri are disappointed to find that they fall short of the descriptions they had read back home in the Bible.

The Lebanese government now protects these trees and has started a massive plan to reseed the mountains with cedars. The cedar has, in fact, become the national symbol of Lebanon and is pictured on the country's stamps and on its flag.

We had naturally wanted to see the Cedars of Lebanon and were delighted when my cousin Jameil Aryain told us that he had made arrangements for us to accompany a political group of which he was president in an all-day trip to Bsharri, where we would picnic and then take a ski lift to the top of the snow-covered mountain to see a magnificent view.

We had been aware since arriving in Lebanon that my cousin's political group, which was made up of Christians, Moslems, and Druze, hoped one day to unite Lebanon, Jordan, Syria, Palestine, Egypt, and Iraq under one flag as it had been in early history.

We had also been aware that this political group was opposed by one made up only of Christians who did not want this to happen, since they are the majority in Lebanon as they are no place else in the Middle East. Neither of these political groups had made any trouble, but we had been told that the Lebanese government was watching both organizations closely.

As I said, my cousin Jameil Aryain was the president of the first political group, and my wife and I were delighted that he had invited us to go along on the outing to see the famous Cedars of Lebanon. At 6 a.m. my wife and I took a taxi to the place where the large group was assembling, then boarded one of the many buses. Each bus was filled to capacity with men, women, and children who were in high spirits and looking forward to a day of fun and good fellowship.

It was a four-hour drive to Bsharri and soon after the buses pulled away, people began eating from the picnic boxes. The sun was shining brightly, and everyone sang happily as we traveled over smooth highways through the beautiful mountains.

In the middle of the morning the buses all halted at the village of Bsharri, the birthplace of the famous Lebanese poet and painter

Kahlil Gibran, and our bus driver informed us that we would have a few minutes rest period and that anyone who wished to visit the Kahlil Gibran Museum could do so.[7]

This was a particular treat for my wife, for she has always been an admirer of Kahlil Gibran's book *The Prophet*. So after paying a small entrance fee, she and I entered the white rock house where he had lived, and a guide escorted us into his workroom. On the walls were his original paintings, and on his desk were ink wells, pens, pencils, writing paper, brushes, tubes of paint, and open books. My wife said she had the feeling that Kahlil Gibran had just gone out for a short walk and would soon return. Seeing the Kahlil Gibran Museum is time and money well spent.

We boarded our bus again, and soon we entered the beautiful park area, which was our destination. At the entry I noticed that the Lebanese government maintained an army post nearby, and I was told that soldiers patrolled the ski area to keep order.

When we reached the picnic area, we all got out of the buses, and many of the men went immediately to the ski lift while the women selected a nice spot away from the parking area and began to spread the picnic lunches. As the men walked along, they talked and laughed, for although some were Christian, some Druze, and some Moslem, they were close friends and called each other "Brother." Each man wore a button on his lapel to signify that he belonged to the political organization which wished to unite all the Arab countries under one flag.

My wife and I spent a happy hour wandering through the grove of stately cedar trees, admiring their massive trunks and wide-spreading branches. Then we walked to a stand where crosses, picture frames, salt and pepper shakers, bowls, and other souvenirs made from cedar were being sold. There we purchased a small bowl and mallet made of cedar, not because it would be useful but because the grain of the wood was especially beautiful and because some of the bark from the tree remained on the bowl.

We went back to join the others, and just as we were about to eat our picnic lunch, we heard gunshots. We could tell from the sound that the gunshots came from the ski lift. Later we learned that many people had been standing in long lines to buy tickets for an afternoon ride on the ski lift when a young man from the all-Christian political organization, which wanted to keep Lebanon separate, had pushed a young man from our group out of the line and taken his place.

Harsh words were exchanged between the two men. Then other members of both organizations got involved, and trouble started in a big way. Fist fights broke out, and there was rock throwing and club swinging. Now, instead of just a few men involved in this commotion, there were dozens of men fighting.

The gunshot my wife and I had heard had been fired by a soldier trying to stop the fighting and restore order. But the warning shots had not stopped the fighting.

In a moment we saw soldiers running from all directions across the parking area and picnic grounds with rifles and revolvers in their hands. They quickly surrounded the ski lift and the parking lot and ordered everyone to stay in their places and remain quiet.

My wife could not believe her eyes that we were right in the middle of a shooting commotion, and I must say that I was pretty surprised.

When order was finally restored, the Christian man who had started the pushing had been severely beaten. The soldiers ordered him to go home, then arrested four men from our group.

Believe me—my wife and I were ready to get out of the park right then and go back to Beirut, but it took an hour or so to get everybody back on the buses.

But we had only driven a short way from the ski area when our buses were stopped by soldiers from the nearby army post and we were told we could go no further. Our driver asked why we were being detained, and one of the soldiers replied, "We do not know, but this order has come down from higher officials."

My cousin and some of the other men left the bus and went to ask the officer why we had been stopped.

"Something has happened you are not aware of," the officer replied in a very serious tone. "We have just received word that the man who started this trouble and was so badly beaten went home as he was ordered to do. But then he took his gun and sat down on the porch with it in his hand. Then when a bus, which had nothing to do with our group, passed through his town, he fired into it and killed an innocent man."

This officer, who was a Druze, then said that feeling was running high in two or three of the Christian towns which we would have to pass through and that he was afraid if our buses drove through these towns before things cooled down, there might be much more shooting and killing.

When my nephew reported this conversation to me—in English—my wife really became frightened. She asked me if there would be any more shooting, and I told her, "I do not know for sure. Maybe not."

Then, since she had been seated by the window and I on the aisle, I made her change seats with me so that she would be safer from flying bullets.

My nephew told the officer that my wife and I were American citizens and suggested that he call the American ambassador in Beirut and ask him to come and take my wife and me out of the trouble area in an official car.

The officer studied upon this suggestion for a while but then shook his head. "No, I am afraid that some young hothead with a gun will fire into the ambassador's car, and we do not want that."

My cousin then said in a loud voice that the officer should call Senator Shebly Aryain who would come in his car with an escort of maybe twenty or twenty-five cars filled with Druze men who would be armed with rifles and ready for trouble.

"That is the last thing I will do," the office said flatly. "To call

Senator Shebly Aryain to come with armed men will only cause worse trouble, for the Christian people in this locality do not have much love for the Druze people."

My cousin then grumbled that he intended to tell Senator Shebly Aryain of this incident and that he in turn would bring this matter up before the Parliament.

For the next three hours we were detained while the officer in charge tried to think of a way to move our buses through the dangerous area. The buses were very comfortable, and the weather was ideal, but one soon tires of waiting and wondering if one is to be shot. It also makes one a little nervous. Especially my wife.

While we were being detained, other cars would slow down as they passed us, and people would shout out their windows, "This is good enough for you. I hope they keep you stranded here all night and all day tomorrow." These people were really having a lot of fun at our expense.

The army officer was sincere in his desire to keep down trouble. While we waited, he told me that when he was appointed commander of this army post, the people in the surrounding Christian towns had objected and said they wanted a Christian officer instead of a Druze in charge. They went so far as to get out a petition with four thousand signatures demanding his removal, but nothing came of this petition when it was presented in the Parliament.

He then told me that when he had taken his pledge to fulfill his duties as commander of the army post, he had put his right hand on the Holy Bible and his left on the Koran and sworn to God, or Allah, to treat all men as brothers, always teaching that there must be no hard feelings because of religious differences, and promising to be fair to all men under his command be they Christian, Moslem, Jew, or Druze. I thought this was very interesting.

He then told me another interesting story: "Once I was invited to a nearby Christian village to make a talk to the people after church, and I took as my subject 'Brotherly Love.' 'We are all Lebanese,' I said, 'be we Christian, Moslem, Druze, or Jew, and there should be no hate between us because of our religious beliefs. Please do not mention to your children about the Druze massacre of the Christians in 1860. Let us all forget the hatred of the past and work together to build Lebanon into a strong country. We all believe in the same God or Allah, let us have unity.'"

"Do you think this talk helped?" Jameil asked the officer.

"I do not know for sure, but I hope so," he replied, then sadly added, "but I do know that every Christian boy over seven years of age has heard of the Druze massacre of Christians in 1860. People should forget this terrible thing in our past and not repeat it to children."

Through all of this talk my poor wife was scared half to death and did not seem at all interested in what the officer was saying. She did not know if we would live to get back to Beirut, much less back to Texas. Sometimes I had my doubts.

Finally, my cousin yelled at the officer, "What are you going to do next?"

"Do not rush me," the officer replied. "I am doing everything I know to do. Just sit down and be quiet while I go into the office and think and study upon what will be best to do."

The officer left, but in a short time he returned and said, "I think I have thought of a solution. At least we will try my plan. I have a very good friend in the next town who happens to be a Catholic priest. Also the preacher and his wife in the town are very friendly toward me, and I believe I can depend on these people to help. Here is what I will do. I will drive into town and talk to the priest and the preacher and the preacher's wife and ask them to come in their car and lead your buses through the overly Christian towns where you may get shot."

The officer drove away but then shortly returned with the priest, the preacher, the preacher's wife, and their son in an

American-made Buick. The preacher's son was driving, and his mother sat beside him in the front seat. The Catholic priest and the preacher sat in the back seat with the windows open so that they could be clearly seen. The boy turned the Buick around in front of the first of our buses, and the Catholic priest waved his hand for the bus drivers to follow closely behind them.

Our buses all followed the car in close formation through the three dangerous Christian villages, and there was no trouble. Outside the third town, the boy pulled the Buick over to the side of the road, and as our buses passed, the Catholic priest and the preacher waved and wished us luck.

Heavenly Days! What a day it had been!

When we finally reached our apartment in Beirut, my poor wife was trembling like a leaf in a strong wind. She made me lock the apartment door and the door of our bedroom. Never, never, have I seen her so frightened!

The headlines of the Beirut morning newspaper carried a long write-up of this Sunday disturbance in Bsharri at the ski head-quarters.

As I told you early in this writing, religious differences have caused more trouble and commotion and hatred in the Middle East than any other problem, especially in Lebanon.

Even today when my wife and I hear the famous Cedars of Lebanon mentioned, our thoughts do not dwell on the beauty of these magnificent trees but upon our terrifying experience that day.

15

Beirut Goodbyes

. . .

I AM OF THE OPINION THAT NOT MANY MEN ARE AWARE OF the time and money their wives spend in beauty shops. In Texas my wife has always had a standing weekly appointment. This is fine and good with me, for I always wanted her to look nice.

So a few days after our arrival in Lebanon, it was time to locate a hairdresser. My cousin suggested we try one of the fine shops in downtown Beirut. So for the first time in our married lives I was taking my wife to the beauty shop and waiting two or three hours, then paying her bill, which was about fifteen Lebanese liras. The price was pretty much in line with what a shampoo and set cost in America.

The beauty shops in Beirut are really something to see. The waiting rooms are elegantly furnished, and there is plenty of reading material. The operators are all young men and women who have received their training in Paris, France. I thought this was very interesting. The operator assigned to my wife spoke excellent English, and he made an extra effort to please her. I can truthfully say I never saw her hair look lovelier.

I knew when we left that shop that this would not be our last trip here. And sure enough—I was right.

After two or three visits to the beauty shop, I felt I could leave her alone while the work was underway, and I walked up and down the busy streets of Beirut. This way the time passed more quickly, and I decided that a weekly trip to the beauty shop was not such a bad ordeal after all.

Each time she left the shop, my wife would tell me that the young operator had asked many questions about America. One day he said, "American Madam, if I could go to America, could I get a job in the shop where you have your work done? Would your friends be willing for me to do their beauty work?"

My wife replied, "If you came to America, I am sure you could do plenty of business."

And why not? He was an excellent operator, and women, being what they are, would be pleased to show off their hair dressing done by this young man.

To me it is a shame that someone like this young hairdresser who would give his right arm to live in America is denied the opportunity. People such as this would make good solid citizens for our country and could make a better life for themselves.

Sometimes when I see so much unrest among the young people who were fortunate enough to have been born in America, I ask myself why are these youngsters so unhappy? So restless and unsettled? To my way of thinking they should be grateful for this birthright and pray to God their thankfulness that they live in America. They take everything so completely for granted and do not seem to realize that to live in America is the fondest dream of so many young people in the Middle East, and I imagine in the rest of the world also.

Throughout Beirut there are quarters where people—French, Jewish, Armenian, Greek, and so on—live together and cling to the ways and traditions of their old countries. But there is also a very beautiful district where Americans live in Beirut.[1] In this district one actually has the feeling of being back in the United States, for there are department stores which are stocked with American goods which are well displayed and plainly marked in English. There are self-service drug stores where American medicines and cosmetics are sold and large, well-lighted supermarkets where an American woman in Beirut can buy anything she could get back home. There is no haggling over prices in these stores. Things run smoothly, and all cash register receipts are printed in English. Banks are operated on the same principles as our banks in America, and deluxe apartments are for rent or sale.

If I had ever considered seriously making Beirut my home, as many friends and relatives urged me to do, I would have settled in this American district, for my wife and I enjoyed going there very much. One day we were wandering through this area when out of a clear blue sky we saw a sign in English: "American Hamburgers Served Here." This was really something to get excited about, for until now we had had no American food since arriving in the Middle East. I knew immediately what we would have for our lunch.

And sure enough, I was right again. We sat at an outdoor table under a red umbrella. The menus were printed in English with American prices, and we promptly ordered hamburgers and Cokes.

When the food came—low and behold—there was also a bottle of catsup! This really seemed a treat. Although generally my wife and I are not overly fond of catsup, that day it seemed to make the hamburgers taste even more delicious.

A few days later we checked our American calendar and were surprised to learn that time had passed so pleasantly that we had not realized we had been in the Middle East four months.

At that time Beirut was experiencing the biggest boom of building apartment houses it had ever known. The most desirable of these apartments were on the Mediterranean coast, and there was such a great demand for these beautiful apartments that an owner could set his own price for rentals. Frequently people said to me, "Mr. Aryain, you should go back to America and convert your assets into cash and bring your children and grandchildren back to Beirut and buy a fine new apartment house overlooking the blue Mediterranean."

This idea sounded fine and good, but I was not interested. Regardless of where a man travels, his thoughts return to his home, children, grandchildren, and friends, and I am no exception. It had been a wonderful experience to visit Lebanon and to see the sights and especially to see my relatives, but America was my home and to America I would return. Especially to Texas.

I have known a few men who lived in America, then took their families back to the Old Country, but these had not proved to be happy moves. In fact, a very good Syrian friend of mine who had lived in West Texas for many years closed out his grocery store at the end of World War II and took his wife and four small children back to Lebanon, where he bought a fruit farm near Beirut. But he had not been happy there, nor had his Lebanese wife, and as his children grew up, they came back to the United States as American citizens. Once, in conversation, this man said to me, "I would give ten years of my life if I could return to America and be buried in Texas."

But each time I mentioned going home to Texas, my sister Hameedie would cry and say, "Brother, please do not leave us again. We are both growing old, and I want us to spend the rest of our lives together. If you leave we may never see each other again."

(And how right my sister proved to be, for during the time of this writing she died after a short illness.)

So I would reply, "All right, Hameedie, we will stay a while longer just to please you." And she would be happy until the word "Texas" came up again.

But my wife and I knew that this uncertainty about when we would leave could not go on indefinitely, so we decided it would be best for all of us if we set a departure date, then followed through on our plans. So one morning I told the family that I was going into Beirut by bus on business and that my wife would remain with them. This was not the first time I had gone into Beirut and left my wife and my sister, for although my wife spoke no Arabic and my sister spoke no English, they had very pleasant days visiting neighbors or just enjoying each other's company.

In Beirut I went to the airline office and made arrangements for us to spend a few days in Egypt, which we had planned to do all along. Then I made reservations for a room in a Beirut hotel, where we would stay after leaving Djedie and wait for our flight. Finally, I went to the bank and arranged for some cash, for I wanted to give my sister a gift of money before we left. When all this was taken care of, I returned to Djedie by bus.

That night as the family sat together, I said, "Today I have made final arrangements for our return to America in a few days."

At this my sister cried, "Brother, you must eat the fruits of Lebanon before leaving. Soon our grapes, apples, and figs will be ripe, and you must not leave Lebanon before tasting the wetness of the fruit grown here."

Hameedie would not be comforted, and all through the night we could hear her walking in the moonlight and praying, "Allah, if my brother must leave us, keep him safe and in good health, and let him and his wife come back to visit us soon."

The following morning my brother-in-law Milhem al-Baraki talked to his wife by telling her, "Your brother must return to America. America has been his home for many years. There his sons and grandchildren live, and a man cannot break family ties. Let us be thankful for this visit with us and pray to Allah he will return.

The next day my wife and I missed seeing Hameedie around the house, and we grew concerned. Then she entered carrying a basket of ripe figs. She had made the rounds of Djedie until she had found some trees with ripe figs, for she was determined that we would taste the figs of Lebanon. Bless her heart. Never has fruit tasted so delicious.

Now we began packing our luggage and found, as most tourists do, that we were taking far more back with us than we had brought from home. Milhem al-Baraki had given us two beautiful Turkish coffee pots, which had been in his family for two hundred years. My cousin Jameil had given us a beautiful brass coffee pot, which I had once given my mother on her birthday. These Turkish coffee pots and matching trays are now on our mantle, where visitors always find them interesting.

Of course, my wife had not been able to resist buying a dozen of the dainty cups for drinking Turkish coffee and boxes and tables inlaid with mother of pearl. All these lovely things had to be carefully packed and shipped ahead to Seminole, Texas.

We would carry with us the beautiful filigree necklace my mother had worn at her marriage and which my sister had insisted my wife must have. Also the women of Djedie had given my wife many pieces of handmade lace and beautiful needlework. These lovely things we still treasure, and they are a constant reminder of the lasting friendships we made with the good people of Djedie.

It is only when one has lived in an Arab home and village that one can truly understand and appreciate the depth of the hospitality for which the Middle East is famous.

All too soon the day came when we had to leave Djedie behind us and move into our hotel in Beirut, but we will never forget the happiness and warmth we had known in this little community.

I had made arrangements with the same taxi driver who had driven us to Damascus and then to Baalbek to take us into Beirut, and it was a sad morning when he arrived. After the luggage was loaded into the car, we said our good-byes to the family. The cries and sobs of my sister could be heard throughout the village, "Please, Mohammed, please, my brother, do not leave us."

All too vividly her cries brought back the painful memory of the sad day almost half a century earlier when I had left my mother, father, and sisters to come to America. There were tears in my eyes and my wife's as we pulled away from the house.

As the cars passed through the village of Djedie, the neighbors were standing in their years waving and calling their farewells.

We called back, "Good-bye, Djedie. Good-bye, our good friends."

Early the following morning the telephone in our Beirut hotel room rang, and my wife answered. "American Madam," the desk clerk said in English, "You have company waiting in the lobby. Is it all right to send them up to your room now?"

My wife said that it would be, and when we answered the knock at the door, there stood Hameedie, her husband, their son Neweff and his wife and two children, their young son Fayze, and our good friend the taxi driver. We were so glad to see them all again that we cried.

Later in the morning my cousin Jameil Aryain and his wife and four small sons arrived. Then another cousin, Adel Aryain, the school teacher in Rashayya, came to spend the day with us in our hotel.

At noon we took our company to the Idriss restaurant, one of the best cafes in Beirut, for lunch.[2] As always the food and service were excellent, and we enjoyed seeing again the beautifully lighted plants, rocks, and indoor waterfall. That day the waiter, learning this was to be our last visit, gave my wife several of the beautiful menus, which were written in Arabic, English, and French. But my poor sister was too grief stricken to eat.

The time of our flight to Egypt was late evening—I will say around ten o'clock, and the check out time in the hotel was two o'clock. When we returned to the hotel after lunch, the manager met us and insisted that we stay until time for our departure to the airport. I thought this was very nice of him.

In the late afternoon I called a taxi service and asked for transportation to the airport for my wife and me and for our fifteen guests. At seven o'clock the desk called to say that our transportation had arrived, and we all went down where I, expecting a limousine, was startled to find a bus waiting. For some reason this struck my wife and me as being very funny, and we did not feel quite so sad as we and our friends boarded our private bus and were off to the airport.

But at the airport as the time grew nearer for us to board the plane, the sadness returned to our group. Farewells were said time and time again. My wife and I kept trying to thank these people for their kindness and hospitality, and they, even the little children, kept saying, "Do come and visit us again."

When our flight number was called, these good people all followed us to the stairs leading down to the boarding area, where more tearful good-byes were said.

It was heartbreaking to tell Hameedie our final good-bye. Like all older Druze women she still kept her face carefully veiled when she was in public, and when I pressed my cheek to hers I noticed that the veil was soaked with tears. This too brought back painfully the memory of the day I had said good-bye to my mother so long ago.

At the bottom of the stairs the heavy gate was closed behind us, and we saw no more of our people.

As sad as I felt when the plane took off and the beautiful lights of Beirut faded below, I took comfort from the thought that God, or Allah, had been good enough to grant me one of the great dreams of my life—I had been permitted to return to my homeland and visit my people. It had indeed been "the trip of a lifetime."[5]

16

Seminole is Home

. . .

ARRIVING IN CAIRO AFTER MIDNIGHT, WE WENT BY TAXI TO
the Nile Hilton, although we had no reservations. The desk clerk
said to us, "You are brave people to come to Cairo at this hour
without hotel reservations, but we try very hard to take good care
of the American tourist." And he gave us a very nice room.

We were exhausted from the emotional strain of leaving our
people in Lebanon, and we went right to bed.

About nine o'clock the following morning we were awakened
by a knock at the door. When we opened it there stood a hotel
porter with a tray holding a pot of American coffee—strong and
hot—and American size coffee cups. We decided right then and
there that the Nile Hilton does indeed take good care of the
American tourist.

My wife poured herself a cup of coffee and wandered out onto
the balcony to drink it. I was just pouring myself a cup of coffee,
when I heard her cry out. I put down my cup and rushed out onto
the balcony to see what in the world was wrong with her.

But nothing was wrong. It was just that from our balcony we
could look across the desert and see the Sphinx and the Pyramids

in the distance. I must say I almost cried out, for seeing the Pyramids and the Sphinx for the first time is like seeing the Grand Canyon—no matter how many pictures you have seen of them, you are not quite ready for the actual sight.

On the tray we found a pamphlet suggesting the things to see in Cairo, and of course my wife immediately checked to see when we could see the Pyramids and the Sphinx. We were both a bit disappointed to find that it was too late to take the tour that day, so we decided just to walk around Cairo and then go to see the Mosque of Sultan Hassan and then the Citadel of the Prophet Mohammed.[1]

During this afternoon of sightseeing we had taken special notice of two black women traveling in our group. We watched how closely they had taken notes in their hand books and the pictures they had taken. It was after we had had our evening meal and were resting in the lobby of the hotel that one of these women came and introduced herself. In no time at all she and my wife were comparing notes and carrying on a steady conversation. She told us she and her traveling companion were school teachers, and they were gathering material in preparation for writing a book on Egypt and the Holy Land.

Early the following morning we were up and ready to see the Pyramids and the Sphinx.

When we reached the bottom of the steps, we noticed some large camels and their drivers waiting for us. "Come ride a camel to the Sphinx," the drivers called to us. "Our camels are very tame animals, and we will walk beside you."

"Why not?" I said to my wife. "This will be fun and an experience we will never forget."

I paid the driver, and he commanded the camel to kneel. Then we mounted these beasts of burden, which are sometimes called the "Ships of the Desert." Across the back of each camel was a brightly colored blanket, and the high saddle placed us high above the heads of the camel driver. Not only were these camels tame, but I think they were well trained to grunt and groan at a given signal as they jog along, for their loads are not all that heavy.[2]

When we were directly in front of the Sphinx, which is a giant stone figure with the head of a man and the body of a lion built for Pharaoh Kharfe in 2500 BC, a photographer approached and cried, "For seven Egyptian dollars I will take your picture on the camel and deliver it to your hotel tonight."

So we posed for the picture. I have always been glad we did, for this picture has been a constant reminder of the fun-filled day we spent at the Pyramids, one of the seven wonders of the world. One of the black schoolteachers was in the picture with us. Over the years we have said so many times that we would like very much to know if these women were successful in writing and having their book on Egypt and the Holy Land published. I sincerely hope so.

Each morning brings the tourist in Cairo another day of excitement, and our third day we visited the Egyptian Museum, which was just across the driveway from our hotel.

Returning to our hotel, we found that a bus was being loaded for a tour of ex-King Farouk's Palace, so we climbed aboard. There is never a dull moment in Cairo, Egypt—there are so many interesting things to see, and transportation is easy to come by.

We had expected to have fun in Egypt, and we had not been disappointed, but at sunrise the next morning we boarded the plane for Rome, Italy. At that time we were undecided about spending a few days sightseeing in Rome, Italy, but by the time we got there, we had decided that we had seen enough Roman ruins to last us a lifetime. What we really wanted to see were some West Texas oil derricks and our little granddaughters. So we just said to heck with it and went on to New York.

We did, however, decide to spend a day or two in New York, since we were there. When the plane stopped at the airport, we took a taxi to a hotel. It was a fine structure standing, I will say, about twenty-five stories tall. When I asked the rate for a room, the desk clerk told me eighteen dollars. I thought this was a shade high, but we moved in. The room was comfortable, and the hotel was in easy walking distance of the places we wished to see, since my wife had never been in New York before.

Now here we were in New York after traveling halfway around the world and making the best of inconveniences one must expect in a foreign country. Well, I went into the bathroom to wash my face and hands, and—lo and behold—the water would not run freely. I had to hold the faucet open with one hand so the water would flow. How in the world could I wash both hands at the same time when it took one hand to keep the water running?

I went down to the lobby and talked to the desk clerk, and he said that for two dollars more I could move to the room across the hall where the water ran freely. So the room for the night cost me twenty dollars. I had the feeling I had been taken in again, just as the merchants and taxi drivers had taken advantage of the American tourists in the Middle East.

The next morning we went to see the United Nations, which was just down the road a little way. As we walked along the crowded streets viewing the shops and stores and gazing up at the tall buildings, our thoughts were not as much upon what we were seeing as on the fact that we were again walking on American soil.

But my thoughts were also upon the day when I had been briefly in New York before, and I felt so happy that this time I would not have to fret and worry about being sent back to Syria because of the breaking out of boils on my face and neck. I was now a part of America. I cannot tell you how joyful this made me feel.

In the next two days we visited the Empire State Building, St. Paul's Cathedral, the oldest church in New York, Grand Central Station, the Cathedral of St. John the Divine, which when completed will be the largest church in the world, and, of course, Macy's Department Store, which we had always heard so much about. We leisurely walked Fifth Avenue and admired the fashionable shops, hotels, and theaters.

But for us the real treat of the stay in New York was the boat ride to the Statue of Liberty. Again my thoughts went back forty-eight years to the first time I had seen this Statue of Liberty in 1913 when I was a young immigrant boy coming to America to make for myself a new and better way of life.

I recalled that the stone lips of the statue had seemed to say to me, "Welcome to America, Mohammed Aryain."

And I remembered that I had thrown my red fez into the ocean and said to myself, "I am a new man in the New World, and I must adjust to the customs of this world."

And now as the boat drove away from the Statue of Liberty, I knew that I had.

Seeing the sights of New York City is fine and good, but give me Texas any old day. So on the third morning, we said to heck with it and boarded a plane for Lubbock, Texas, our starting point for this long dreamed of trip to the Middle East.

We had been away from Seminole four months and four days, and it had indeed been the trip of a lifetime and everything I had hoped it would be. But how wonderful it was to be back in the country we loved with our family and our good friends and neighbors. And how good it was to sleep in our own bed again.

We had been back in Seminole only a short time when out of a clear blue sky my wife brought out the house plans books again. This really surprised me, for I had thought I had settled this matter once and for all when I had given her the choice of building a new house or making the trip to the Middle East.

But a woman always has the last word, so in the spring of 1963 the foundation was laid for the home of her dreams, a brick house with three bedrooms, two bathrooms, separate living room, combination den and kitchen with a fireplace, a utility room, and a double garage.

I have made the remark many times, "A man cannot live with these women, but he cannot live without them." And for sure I would not want to live without this wife of mine.

Just as the oxen teams, which once pulled the heavily loaded wagons of settlers west across this great country of ours, and the wood burning locomotives and riverboats have all given way to modern machinery, so has the day of the immigrant peddler slipped into history.

Never again will a housewife in some remote area answer a knock at her door and find some young man, who can scarcely speak enough English to make himself understood, asking for the privilege of entering her home to show her this merchandise he carries on his back and then later hesitantly asking if he might spend the night with her family.

That era is gone forever.

Young men and women from the Middle East arriving in America in this day and age come as exchange students. They live with American families while they attend our colleges and universities, and they find a place in our communities. With their intelligence and education and willingness to work hard, they make a contribution wherever they live, and they are far more readily accepted than the people of my generation were.

At the time of this writing, 1973, I have lived a full lifetime—sixty years—in the United States of America. I would not trade America for any other place in the world. With all the struggles and hardships and setbacks I have endured, America has been good to me.

Our sons, Edward and Jameil, have made their places in the world.

My children and grandchildren will never inherit an estate of a million dollars from me, but I have tried to leave them a heritage they will never be ashamed of.

For our ages my wife and I are in good health. Our bones may ache at times, but we are thankful that we have had the physical strength and mental ability to write this story for you.

We hope you have enjoyed it.

It has been a long, long road from Henna, Syria, to Seminole, Texas, but it has been worth it. After living thirty-four years in Seminole, it will always be my home, just as America will always be my country.

When I was trying to persuade my father to permit me to come to America, I said, "God will look after me."

God has been good to me and my family.[5]

I am grateful.

Afterword

. . .

EDITOR'S NOTE

Once they realized that their father's story really would be published, Eddie and Jameil Aryain wanted to make a few comments about their father and mother themselves. Eddie, who never married, moved to Los Angeles in 1948 and managed a Farmers' Market bookstore and later was in the catering business before his retirement. Presently he is pursuing his lifelong avocation of creative writing. Jameil operated Aryain's Dry Goods store for twenty years before selling it in 1972 and then served as the business manager for the Seminole Medical and Surgical Clinic for twenty more years until his retirement. Citizens of Seminole named Jameil Citizen of the Year in 1989 following twelve years of service to the city—six on the city council (1976–82) and six as mayor (1982–88).

EDWARD (EDDIE) ARYAIN

Years ago a friend was curious about how my father got from a tiny village in Syria to a small oil field town in West Texas. I tried to explain that when I was a boy, many small towns in Texas, New Mexico, and Oklahoma had a dry goods store run by a Syrian family, another by a Jewish family, and a restaurant run by a Greek family. When I was in grade school in Brownfield, Texas, there

was a tiny food stand on the Seagraves Highway owned by a man from Greece named Alex. Even in the Great Depression there were always people waiting in line to be served. Half a century later, my mouth still waters at the memory of Alex's ten-cent hamburgers and chili dogs.

Edward (Eddie) Aryain,
2005. Photo by Hector Elias,
Hollywood, California.

My friend kept asking questions I could not answer, so the next time I was in Seminole I questioned my father about his life. It was like opening a flood gate. My mother and I sat fascinated as he began to talk. I was especially interested in his stories of the Turkish oppression of Syria before the First World War, and I suggested he tell these stories to my mother and that she type them on her old Underwood typewriter just as he told them.

So my father, who had taught himself to read English so he could devour the *Seminole (TX) Sentinel* and the *Lubbock (TX) Avalanche-Journal* but had never learned to write English, became an author. (Actually, that last is not entirely true, for my fourth grade teacher—a marvelously kind lady named Mrs. Renfro—used to come to our house for supper and then prepare my father for his American citizenship papers. She taught him to write his name, so he could at least sign his checks, a skill I was very grateful for when I reached my teens.)

When my parents completed a few pages, they would send them to me in Los Angeles, and I would roar with laughter and then weep. I also shared these pages with my friends, a somewhat literate group, and they were as enthralled as I, and for months I dined out on my parents' pages.

Finally, one of my friends said, "This is a wonderful bit of Americana!"

I was so impressed by this comment that I reread the pages and was stunned to realize my friend was right. My father was a very observant man with a lively curiosity, and even when he was quite old, he viewed the world with the excited eyes of a young immigrant boy. For instance, he would drive me miles to show me a new oil well being drilled. This bored me, for I felt when you had seen one oil well, you had seen them all. But he enjoyed doing this, so I grinned through clenched teeth and am now glad that I did.

I was astonished when I realized my parents' stack of pages had grown into a small book. I corrected the spelling and trimmed out some repetitions but tried to keep the flavor of what they had written. I cannot know if I succeeded in this last, for when I read what they wrote I hear my father's guttural Arabic accent colored by a West Texas twang that brings tears to my eyes.

My father was a complicated man, and certainly my relationship with him was often complicated, but it never occurred to me that he did not love me deeply, and I trusted him completely to be there if I needed him. Things were very difficult for our family during the Great Depression, and I was haunted by the fear we might not make it financially. But I was confident I would not go down alone—I knew my family would be there. I am awed by my father's courage to go on struggling for his family when everything seemed so hopeless and he felt so inadequate. I don't think I could have done it.

I will let his book about his life stand by itself and only say that his health failed, and he died at the age of seventy-seven. I, of course, caught the next plane for West Texas, and the next day my mother, brother, and I went to the funeral parlor to make the decisions about a casket and services. As we came out of the funeral home, a cowboy rode by on his horse. The cowboy reined in his horse and raised his Stetson hat to our family. His simple dignified gesture of respect spoke volumes about what my father had accomplished—what his life had been about.

My mother's story continued for a number of years after my father's death. Although she and my father had always loved to travel, it was difficult for her to think about going alone. Nevertheless, she came to Los Angeles to visit me after his death. I took her to Disneyland, Marineland, the Los Angeles Art Museum, and the Huntington Library, all of which she adored. (I remember it used to irritate me when Dad told people I lived in San Angelo, California! Now it brings a lump to my throat.)

After all their years of struggle, my parents had been able to enjoy the fruits of all their hard work in their later years. Their trip back to Syria, their travels in the States, and their home on a street lined with the homes of their friends all were great pleasures for them.

As the years progressed, my mother's health began to fail, but she continued to live in the house she and Dad had so proudly designed and built together. One Friday she went to the beauty parlor, so her hair would look nice for Sunday school. That Saturday night she got sick and died a few hours later.

Some years later my niece Linda and her husband, Scott Robins, treated me to a trip to New York. I think we saw five Broadway shows in one weekend. We also went out to visit the Statue of Liberty and Ellis Island. We found the plaque with Dad's name and the date of his entry into the United States, which was put up after we made a contribution to the restoration and preservation of Ellis Island through which so many millions of frightened but courageous immigrants entered America. My niece, her son Jeffrey, and I—three generations of my father's American descendants—were photographed beside his plaque with the New York skyline behind us. Until recently I thought that nothing could have pleased Ed Aryain more. Now, I think this publication of his story by Texas Tech University Press would have pleased him far more.

My father loved America, but the part of America he loved best was West Texas.

JAMEIL (DINK) ARYAIN

From my earliest memories, an expression I heard from my father was "What a great country." He instilled in his sons a love for this "great country," the United States of America. I have wondered at times if descendants of foreign-born citizens have a greater appreciation for America than natural-born citizens. But then, we are all "A Nation of Immigrants."

Another expression I heard from my father was "What a beautiful country." In his later years after they had the time and money, he and my mother traveled extensively. Regardless of the places they visited—national parks, the California coast, the mountains of Colorado, the Ozarks of Missouri, or New York City—his expression was always "What a beautiful country." He was always amazed at the great beauty he saw in his adopted country.

As I have grown older, my admiration for my father's courage and determination has continued to grow. I cannot imagine the desire that seemed to burn in his heart, the desire to come to America. He came as a fifteen-year-old boy, without money or close relatives waiting for him. On Ellis Island he was alone though surrounded by people. He could neither read nor write the English language.

He never saw his parents again and waited nearly fifty years before he could return to the Old Country. I have often asked myself, "Could I have done this?" I doubt that I would have had the courage. This is a story that happened millions of times in America. This is one of the things that makes this country so great.

I once asked a knowledgeable person who had admired my father's story why it was so unique. Millions of people came to America in just this way. "That is true," he said, "but the difference is he chose to write and record his story."

I also marvel at the courage and strength of my mother. She was born and raised in Missouri. Her family could trace their ancestors back to the signers of the Declaration of Independence. She came to Lamesa, Texas, to work for an aunt who had married a Syrian immigrant. She met my father at this point, and they married shortly thereafter.

Jameil Aryain, October, 2004.

They began a long career in the retail dry goods business. They experienced success, failure, devastating sandstorms, and the Great Depression. They moved to several towns, eking out a living. They were subjects of some discrimination, which my father could not understand.

In 1939 they moved to Seminole, Texas. It was a small farming and ranching town that was beginning to experience an oil boom. They opened their dry goods store, and it prospered. They were so proud when they were able to buy the building their store was in. A short time later they built and in two years paid for the first home they had ever owned. They soon knew that Seminole would always be their home.

This story could have been written in a hundred small towns in Texas and Oklahoma. I am forever indebted to the people of Seminole. The people in this town accepted my parents. They prospered and were proud to call Seminole their home.

My father would be greatly troubled by the situation that exists today in the Middle East. I know he would want his adopted country and his native country, Syria, to be on friendly terms. This was the case for many years after he arrived in the United States. He would be saddened by the situation that exists today, but his undying love would be with the United States of America.

Thousands of young men of Arabic descent have served with honor in the armed forces of the United States. My brother and I are included in their group.

I think my parents would be pleased and honored to know that their descendants have represented them well. I know that each of our children has an undying love for this great country, in part because of my father's incredible sacrifices.

Notes

. . .

Plainsword

1. "Meet Lincoln's New Millionaires," *Lincoln* [NE] *Journal Star*, February 23, 2005.

2. Ed Aryain, *From Syria to Seminole: Memoir of a High Plains Merchant*, J'Nell Pate, ed. (Lubbock: Texas Tech University Press, 2006), 121.

Introduction

1. Wallach, *Desert Queen*, 73.

2. Eddie Aryain (son of Ed Aryain), telephone interview with J'Nell Pate, Los Angeles, July 17, 2003, March 17, 2004.

3. Undated, handwritten letter from Etta Aryain to Eddie Aryain about the manuscript she and her husband had just finished writing. Letter is included with first typed draft of the manuscript in possession of Jameil Aryain.

4. Quilliam, *Syria and the New World Order*, 33; Haddad, *Fifty Years*, 1; Kayal and Kayal, *Syrian-Lebanese in America*, 28, 50; Goodwin, *Lords of the Horizons*, 94–95.

5. Tibawi, *Modern History of Syria*, 201; Kinross, *Ottoman Centuries*, 577–78; Haddad, *Fifty Years*, 35.

6. Glass, *Tribes with Flags*, 74.

7. Quilliam, *Syria and the New World Order*, 32.

8. Inalcik and Quataert, *Economic and Social History*, 775; Wallach, *Desert Queen*, 76.

9. Tibawi, *Modern History of Syria*, 178; Hourani, *Syria and Lebanon*, 28; Hitti, *Syrians in America*, 28.

10. Fedden, *Phoenix Land*, 5; Haddad, *Fifty Years*, 2.

11. Haddad, *Fifty Years*, 19–18.

12. Hitti, *Origins of the Druze People*, i.

13. Dana, *The Druze in the Middle East*, xii

14. Orfalea, *Before the Flames*, 56; Abu-Izzeddin, *Druzes*, 85, 101; Makarem, *Druze Faith*, 132.

15. Fedden, *Phoenix Land*, 88; Gilmour, *Lebanon*, 24.

16. Abu-Izzeddin, *Druzes*, 221–22; Fedden, *Phoenix Land*, 88.

17. Abu-Izzeddin, *Druzes*, 117.

18. Quilliam, *Syria and the New World Order*, 42; Mackey, *Passion and Politics*, 281; Naff, *Becoming American*, 241.

19. Walbridge, "Middle Easterners and North Africans," 399.

20. Encyclopedia.com, s.v. "Ibrahim Pasha," http://encyclopedia.com/html/i/ibrahimp1.asp (accessed December 1, 2003); Firro, *History of the Druzes*, 69–70, 72.

21. Firro, *History of the Druzes*, 85–86; Ma'oz, *Ottoman Reform*, 124–25.

22. Firro, *History of the Druzes*, 110–11, 186.

23. Ma'oz, *Ottoman Reform*, 125.

24. Tibawi, *Modern History of Syria*, 123, 127; Kayal and Kayal, *Syrian-Lebanese in America*, 62-63; Glass, *Tribes with Flags*, 183; Orfalea, *Before the Flames*, 57.

25. The United States sent $35,000. Orfalea, *Before the Flames*, 55; In seeking protectorates in the Middle East, Britain and France were in competition. Fedden, *Phoenix Land*, 220.

26. Dinnerstein and Reimers, *Ethnic Americans*, 36.

27. Daniels, *Not Like Us*, 61.

28. Namias, *First Generation*, 2; Naff, *Becoming American*, 90; Wakin, *Lebanese and Syrians*, 17.

29. Orfalea, *Before the Flames*, 61.

30. Hitti, *Syrians in America*, 51.

31. Dinnerstein and Reimers, *Ethnic Americans*, 38; Wakin, *Lebanese and Syrians*, 17; Hitti, *Syrians in America*, 51.

32. *Syrian and Lebanese Texans*, 1; Naff, *Becoming American*, 2, 112; and Hitti, *Syrians in America*, 36.

33. Caldwell, "Syrian-Lebanese in Oklahoma," 17.

34. Wakin, *Lebanese and Syrians*, 5.

35. Kayal and Kayal, *Syrian-Lebanese in America*, 67, 70; Walbridge, "Middle Easterners and North Africans," 393; *Syrian and Lebanese Texans*, 1. Also "List or Manifest of Alien Passengers for the United States," SS *Niagara* sailing from Havre [Le Havre, France], June 7, 1913, line 30, "Mohamed Aryen [*sic*]"; Pat Aryain (daughter-in-law of Ed Aryain), interview with J'Nell Pate, July 2005, August 2005.

36. Handlin, *Uprooted*, 4.

37. Naff, *Becoming American*, 13; Wakin, *Lebanese and Syrians*, 37.

38. Wakin, *Lebanese and Syrians*, 14.

39. Dinnerstein and Reimers, *Ethnic Americans*, 72.

40. Reeves, *Ellis Island*, 135; Jacobs, *Ellis Island*, 23.

41. Jacobs, *Ellis Island*, 19; Reeves, *Ellis Island*, 9; Corsi, *In the Shadow of Liberty*, 4; Jameil Aryain and Pat Aryain, interview with J'Nell Pate, Seminole, Texas, July 16, 2003.

42. Jacobs, *Ellis Island*, 6–7, 10; Reeves, *Ellis Island*, 60. SS *Niagara* Manifest, line 30. Entries are as follows: family name: Aryen [*sic*], given name: Mohamed, age: 20, sex: m, married or single: s, calling or occupation: blank, able to read: yes, nationality: Syrian, race or people: Syrian, last permanent residence: Syria, Haina [*sic*], the name and complete address of nearest relative or friend in country whence alien came: Father: Hussain Aryen [*sic*], final destination: Pa, Rochester.

43. Reeves, *Ellis Island*, 95; Speranza, "Victims of Fraud and Deceit," 51.

44. Handlin, *Uprooted*, 170; Naff, *Becoming American*, 92, 138–39, 215; Daniels, *Coming to America*, 207.

45. Wakin, *Lebanese and Syrians*, 6; Kayal and Kayal, *Syrian-Lebanese in America*, 95.

46. Kayal and Kayal, *Syrian-Lebanese in America*, 91.

47. Naff, *Becoming American*, 1, 270.

48. Kayal and Kayal, *Syrian-Lebanese in America*, 100.

49. Leach, *Land of Desire*, 266.

50. Jaffee, "Peddlers of Progress," 529; Naff, *Becoming American*, 90, 139; Wakin, *Lebanese and Syrians*, 21; Rosenberg, *Sangers' Pioneer Texas Merchants*, 10.

51. Naff, *Becoming American*, 163, 169–70.

52. Golden, *Forgotten Pioneer*, 24; Orfalea, *Before the Flames*, 81.

53. Walbridge, "Middle Easterners and North Africans," 394; Kayal and Kayal, *Syrian-Lebanese in America*, 104, 111.

54. Banks, *First Person America*, 32; Hitti, *Syrians in America*, 87.

55. Banks, *First Person America*, 33.

56. Erdman, *Life Was Simpler Then*, 154.

57. Van Steenwyk, *Saddlebag Salesmen*, 52–56.

58. Jameil Aryain (mayor of Seminole, Texas), letter to the editor, *Seminole (TX) Sentinel*, May 17, 1987.

59. Jameil Aryain and Pat Aryain, interview; Jameil Aryain, letter to the editor.

60. Jameil Aryain and Pat Aryain, interview; Higham, *Strangers in the Land*, 267.

61. Higham, *Strangers in the Land*, 281, 284.

62. Higham, *Strangers in the Land*, 286–87; Dinnerstein and Reimers, *Ethnic Americans*, 69; Daniels, *Not Like Us*, 129.

63. Wakin, *Lebanese and Syrians*, 38; Naff, *Becoming American*, 247; Caldwell, "Syrian-Lebanese in Oklahoma," 97; Kayal and Kayal, *Syrian-Lebanese in America*, 110.

64. Jameil Aryain and Pat Aryain, interview; Jameil Aryain, telephone interview with J'Nell Pate, August 26, 2003.

65. Jameil Aryain and Pat Aryain, interview.

66. *New Handbook of Texas*, s.v. "Seminole, Texas."

67. Jameil Aryain and Pat Aryain, interview; Glass, *Tribes with Flags*, 179; Ma'oz, *Syria and Israel*, 119.

68. Obituary of Ed Aryain, *Seminole Sentinel*, October 12, 1974; Obituary of Etta E. Aryain, *Seminole Sentinel*, November 22, 1981. (Dates cited are dates of death, not necessarily the date the obituaries appeared in the newspaper.); Jameil Aryain and Pat Aryain, interview.

69. Jameil Aryain and Pat Aryain, interview.

70. Nan Shelton Wallen and Harvey N. Wallen, letter to the editor, *Seminole (TX) Sentinel*, May 6, 1987.

71. Jameil Aryain, letter to the editor, *Seminole (TX) Sentinel*, May 17, 1987.

72. Etta Aryain, letter to her son Eddie, 1973.

1. Growing up in Henna

1. Henna is located on the side of Mount Hermon southwest of Damascus not far from the present border between Syria and Lebanon. *National Geographic Atlas of the Middle East*, 42.

2. It was Mount Hermon, the home of the Druze. Hitti, *Origins of the Druze People*, 2; Badih Jameil Aryain to Jameil Aryain, August 8, 2000.

3. Syrian bread, considered the "staff of life," is flat, unleavened, and looks like a flour tortilla. Pat Aryain, interview; Naff, *Becoming American*, 213; Hitti, *Syrians in America*, 46.

4. Hummus was a paste of mashed chick peas, or garbanzo beans, made with salt, pepper, olive oil, and sesame seeds and served as a dip. Other Syrian foods are audis (lentils), tabouleh (olive oil and dried meat), and lebeneh (white cheese). Pat Aryain, interview; Glass, *Tribes with Flags*, 18; Wallach, *Desert Queen*, 104.

5. See the introduction for a fuller explanation of the Druze sect. See also Abu-Izzedden, *Druzes*; Makarem, *Druze Faith*. Although Ed's spelling of *Moslem* has been replaced in the last few decades by *Muslim*, the usage during his time has been retained in this manuscript.

6. One historian comments that "hospitality" is "the most celebrated custom of all." Betts, *Druze*, 50.

7. One theory is that in the Ottoman Empire, the rulers forced the Druze, Jews, Muslims, and Christians to get along. When France began to intervene, it wanted to create quarrels among the minorities to get some of them on their side. Glass, *Tribes with Flags*, 67.

8. The editor has been unable to determine just which Russian czar's burial caused this Russian-Turkish crisis. The editor examined several texts on Russian history and failed to find this confrontation.

9. In the name of nationalism young Turkish university students and young men from the Ottoman military academy in 1908 forced Abdul

Hamid to reinstate the constitution and then to resign. Wallach, *Desert Queen*, 95, 132.

10. Italian occupation of Libya lasted from 1912 to 1942. Ibrahim Ighneiwa, "Libya: Mohammad 'Idris I' al-Sanousi King of Libya (1951–1969)," http://www.ourworld.compuserve.com/homepages/dr-ibrahim -ighneiwa/idris.htm (accessed July 24, 2003).

11. Amir Sayyid Mohammad Idris, who became the king of Libya on December 24, 1951, was vacationing in Turkey when armed forces led by Mu'ammar al-Qadhafi overthrew his government on September 1, 1969. Ed Aryain didn't know that Qadhafi's government would not be democratic. When this was written, King Idris would have still been alive as Ed assumed. King Idris lived in exile in Egypt until his death on May 25, 1983. Ighneiwa, "Libya."

12. Kurds are defined as those who use one of the two chief Kurdish dialects, Zaza in the north and Kermanji in the center or south. They are located in the mountains north of an area that once was Greater Syria before twentieth-century boundary divisions. Quilliam, *Syria and the New World Order*, 43; Arfa, *Kurds*, 1.

2. A Famous Aryain Ancestor

1. See comments about Ed Aryain's famous ancestor in the introduction. A great-nephew of Ed, Badih Jameil Aryain, wrote Ed's son Jameil a letter about their common ancestor, Shibli al-Aryan, confirming that he was mentioned in the history books in the schools because he fought against the Egyptians and the Turks. Al-Aryan reached the highest rank of Basha. Badih Jameil Aryain to Jameil Aryain, October 19, 2000.

2. In 1831–32 Ibrahim Pasha, son of Muhammad Ali, ruler of Egypt, occupied Syria with the permission of the Ottoman sultan. Not until 1840 when the British intervened was Ibrahim driven from Syria, although Shibli al-Aryan led the Druze in revolt against him in 1838. Hourani, *Syria and Lebanon*, 28–29; Hitti, *Origins of the Druze People*, 8.

3. The Ottoman sultan from 1839 to 1861 was Abdul Medjid; most likely, it was he (or one of his agents) who met with Shibli al-Aryan. Pavlowitch, *Anglo-Russian Rivalry*, 152.

4. Unfortunately, the editor has not located a source for this story of Shibli al-Aryan's meeting with the sultan. Two English-language Druze books mention Shibli al-Aryan and his fighting but not in the detail of Ed's account. These are Firo, *History of the Druzes*, 69–86, and Abu-Izzeddin, *Druzes*, 218–20; also mentioning al-Aryan is Ma'oz, *Ottoman Reform*, 124–28. Dates that Shibli al-Aryan was Bashir the Great have not been documented.

5. Following the collapse of communism in the area, Yugoslavia also disappeared from the map of Europe. The bulk of the former Yugoslavia has been replaced by Serbia-Montenegro. The Balkans region remains troubled by conflict as of the date of this publication.

6. Rashayya—also spelled "Rashaiya" or "Rashaya"—is located on the western slope of Mount Hermon. The al-Aryan family was the principal Druze family of Rashayya in the mid-nineteenth century, and members of the Middle Eastern branch of the Aryain family live there still. Leila Tarazi Fawaz, *An Occasion for War*, 63.

7. A Druze army of five thousand men advanced on Rashayya by mid-June 1860, and over eight hundred Christians died there and in surrounding villages. Druze surrounded Hasbayya on June 3, 1860, and greatly outnumbered the Christians. Within a day one thousand Christians perished, according to the story of the massacre of Hasbayya that has been passed down generation to generation. Fawaz, *An Occasion for War*, 62–64.

8. Zalah was the most important town of Mount Lebanon and the only remaining Christian stronghold by 1860. They feared a Druze attack, which came on June 18, 1860, and the city fell within hours. Fawaz, *An Occasion for War*, 64–67.

9. A band of Druze fired on ten muleteers from Dahr al-Ahmar, killing two, initiating the conflict at Rashayya. Fawaz, *An Occasion for War*, 63.

10. Ed Aryain was writing in 1973 before there was an increased emphasis on multiculturalism and diversity in the United States and before a call for reparations for slavery gained some support among black Americans. He did not anticipate the emergence of a divisive political issue.

11. The Druze for many years had been "a thorn in the side of the Turks." Hitti, *Origins of the Druze People*, 2.

3. Leaving Syria for America

1. Another theory for the association of the calf with the Druze religion centers on Caliph Al-Hakim. In 1008 A.D., Caliph Al-Hakim, whom the Druze believe to be the tenth incarnation of God, pressured all non-Muslims, Jews, and especially Christians, to convert. He is said to have forced Jews to wear a replica of a golden calf around their necks. The Jewish Agency for Israel, *History of the Jewish People*, s.v. "1000–1099," http://www.davidsconsultants.com/jewishhistory/history.php?startyear=1000&endyear=1099 (accessed August 25, 2003). There are many other theories of the origin of the calf, none of which can be substantiated. Betts, *The Druze*, 31.

2. While wearing headgear was a symbol of Islamic belief that Mohammed the Prophet began, the fez was adopted in 1828 as a reform measure by Ottoman sultan Mahmud II (1808–39), also called Mahmud the Reformer. Kinross, *Ottoman Centuries*, 438–66.

3. Ed is referring to the Turkish-perpetrated massacres that occurred between 1894 and 1896 under Sultan Abdul-Hamid II. The later massacres of 1915 and 1916, under the Young Turk government, were even worse—the campaign of starvation against the Armenian Christians killed an estimated one million people. Neipage, Memoirs and Diaries: "The Armenian Massacres", http://www.firstworldwar.com/diaries/armenianmassacres.htm (accessed September 18, 2003); see also *Encyclopedia Britannica Online*, s.v. "Armenian Massacres," http://www.britannica.com (accessed September 18, 2003); Armenian National Institute, *Encyclopedia Entries on the Armenian Genocide*, s.v. "Hamidian (Armenian) Massacres" (by Rouben Paul Adalian), http://www.armenian-genocide.org/encyclopedia/hamidian.html (accessed September 18, 2003).

4. Peddling in the Midwest

1. Located thirty-nine miles south of Lincoln, Nebraska, Beatrice was on the Burlington Railroad. It is the county seat of Gage County and a major retail center for the surrounding area. Information on most of the Midwest towns Ed Aryain visited was located online at Online Highways, *Online Highways Travel Guide: USA*, http://www.ohwy.com.

2. Fort Worth, thirty miles west of Dallas on the Texas and Pacific Railroad, formed a junction of ten different railroad lines because of its stockyards terminal market. Pate, *North of the River*, 154.

3. Waxahachie, the county seat of Ellis County, is thirty miles south of Dallas. By 1920 it had two hundred businesses and a population of 7,958. Online Highways, s.v. "Waxahachie, Texas," http://www.ohwy.com (June 30, 2003).

4. Although the state had no anti-peddling law, individual towns, at the urging of town merchants, sometimes would pass a license requirement to hamper the peddlers, whom they saw as their competition. Naff, *Becoming American*, 174.

5. Eastern Bell County, in which Temple is located, was populated heavily by Germans and Czechs. Ed could have meant any of the following communities: Seaton, Ratibar, Zabcikville, or Westphalia, although Westphalia was in Falls County near the Bell County line. He also could have meant Heidenheimer, located five miles southeast of Temple on the Atchison, Topeka, and Santa Fe Railroad, which was named for a director of the railroad, S. Heidenheimer, but the town was not German or Czech. It had a peak population of 250 in 1925. Michael Kelsey (Temple Public Library), telephone interview with J'Nell Pate, August 11, 2003; also *New Handbook of Texas*, s.vv. "Seaton, Texas," "Westphalia, Texas," "Zabcikville, Texas"; *Handbook of Texas Online*, s.v. "Heidenheimer, Texas," http://www.tsha.utexas.edu/handbook/online (accessed June 27, 2003).

6. Corsicana lay fifty-eight miles southeast of Dallas on the Houston and Central Texas Railroad, which had arrived in 1871. Texas's first significant discovery of oil, and the first oil found west of the Mississippi, came in Corsicana in 1894. A new oil boom came to Texas in 1923, when wildcatters discovered the Powell Oil Field near Corsicana. The population of the Navarro County town swelled to twenty-eight thousand at the height of the short-lived boom. *Handbook of Texas Online*, s.v. "Corsicana, Texas," http://www.tsha.utexas.edu/handbook/online (accessed June 30, 2003).

7. Dallas, established in 1841 on the East Fork of the Trinity River, had developed into a busy merchandizing city serving East Texas.

8. Ed's sons do not remember their father ever having a gold watch and chain, so he was forced to sell it during the difficult times of the Depression. Pat Aryain relating information from Eddie and Jameil Aryain, interview with J'Nell Pate, February 14, 2006.

9. Sherman, county seat of Grayson County and located seventy-five miles north of Dallas, was on the Missouri, Kansas, and Texas Railroad after 1880. Its population in the mid-1920s was approximately fifteen thousand. *Handbook of Texas Online*, s.v. "Sherman, Texas," http://www.tsha.utexas.edu/handbook/online (accessed June 30, 2003).

10. St Joseph is located on the far northwestern edge of Missouri, near the Midwestern states the Syrian peddlers favored. French fur trader Joseph Robidoux established a trading post in 1826 that later was named after his own patron saint, St. Joseph. It is thirty miles north of Kansas City in Buchanan County. http://www.stjomo.com/new_history_1.htm (accessed February 8, 2006) and http://www.ohwy.com/mo/s/stjoseph.htm (accessed February 9, 2006)

11. Topeka is located in Shawnee County on the banks of the Kansas River. Online Highways, s.v. "Topeka, Kansas," http://www.ohwy.com (accessed June 27, 2003).

12. Salina, on the banks of the Smoky Hill River, is the county seat of Saline County. Online Highways, s.v. "Salina, Kansas," http://www.ohwy.com (accessed June 27, 2003).

13. Colby is the county seat of Thomas County in far northwest Kansas. Online Highways, s.v. "Colby, Kansas," http://www.ohwy.com (accessed June 21, 2003).

14. Akron is the county seat of Washington County. Limon, eighty-five miles southeast of Denver, is in eastern Colorado. Online Highways, s.vv. "Akron, Colorado," "Limon, Colorado," http://www.ohwy.com (accessed June 27, 2003).

15. Wray, Colorado, is the county seat of Yuma County. Online Highways, s.v. "Wray, Colorado," http://www.ohwy.com (accessed November 13, 2003).

16. Dodge City, Kansas, settled in 1872, is in the southwestern part of Kansas on the Arkansas River. It is the county seat of Ford County. Online Highways, s.v. "Dodge City, Kansas," http://www.ohwy.com (accessed November 13, 2003).

17. English immigrant Fred Harvey signed a contract with the Santa Fe
    Railroad to sell meals to passengers on Santa Fe trains at restaurants
    along the route and would feed Santa Fe Railroad employees at half
    price. In exchange, the railroad built the restaurants and transported
    Harvey's supplies for free. By 1917 one hundred Harvey Houses served
    Santa Fe's customers in towns across the West. Morris, *Harvey Girls*; see
    also Poling-Kempes, *Harvey Girls*.

18. Heaves is a chronic, non-infectious respiratory disease of horses charac-
    terized by difficult breathing, coughing, nasal discharge, and lack of
    stamina. Dr. Jimmie E. Gill, DVM, interview with J'Nell Pate, Fort
    Worth, Texas, August 14, 2003.

19. Shawnee, named after the Indian tribe, became the main city for the
    Greater Seminole Field (Oklahoma) boom and was the supply area for
    one of the largest and most productive oil fields in the world at that
    time. Shawnee was the county seat of Pottawatomie County and estab-
    lished a post office in 1892. *Oklahoma*, 206; Shirk, *Oklahoma Place
    Names*, 218.

20. Its post office established in 1829, Chickasha, Oklahoma, is the county
    seat of Grady County in the south central part of the state. Shirk,
    Oklahoma Place Names, 49; also Online Highways, s.v. "Chickasha,
    Oklahoma," http://www.ohwy.com (accessed June 30, 2003).

21. Named after the Waco Indians, this county seat of McLennan County is
    located seventy miles south of Dallas and Fort Worth. "Waco, Texas,"
    The New Handbook of Texas, 776; also at http//:www.ohwy.com/tx/w
    /waco.htm.

22. The editor has been unable to locate the title or more of the verses of
    this song and has reached the conclusion—after examining hundreds of
    railroad songs—that the railroad men made up the song themselves,
    knowing how much money the railroads were making. See Baker and
    Kunz, *The Collector's Book of Railroadiana;* Carpenter, "The Railroad in
    American Folk Song, 1865–1920" in *Diamond Bessie and the Shepherds*,
    edited by Wilson M. Hudson; Cohen, *Long Steel Rail: The Railroad in
    American Folksong;* and Douglas, *All Aboard: The Railroad in American
    Life*. Also a three CD set of western railroad songs with historical narra-
    tion by Keith and Rusty McNeil. WEM Records, Riverside, California,

1994. "Train 45 Railroad Songs of the Early 1900s," Rounder Records Corp., 1998.

23. Charlie Cabool would be a partner with Ed in Navarro, Texas. Later Cabool "operated a very successful dry goods store for many years in O'Donnel, Texas." Charlie's uncle, Casey Cabool, became a friend of Ed's as well. Casey and his wife, also named Mary, operated stores in Jal, New Mexico, and Levelland, Texas. They were still in Levelland in 1987. Jameil Aryain, letter to the editor, *Seminole (TX) Sentinel,* May 17, 1987.

24. Numerous Syrian suppliers kept the peddlers busy with plenty of merchandise. Salem Bashara and two brothers settled in Fort Wayne, Indiana, in 1887 and provided goods to a network of Syrian peddlers. A Druze supplier opened a store in Hannibal, Missouri, about 1890 and helped other Druze get started. He perhaps was the Joseph Izzam that Ed mentions, although no Izzam appeared in the Hannibal City Directories after Ed arrived in the United States. No Ahmeed or Hameed appeared in the Fort Smith city directory, but a Kassam Hammet owned a wholesale dry goods store at 115 N. Third during the years that Ed Aryain peddled. Naff, *Becoming American,* 42, 158; Sharon Lambersen (Hannibal Free Public Library, Hannibal, Missouri) to J'Nell Pate, July 9, 2003; Billie Bair (Fort Smith Public Library, Genealogy Department, Fort Smith, Arkansas) to J'Nell Pate, July 14, 2003; city directories for Fort Smith, Arkansas, 1914, 1918, 1919–20, 1921–22, 1925–26, 1928–29.

25. Colorado Springs, Colorado, established by gold miners in 1859, was originally called El Dorado. The county seat of El Paso County, it was renamed after mineral springs found nearby. Online Highways, s.v. "Colorado Springs, Colorado," http://www.ohwy.com (accessed November 13, 2003).

26. Ed is most likely describing the Antlers Hotel. General William Jackson Palmer, who built the railroad into and created the town of Colorado Springs, constructed the posh hotel in 1883. It burned, and a new one opened in 1901. Later, Spencer Penrose, a wealthy businessman who grew rich from Cripple Creek, Colorado, gold and a Utah copper mine, completed the Broadmoor Hotel in 1918. It quickly

became a playground for the wealthy. Noel and Norman, *Pike's Peak Partnership*, 72.

5. *Visiting Uncle Ollie*

1. Brush, Colorado, was named for Jared L. Brush, a Colorado cattle pioneer. Located nine miles to the west of Brush was Fort Morgan, once a station on the Oregon Trail from the Missouri River to Denver. It became ranching and farming country. Online Highways, s.vv. "Brush, Colorado," "Fort Morgan, Colorado," http://www.ohwy.com (accessed June 20, 2003).

2. Located in Laramie County, Cheyenne, Wyoming, became a stop on the Union Pacific Railroad in 1867 and was named after the local Cheyenne tribe. Ed would have found easy access to the town by rail. Online Highways, s.v. "Cheyenne, Wyoming," http://www.ohwy.com (accessed February 2, 2004).

3. Laramie, located in southeastern Wyoming on the banks of the Laramie River, became a railroad town in 1868. Online Highways, s.v. "Laramie, Wyoming," http://www.ohwy.com (accessed June 27, 2003).

4. Named for ranch proprietor Nels Morris, Morristown, South Dakota, the town on the border between North Dakota and South Dakota, supplied surrounding ranching families. *South Dakota Guide*, s.v. "Morristown, South Dakota."

5. Denver is located in central Colorado on the plains at the junction of the South Platte River and Cherry Creek. Online Highways, s.v. "Denver, Colorado," http://www.ohwy.com (accessed November 13, 2003).

6. The county seat of Lincoln County, North Platte, Nebraska, is located on the banks of the Platte River, where William Peniston from Yorkshire, England, and A. J. Miller built a general store just west of the junction of the North Platte and South Platte rivers in 1868 when they heard the railroad was coming. Online Highways, s.v. "North Platte, Nebraska," http://www.ohwy.com (accessed June 20, 2003).

7. The state capital of South Dakota, Pierre, on the east bank of the Missouri River, was named after Pierre Chouteau, an early fur trader. Online Highways, s.v. "Pierre, South Dakota," http://www.ohwy.com (accessed June 20, 2003).

8. Burghol is wheat with its husk removed, that is steamed, dried, and crushed. It has a nutty flavor, a chewy texture, and is used in salads, pilafs, and soup. Naff, *Becoming American*, 39. and http://www.ethnic-grocer.com/commerce/catalog/product (accessed February 11, 2006).

9. Ed is referring to the Standing Rock Indian Reservation, established in 1889 west of the Missouri River. *State Farm Road Atlas*, s.v. "South Dakota," 93.

6. Oklahoma Oil Towns

1. Drumright, located in northwest Creek County near Tulsa, was named for Aaron Hatcher Drumright, who bought 120 acres of land six months before oil was discovered on it in 1912; a townsite boomed the next year. Eventually three hundred or more producing rigs dotted the landscape. Unfortunately, Drumright also attracted bootleggers, gamblers, and other criminal types. Glasscock, *Then Came Oil*, 222; Shirk, *Oklahoma Place Names*, 73; *Oklahoma*, 466; OKGenWeb, s.v. "Drumright, Oklahoma," http://www.rootsweb.com/~okcreek/towns/drumright.htm (accessed June 22, 2003).

2. One of these Syrians was George Massad, who operated a grocery and dry goods store. In 1917 George and two of his brothers, Amos and Phillip, opened Massad Mercantile. Caldwell, "Syrian-Lebanese in Oklahoma," 116.

3. One-fourth of all Syrian-Lebanese in Oklahoma (approximately fifty) congregated in Drumright during the oil boom of the teens and 1920s, so it is natural that they sought out one of their number who prepared traditional meals. Tom Caldwell, telephone interview with J'Nell Pate, Drumright, Oklahoma, June 23, 2003; also Caldwell, "Syrian-Lebanese in Oklahoma," 75.

4. The gunfight erupted on May 1, 1918, when Joe Naufal and his wife, Sadie, began arguing with Alex Francis and his son John about rent the Francises owed. Since no one but the participants saw the shooting in which Sadie Naufal was killed, the facts were difficult for the law enforcement officers to grasp. Because the gun belonged to Joe Naufal, he was first charged; later the police dropped Naufal's charges and arrested both Francis men. Alex Francis was found guilty of murder,

but upon appeal, the charge was dismissed on February 24, 1923, because a witness had lied under oath. "Naufal Charged with Murder," May 3, 1918; "Requests Francis Arrest," June 21, 1918; "Aftermath Death of Mrs. Naufal Results in Arrest of Two," June 28, 1918; "Father and Son Are Held Bonds $10,000 on Charge of Murder," July 5, 1918; "Father and Son Arraigned on Charge of Murder of a Syrian Woman," November 15, 1918; "Coal for Sale at Francis' Grocery at $10. Per Ton," December 27, 1918, all in *Drumright (OK) News*. See also *State of Oklahoma v. A. Francis*, State of Oklahoma, Superior Court of Creek County, Drumright Division: Criminal Cases, Roll No. 1-2555, Case of John Francis and Alex Francis, 1918–21; *A. Francis v. State of Oklahoma*, State of Oklahoma, Criminal Court of Appeals of Oklahoma, Case of A. Francis, A-3619, 1922–23.

5. Sapulpa, Oklahoma, twenty-five miles east of Drumright, is the county seat of Creek County, in which Drumright is located. Both communities are southwest of Tulsa. Online Highways, s.v. "Sapulpa, Oklahoma," http://www.ohwy.com (accessed December 1, 2003).

6. Many Americans called the German leader "Kaiser Bill." In Drumright the oil boom began to wane shortly after World War I, but in 1919 Drumright produced seventeen percent of all the oil marketed in the United States. Caldwell, "Syrian-Lebanese in Oklahoma," 73–75.

7. Bedouins had no political boundaries or permanent lands, roaming across the region of Greater Syria freely. In modern times it has been difficult for the Bedouin nomads to maintain their existence, and the government is trying to find lands to give them on which to settle. Kayal and Kayal, *Syrian-Lebanese in America*, 49; Fernea and Fernea, *Arab World*, 353.

8. In September 1918, Lawrence and Arab prince Feisal I entered Damascus ahead of British general Edmund Allenby, opening the way for the British occupation of Syria and Lebanon. T. E. Lawrence, a British adventurer, soldier, and author, had joined the British Military Intelligence Service in Cairo and helped the Arabs revolt against their Turkish overlords in World War I. Born in North Wales in 1888, Lawrence was well educated and spoke several languages. Short, having a fair complexion and blue eyes, Lawrence, an archaeologist by training, loved the desert.

He wore a white robe like the Arabs, fought guerilla style, blew up trains, and made lightning-fast raids. When World War I erupted he was working for the Arab Bureau in Cairo as a British intelligence officer. The British wanted Arab help against the Ottoman Empire. Lawrence met Feisal, the third son of the Sharif Hussein, at Arab headquarters in Hama in Syria. The Arabs wanted to overthrow the Turks. Crossing the desert on camels, Lawrence and the Arabs attacked the Turkish port of Aqaba at the head of the Red Sea, which became a major victory for the Allies. Bender and Leone, *Middle East*, 34; Graves, *Lawrence and the Arabs*, 12–13, 41, 337; Mackey, *Passion and Politics*, 86–87.

9. The French entered and established a mandate over Syria that did not expire until after World War II. http://uploader.wuerzburg.ed/gym-fkg/schule/fachber/englisch/joel/strophe4/lawr.html (accessed September 18, 2003). "Lebanon's History: French Intervention," Federal Research Division —Library of Congress, http://www.rimbaud.freeserve.co.uk/lebanon_french.htm (accessed September 19, 2003).

   The Sykes-Picot Agreement between the British, French, and Russians divided the Ottoman Empire after World War I. Britain took control over Palestine and France over the area that is now Lebanon and Syria. Friedman, *From Beirut to Jerusalem*, xi.

10. A day of thanksgiving is April 17, commemorating the day the French handed over airports and other public facilities. The last units of the French army left by the fall of 1946. Longrigg, *Syria and Lebanon*, 355.

11. Opened in 1921, the Tonkawa Field in southwestern Kay County, Oklahoma, was located near the town of the same name established in 1893 and named after the Tonkawa Indians. By 1923, when the boom was at its height, the town held approximately ten thousand people and had over 150 new businesses, more than 100 of them cafes and eating places. E. W. Marland drilled the discovery well that became the Tonkawa Field. Mathews, *Life and Death of an Oilman*, 117, 145; Shirk, *Oklahoma Place Names*, 238; Gilbert, *Three Sands*, 45–46.

12. A new town created in Noble County sprang up in late 1922 because of the oil boom. The name came from the three sand levels from which the oil developed. Shirk, *Oklahoma Place Names*, 235; *Oklahoma*, 422; Gilbert, *Three Sands*, 33–34.

13. Eddie Swyden, perhaps a descendant of Moses Swaydan (although the spelling of the name is different), told an interviewer in Tulsa on October 28, 1983, that second-generation children of Syrian immigrants in the Oklahoma oil fields went to college and engaged in professions. Caldwell, "Syrian-Lebanese in Oklahoma," 47.

14. The policeman's name was John Middleton. He was the county deputy in Three Sands during the spring of 1923 and carried a Colt 45 on each hip. Gilbert, *Three Sands*, 38.

15. Carter Oil Company later became an affiliate of Standard Oil of New Jersey. In 1959 it was incorporated into Humble and in 1973 began to be marketed as Exxon. *Handbook of Texas Online*, s.v. "Exxon Company, U.S.A.," http://www.tsha.utexas.edu/handbook/online (accessed September 18, 2003).

16. The Masons date back hundreds of years to when stone masons and others in the building trades gathered in shelter houses or lodges. Eventually the gathering changed and members became bound together, not by trade, but by their desire to be fraternal brothers. Shriners grew out of Freemasonry over a century ago. To be a member of a Shrine, a man must first be a Master Mason in the Masonic fraternity. http://www.shrinershq.org/shrine/affmason.html (accessed February 11, 2006).

17. Oilfield worker Jackson Burns, a full blood Choctaw with a wife and three children, refused to pay protection money to Deputy John "Two Gun" Middleton and his assistant George "Hookey" Miller (who had a hook on his right arm following a dynamite explosion). Even though the two deputies chained Burns to a bedpost in a boarding house, beat him, and ordered him to leave town, Burns did not leave. He was sitting in the Blue Front Café at 12:20 p.m. on Saturday, July 21, 1923, when Middleton and Miller approached him and went for their guns. Burns was faster and put three bullets in each deputy with a .38 Special. At the trial Burns was acquitted of both killings on a self-defense plea. Burns later died in a boiler explosion at a drilling rig. Gilbert, *Three Sands*, 39; Conaghan, *Three Sands*, 8; Betty Lane, "Oil Bearing Strata Yield More Than Petroleum: A Bustling City, Three Sands" *Newkirk (OK) Herald*, June 2002; also Office of Court Clerk, Kay County,

Newkirk, Oklahoma, Criminal Appearance Docket, Case Numbers 3868 and 3869 Jackson Burns, July 25, 1923; District Court In and For Kay County, State of Oklahoma, Case Numbers 1557, 1558, Filed September 28, 1923, Verdict: Not Guilty.

18. Ed was choosing not to use the more specific terms of *prostitute* and *venereal* disease. Like mining towns in the Old West, oil boomtowns attracted such women.

19. Editorials in the local newspaper urged officials "to "clean up the town," so federal marshals cooperated with the county sheriff to raid businesses to enforce laws against drunkenness, vagrancy, and prostitution. State health officers checked cafes and restaurants for tuberculosis among their workers and also checked the women of the boarding houses for venereal disease. After several raids, nearly all the houses of ill repute in Three Sands closed down, and the prostitutes went elsewhere. Gilbert, *Three Sands*, 38–40.

7. Storefronts in Texas

1. Like the Oklahoma oil towns, the Texas oil boomtowns had temporary buildings, shotgun houses, tents, and sheet iron buildings thrown up on narrow, muddy streets. Restaurants, banks, and drug stores stayed open twenty-four hours a day. Each town looked like the one the traveler had just left. Tuckertown, established about 1900, was located six miles southeast of Corsicana in the Powell Oil Field in eastern Navarro County. It flourished only during the oil boom. Whitney, twelve miles southwest of Hillsboro in western Hill County, was established in 1876 when the Houston and Texas Central Railroad built northward. It was named after Charles A. Whitney, a brother-in-law of J. P. Morgan, a major investor in the railroad. The population was about 750 in the 1930s. Navarro, located eight miles southeast of Corsicana in Navarro County, was established in the early 1880s but had no post office until 1908. The population was 75 in the 1930s. Olien and Olien, *Life in the Oil Fields*, 35, 43; *New Handbook of Texas*, s.vv. "Navarro, Texas," "Tuckertown, Texas," "Whitney, Texas."

2. Prohibition, making the manufacture, transportation, or importation of intoxicating alcohol illegal in the United States, was established by the

Eighteenth Amendment to the U.S. Constitution, going into effect in January 1920. *Oxford Companion to American History*, s.v. "Eighteenth Amendment," 217.

3. Sam and Luma Hameed would later become relatives of Ed when he married Luma's niece. The Hameeds operated a store in Lamesa, Texas, then one in Roswell, New Mexico. In the 1950s, they moved to Levelland, Texas, and operated a dress shop. They retired in Levelland, where a Sam Hameed Golf Tournament was named for him. Jameil Aryain, letter to the editor, *Seminole (TX) Sentinel*, May 17, 1987.

4. San Angelo was a community that developed near Fort Concho, one of the Texas frontier forts established in 1867, as more and more settlers began moving westward after the Civil War. Big Lake, located eighty-three miles southwest of San Angelo, developed when the Santa Rita well no. 1 blew in on May 28, 1923. Rundell, *Oil in West Texas*, 21–22.

5. Lamesa was located sixty miles south of Lubbock on the Santa Fe Railroad. The town was platted in 1903 and so named because of its tablelike flatness. *New Handbook of Texas*, s.v. "Lamesa, Texas."

6. Best began in 1924 on the Santa Fe Railroad in southwestern Reagan County after oil was discovered the year before. *New Handbook of Texas*, s.v. "Best, Texas."

8. Marriage to Etta

1. Located in west-central Lamb County, Amherst began in 1913 as a rail station for the Pecos and Northern Texas Railway. When the townsite was platted in 1923, a railroad official named it for Amherst College. Littlefield, the county seat of Lamb County, was named for George W. Littlefield, a local rancher and financier who had acquired 235,858 acres of the Yellow House Division of the XIT Ranch and added it to other holdings. Littlefield formed a land company and had surveyors lay out a town after he learned that the Santa Fe Railroad would pass through the area. By 1913 the town was a station on the railroad. Sudan, once a part of the 77 Ranch, was located in west-central Lamb County on the Santa Fe Railroad and was developed in 1917–18. The first postmaster suggested the name. *New Handbook of Texas*, s.vv. "Amherst, Texas," "Littlefield, Texas," "Sudan, Texas"; Peterman, *Pioneer Days*, 59.

2. Littlefield was incorporated in 1924 and began growing, reaching a population of 3,500 by 1930. *New Handbook of Texas*, s.v. "Littlefield, Texas"; also Peterman, *Pioneer Days*, 64.

3. The Yellow House Ranch covered 312,175 acres in Lamb, Hockley, Bailey, and Cochran counties. George W. Littlefield named it for the southern, or Yellow Houses, division of the XIT Ranch, which he purchased in 1901. The name originated when the Spanish called a yellowish limestone bluff with caves "las Casas Amarillas" (the Yellow Houses), which from a distance appeared to be a city. *New Handbook of Texas*, s.v. "Yellow House Ranch."

4. William Monnig, who came to Fort Worth with his brother George and opened a dry goods store in 1889, was born in Hermann, Missouri. His father, Otto, came to the United States from Germany in 1848. The name Monnig, sometimes spelled "Moennig" or "Maennich," apparently was German or Prussian, not Syrian. Morrow and Monnig, *Monnig Family History*.

5. Reuben Tobolowsky, a Jewish resident of Dallas, served as secretary-treasurer of the Willard Hat Company and the Davis Hat Company, both owned by Henry P. Willard. Carol Roark (manager of the Texas/Dallas History and Archives Division, Dallas Library) to J'Nell Pate, August 19, 2003; *Dallas City Directory*, 1927, 1929, 1931, 1933.

6. F. A. Brown was president of the Graham-Brown Shoe Company, located at 708–14 Main Street in Dallas, which manufactured shoes and golashes. In addition, the store was a distributor of Dr. Austin's Arch Support Shoes. *Dallas City Directory*, s.v. "Graham-Brown Shoe Company, Inc.," 1925–26, 1928, 1930, 1932.

7. Unfortunately, the people apparently succeeded in making Replin leave Littlefield, for he closed his business in March 1926. Going out of business advertisement, *Lamb County (TX) Leader*, March 11, 1926, p. 6.

8. Ads in the Littlefield newspaper, the *Lamb County Leader*, were for a Chili King Café, not Hamburger King Café. The owner was V. A. Valles. *Lamb County (TX) Leader*, September 4, 1924, p. 2.

9. The "New Immigration" brought thirty million people from central and eastern Europe and the Middle East in less than twenty-five years. They settled in cities and were willing to work menial jobs. This rapid

influx led to a restoration of the Ku Klux Klan that had emerged in the
South after the Civil War. On a snowy March day in 1924, thirty "robed
and hooded" Klansmen marched in the streets, the first appearance of
the Klan in Littlefield. The Klan made a great show of giving twenty-
five dollars to a widow with five children. "White Robed Klans Men
Parade Streets As Snow Is Falling," *Lamb County (TX) Leader*, March
20, 1924.

10.   With fifty-mph winds, a fine dust from the northwest started at 4 a.m.
and blew until sundown on Thursday, November 25, 1926, creating
thousands of dollars worth of damage. Small barns and houses were
blown over, and the wind forced cotton out of ripe bolls. Awnings and
store signs came down as well. Dust covered everyone's Thanksgiving
dinner. No one in Littlefield died, as was the case on the Great Plains,
where fifty lost their lives. "Folks Thankful When Thursday Wind Was
Over," *Lamb County (TX) Leader*, December 2, 1926, p. 1.

11.   Relief for farmers came June 6, 1927, when the rains came and continued weekly for a while. And 1928 was a better year. Peterman, *Pioneer
Days*, 11–12.

12.   Jewish manufacturing firms in Dallas at this time included Benno
Manufacturing Company, founded by Benjamin Benno in 1911, which
made shirts, covered buttons, and maids' and waitresses' uniforms.
August Lorch owned a ladies' clothing manufacturing firm. Others were
Sweet Cap and Tie Company; Max Friedmen's Home Industrial Tailors;
H. Bark's Pants Factory; March Lee Manufacturing Company; H.
Schwartz Lion Manufacturing Company; Model Tailors; David Fair, tai-
lor; and Koenigsberg and Cohen, makers of fine coats and suits.
Biderman, *They Came to Stay*, 33, 244, 246; also "Weiss Dies, Dallas
Civic Leader, 92," *Dallas Morning News*, November 3, 1957, p. 1, 11;
Dallas City Directory, s.v. "Milliners' Supply Co.," 1928.

13.   One of the best-known Jewish milliners was Martin Weiss, an immigrant from Hungary who had begun his career in the United States as a
peddler after his mother put him on a boat to America in 1888 with
eighty-four dollars. He had arrived in Dallas in 1911 and later bought
the stock of a bankrupt millinery store, Milliners' Supply Company,
located at 909–11 Elm. His philanthropy and generosity in Dallas

became well known over the years. Since the store Ed visited (as he recalled) was on Commerce, it could have been one of a number of Jewish people who were in the millinery trade in Dallas. Biderman, *They Came to Stay*, 219, 251; "Weiss Dies, Dallas Civic Leader, 92," *Dallas Morning News*, November 3, 1957, p. 1, 11.

9. Difficult Depression Years

1. A ranching family named Brownfield in Terry County inspired the name of the town founded in 1903 on land that had been their ranch. The family donated town lots to voters and land for a courthouse, school, and churches. The population in the early 1930s when Ed and his family moved there was about three thousand. Several old ranching families proved clannish in the well-established community. *New Handbook of Texas*, s.v. "Brownfield, Texas"; Jameil Aryain and Pat Aryain, interview.

2. This work program was a part of Franklin D. Roosevelt's New Deal, the Works Progress Administration created on April 8, 1935, to end direct federal relief payments but to continue to provide money by employing workers on public projects. *Webster's Guide to American History*, "Chronology 1935, April 8," 455.

3. A two-page spread in the *Terry County (TX) Herald* cited men's leather suede jackets, $3.98; ladies dresses, $2.98 and $3.98; and men's dress shirts 98¢. Ed even tried Green Stamps. In 1934 he quit calling his store The Fair Store and changed the name to Aryain's Dry Goods. Advertisements, *Terry County (TX) Herald*, September 14, 1934 (The Fair Store), September 28, 1934 (Aryain's), December 10, 1937, October 28, 1938.

4. Charlie Shebly died shortly thereafter. His wife, Mary, married Casey Cabool. Jameil Aryain, letter to the editor, *Seminole (TX) Sentinel*, May 17, 1987.

5. United States, Certificate of Citizenship, Ed Aryain. May 16, 1939. No.4482648 in posession of Jameil Aryain, Seminole, Texas.

10. Fresh Start in Seminole

1. Seagraves in northern Gaines County was established in 1918 as the terminus of the Santa Fe Railroad spur from Lubbock. It was named after

railroad executive C. L. Seagraves and became a major cattle shipping point. *New Handbook of Texas*, s.v. "Seagraves, Texas"; Texas Online, s.v. "Seagraves, Texas," http://www.texas-on-line.com/graphic/seagraves (accessed July 24, 2003).

2. See the introduction for more information on Seminole. A news story appeared in the *Terry County (TX) Herald* in Brownfield that Ed Aryain was leaving soon to go to Seminole "to enter business in that coming oil center." The writer continued, "The *Herald* joins other business interests of town in recommending the Aryain family to the good people of Seminole." "This Week We Give You—Aryain D.G," *Terry County (TX) Herald*, March 24, 1939, p. 1.

3. Born in Salonika in 1881, Mustafa Kemal entered a military school at age twelve, finished the Staff College, and was commissioned a captain in 1905 at age twenty-four. He began to see a need for the influences of Western civilization because of his military assignments in Europe. A hero in World War I, he became involved in a nationalist movement for Turkey, and by 1922 ushered in the Republic, making Turkey a secular state. A new law he approved required everyone to have surnames; thus, on November 29, 1934, he dropped his Arab name of Mustafa and became Kemal Ataturk. Ataturk meant "Father Turk." He had made himself the father of Turkey, creating the modern nation from the remnants of the Ottoman Empire. Kinross, *Ataturk*, 7, 14, 25, 430–31, 494, 501–2, 538, 578.

4. Mustafa Kemal (Ataturk) adopted several children, some of them war orphans. Sabiha Gokeen was the military pilot. One story is that Sabiha herself approached Ataturk and asked for help in her schooling. She trained in Russia as a military pilot, and later in 1937 she took part in a bombing raid against Kurdish rebels in the Tunceli Mountains. Ataturk loved to brag about her and show off her skills. Kinross, *Ataturk*, 535–36; Mango, *Ataturk*, 298–99, 439, 514.

5. Order of the Eastern Star is the largest fraternal organization in the world to which both men and women may belong, but it is typically the organization women join when their husbands become Masons. http://www.easternstar.org/oes/home.html (accessed February 11, 2006).

6. Following World War II, France surrendered its mandate, and Syria gained its independence in 1946. Lebanon was recognized as an inde-

pendent entity in 1943. Kinross, *Ottoman Centuries*, 14; Mackey, *Passion and Politics*, 282; Hitti, *History of Syria*, 704.

7. Ed's son Jameil remembers that at the time he often had trouble persuading his father to spend the money on the remodeling and introductions of new ideas. Jameil Aryain and Pat Aryain, interview.

11. Middle Eastern Welcome

1. The family remembers Ed and Etta visiting a very ill Safaka early in the trip, but she barely knew Ed. Pat Aryain, interview. February 14, 2006.

2. Shebly Aryain represented Rashayya in the Lebanese parliament for several years. He died in 1995.

3. Jameil Aryain's son, Badih Jameil Aryain, has corresponded with Ed's son Jameil. Badih Jameil Aryain to Jameil Aryain, August 8, 2000.

4. Kamal Jumblatt (1917–77) was the traditional chief of Lebanon's Druze minority and a lawyer who led the Lebanese Nationalist Movement. In 1949 he founded the Progressive Socialist Party. He was elected a deputy for Mount Lebanon beginning in 1943 and continued to be elected over and over. He was elected for the eighth time in 1972. Jumblatt was assassinated March 16, 1977, at the gates of his headquarters in the Shouf District. His son Walid Jumblatt succeeded him as Druze leader. Moubayed, "Syria Loses Its Former Ally in Lebanon, Druze Leader Walid Jumblatt," *Washington Report On Middle East Affairs*, January/February 2001, http://www.washington-report .org/back-issues/010201/0101035.html (accessed September 19, s003); also Lebanese Progressive Socialist Party, "Kamal Jumblatt," http://www.psp.org.lb/kamal%20jumblatt-english.htm (accessed June 20, 2003).

5. Jumblatt had a palace in Mukhtara. Glass, *Tribes with Flags*, 432.

6. Established by American missionaries in 1866 with sixteen students, the American University of Beirut is a private, independent, non-sectarian institution with a charter from the State of New York and a private, autonomous board of trustees. Presently coeducational, instruction is in English. It was originally called the Syrian Protestant College, but the present name change came in 1920. It is open to students of all races,

nationalities, and beliefs. American University of Beirut, "History of AUB," http://www.aub.edu.

12. Holy Land Tourists

1. The granddaughters did carry the white Bible at their wedding ceremonies. Jameil Aryain and Pat Aryain, interview.
2. For the story of Abraham and Isaac, see Genesis 22.

13. Cutting Ties in Henna

1. Jamal Pasha (1872–1922), military governor of Syria in World War I, was called Jamal the Butcher in the Arab world. He commanded the Ottoman army in Syria from 1915 to 1917 and executed Syrian leaders on May 16, 1916, in both Damascus and Beirut. The day is commemorated in Syria and Lebanon as Martyrs' Day. A blockade that Pasha ordered on the entire eastern Mediterranean coast to thwart the British kept money and mail from arriving in Syria for many months. Damascus Online, "Jamal Pasha (1872–1922)," http://www.damascus-online.com/se/ SE-main.htm (accessed June 20, 2003). See also Haddad, *Fifty Years,* 46–47; Wallach, *Desert Queen,* 202; "Lebanon's History: French Intervention," Federal Research Division—Library of Congress, http://www.rimbaud.freeserve.co.uk/lebanon_french.htm (accessed September 19, 2003).
2. Jezzine is located on cliffs overlooking a picturesque valley of forests and waterfalls. Once a resort city of eighty thousand people, the Lebanese civil war in the 1980s caused seventy-five thousand to leave. Criminals and prostitutes moved in, but many empty stone houses still remained. Andjelic, "City of Whores."

14. Gunshots in Lebanon

1. For the story of Paul's blindness on the road to Damascus, see Acts 9.
2. Originally called the Cathedral of St. John the Baptist, the Omayyad Mosque in Damascus was built in 705 A.D. by the Omayyad Caliph al-Walid ibn Abdul Malek and took ten years to complete. It is sometimes spelled "Ummayad" or "Umayyad." Glass, *Tribes with Flags,* 185; also

Wallach, *Desert Queen*, 76; "Landmarks of Old Damascus The
Omayyad Mosque," http://www.syriatoday.ca/b-landmarks-old
-damascus.htm (accessed February 12, 2006).

3. Located in eastern Lebanon northeast of Beirut, Baalbek's history dates
    back over five thousand years to 1900–1600 B.C. in the Middle Bronze
    Age and even perhaps earlier to 2900–2300 B.C. in the Early Bronze
    Age. In the Greek and Roman periods 323–64 B.C. and 64 B.C.–312
    A.D., it was called Heliopolis. Baalbek consists of a great temple com-
    plex on a high point in the Bekaa Valley. The word "Baalbek" may
    mean "god of the Bekaa Valley" or "god of the town" and represents
    the Phoenician worship of Baal. Six columns remain from the Greek
    Temple of Jupiter. Sacred Sites, "Baalbek, Lebanon," http://www
    .sacredsites.com (accessed June 20,2003). See also Haddad, *Fifty Years*,
    239.

4. Located between two parallel mountain ranges, this fertile valley, irri-
    gated by the Litany River, is the largest agricultural area in Lebanon.
    Phoenician writings from 1400 B.C. call the valley the "Place for the
    Gods." The valley has monuments all over it, including Baalbek and the
    Temple of Bacchus. Libanmall.com, "Bekaa Valley," http://www
    .libanmall.com (accessed June 20, 2003). See also GreatBuildings.com,
    "Temple of Bacchus," http://www.greatbuildings.com (accessed June
    20, 2003).

5. Located at Baalbek, Lebanon, the style of the Roman Temple of
    Bacchus, 150 A.D., is ancient Roman Corinthian. Of the forty-two origi-
    nal columns, nineteen are still standing. GreatBuildings.com, "Temple
    of Bacchus," http://www.greatbuildings.com (accessed June 20, 2003).

6. The Temple of Venus at Baalbek dates from the third century A.D.
    Encyclopedia Britannica Online, s.v. "Temple of Venus at Baalbek, Third
    Century, A.D.," http://www.britannica.com/ebe/art (accessed
    September 18, 2003).

7. Kahlil Gibran (1883–1931) was born in Bsharri, Lebanon, of Christian
    parents and became a world-famous Lebanese mystic, philosopher,
    artist, and poet. He lived in an apartment in New York City for twenty
    years before he died, and his books sold well in the United States even a
    half-century after his death. Gibran's body was carried back to Bsharri
    for burial. Hilu, *Beloved Prophet*, 4–5; Glass, *Tribes with Flags*, 318.

15. Beirut Goodbyes

1. The district where Americans lived would have been in the Christian section in East Beirut. Glass, *Tribes with Flags*, 273.

2. Later, during the Lebanese civil war, the Muslim area of West Beirut where the Idriss was located saw many hotels and clubs destroyed. Glass, *Tribes with Flags*, 386.

3. Ed didn't live to learn of the civil war in Lebanon in the 1980s and what happened to the beautiful Beirut he and Etta had visited. Buildings were gutted at the central square, the Place des Martyrs. Glass, *Tribes with Flags*, 402.

16. Seminole is Home

1. One reason why Ed and Etta could write about this visit with so much detail was that Etta kept a journal of her trip. Later when Ed was telling his story to Etta, they consulted her notes to refresh their memories. Their trip to Egypt reads more like the journal of a tourist than the visit home of a returning son of Syria, so some of the detail has been condensed. Eddie Aryain, interviews; Jameil Aryain, interviews.

2. At least toward the end of the long trip, Ed's humor was intact.

3. Throughout the manuscript Ed repeatedly said "Allah, or God." Here at the close of his story he only said "God," which seems to indicate his American and religious transformation.

Bibliography

. . .

BOOKS AND ARTICLES

Abu-Izzeddin, Nejla M. *The Druzes: A New Study of Their History, Faith, and Society.* Leiden: E. J. Brill, 1984.

Anderson, Agnes Martin. "Ed and Etta Aryain." In *The Gaines County Story: A History of Gaines County, Texas,* edited by Margaret Coward. Compiled by Gaines County Historical Survey Committee. Seagraves, TX: Pioneer Book Publishers, 1974.

Andjelic, Zoran. "City of Whores: The Brothels and Bunkers of Jezzine." *Diacritica Press* and *Sobaka Magazine,* http://www.diacritica.com/sobaka/archive/jezzine.htm.

Arfa, Hassan. *The Kurds: An Historical and Political Study.* London: Oxford University Press, 1966.

Baker, Stanley L., and Virginia Brainard Kunz. *The Collector's Book of Railroadiana.* Secaucus, NJ: Castle Books, 1976.

Baker, William G. *The Cultural Heritage of Arabs, Islam, and the Middle East.* Dallas, TX: Brown Books, 2003.

Banks, Ann, ed. *First Person America.* New York: Alfred A. Knopf, 1980.

Bender, David L., and Bruno Leone, eds. *The Middle East: Opposing Viewpoints.* San Diego, CA: Greenhaven Press, 1992.

Betts, Robert Brenton. *The Druze.* New Haven, CT: Yale University Press, 1988.

Biderman, Rose G. *They Came to Stay: The Story of the Jews of Dallas, 1870–1997*. Austin, TX: Eakin Press, 2002.

Caldwell, Tom Joe. "The Syrian-Lebanese in Oklahoma." Master's thesis, University of Oklahoma, 1984.

Carpenter, Ann Miller. "The Railroad in American Folk Song, 1865–1920." In *Diamond Bessie and the Shepherds*, edited by Wilson M. Hudson, 103–19. Austin, TX: Encino Press, 1972.

Churchill, Charles Henry. *The Druzes and the Maronites under the Turkish Rule from 1840 to 1860*. London: Bernard Quaritch 15 Piccadilly, 1862.

Cohen, Norm. *Long Steel Rail: The Railroad in American Folksong*. Urbana: University of Illinois Press, 1981.

Conaghan, B. F. *Three Sands*. Tonkawa, OK: Tonkawa Centennial Committee, 1994.

Copeland, Paul W. *The Land and People of Syria*. Philadelphia, PA: J. B. Lippincott, 1964.

Corsi, Edward. *In the Shadow of Liberty: The Chronicle of Ellis Island*. 1935. Reprint, New York: Arno Press, 1969.

Cristol, Gerry. *A Light in the Prairie: Tempel Emanu-El of Dallas, 1872–1997*. Fort Worth: Texas Christian University Press, 1998.

Crocchiola, Stanley, F. *The Early Days of the Oil Industry in the Texas Panhandle, 1919–1929*. Borger, TX: Hess, 1973.

Dana, Nissim. *The Druze in the Middle East: Their Faith, Leadership, Identity, and Status*. Brighton: Sussex Academic Press, 2003.

Daniels, Roger. *Coming to America: A History of Immigration and Ethnicity in American Life*. New York: Harper Collins, 1990.

————. *Not Like Us: Immigrants and Minorities in America, 1890–1924*. Chicago: Ivan R. Dee, 1997.

Dinnerstein, Leonard, and David M. Reimers. *Ethnic Americans: A History of Immigration and Assimilation*. New York: Harper & Row, 1975.

Douglas, George H. *All Aboard: The Railroad in American Life*. New York: Paragon House, 1992.

"Ed Aryain Is Seeing Realization of Vision," *Seminole (TX) Sentinel*, February 22, 1940.

Erdman, Loula Grace. *Life Was Simpler Then*. New York: Dodd, Mead, 1963.

Esposito, John L. *The Islamic Threat: Myth or Reality?* 1993. Reprint, Oxford: Oxford University Press, 1999.

Fawaz, Leila Tarazi. *An Occasion for War: Civil Conflict in Lebanon and Damascus in 1860.* Berkeley: University of California Press, 1994.

Fedden, Robin. *The Phoenix Land: The Civilization of Syria and Lebanon.* New York: George Braziller, 1965.

Fernea, Elizabeth Warnock, and Robert A. Fernea. *The Arab World: Forty Years of Change.* 1985. Reprint, New York: Doubleday, 1997.

Firro, Kais M. *A History of the Druzes.* New York: E. J. Brill, 1992.

Forbes, Gerald. "Southwestern Oil Boom Towns." *Chronicles of Oklahoma* 17 (December 1939): 393–400.

Friedman, Thomas L. *From Beirut to Jerusalem.* New York: Farrar Straus Giroux, 1989.

Gambill, Gary C., and Daniel Nassif. "Walid Jumblatt: Head of the Progressive Socialist Party (PSP). *Middle East Intelligence Bulletin* 3, no. 5 (May 2001).

Geniesse, Jane Fletcher. *Passionate Nomad: The Life of Freya Stark.* New York: Modern Library, 1999.

Gilbert, James Leslie. *Three Sands: Oklahoma Oil Field and Community of the 1920s.* Tonkawa, OK.: Tonkawa Centennial Committee, 1994.

Gilmour, David. *Lebanon: The Fractured Country.* New York: St. Martin's Press, 1983.

Glass, Charles. *Tribes with Flags: A Dangerous Passage through the Chaos of the Middle East.* New York: Atlantic Monthly Press, 1990.

Glasscock, Carl B. *Then Came Oil: The Story of the Last Frontier.* Indianapolis: Bobbs-Merrill, 1938.

Golden, Harry. *Forgotten Pioneer.* Cleveland, OH: World Publishing, 1963.

Goodwin, Jason. *Lords of the Horizons: A History of the Ottoman Empire.* New York: Henry Holt, 1998.

Graves, Robert. *Lawrence and the Arabs.* 1928. Reprint, New York: Paragon House, 1991.

Haddad, George. *Fifty Years of Modern Syria and Lebanon.* Beirut: Dar-al-Hayat, 1950.

Handlin, Oscar. *The Uprooted: The Epic Story of the Great Migrations that Made the American People.* Boston: Little, Brown, 1951.

Helgesen, Sally. *Wild-Catters: A Story of Texans, Oil and Money.* New York: Doubleday, 1981.

Higham, John. *Strangers in the Land: Patterns of American Nativism, 1860–1925.* 1963. Reprint, New York: Atheneum, 1966.

Hilu, Virginia, ed. *Beloved Prophet: The Love Letters of Kahlil Gibran and Mary Haskell, and Her Private Journal*. New York: Alfred A. Knopf, 1974.

Hitti, Philip K. *History of Syria, Including Lebanon and Palestine*. New York: Macmillan, 1951.

————. *The Origins of the Druze People and Religion*. New York: Columbia University Press, 1928.

————. *The Syrians in America*. New York: George H. Doran, 1924.

Hourani, Albert Habib. *A History of the Arab Peoples*. Cambridge, MA: Belknap Press of Harvard University Press, 1991.

————. *Syria and Lebanon: A Political Essay*. London: Oxford University Press, 1946.

Inalcik, Halil, and Donald Quataert, eds. *An Economic and Social History of the Ottoman Empire, 1300–1914*. 1994. Reprint, Cambridge: Cambridge University Press, 1996.

"Is Bound Over to Superior Court after Preliminary Hearing before Justice Ham Here This Morning," *Drumright (OK) News*, January 13, 1922.

Jacobs, William Jay. *Ellis Island: New Hope in a New Land*. New York: Charles Scribner's Sons, 1990.

Jaffee, David. "Peddlers of Progress and the Transformation of the Rural North, 1760–1860." *The Journal of American History* 78 (September 1991): 511–35.

Kayal, Philip M., and Joseph M. Kayal. *The Syrian-Lebanese in America: A Study in Religion and Assimilation*. Boston: Twayne Publishers, 1975.

Kinross, John Patrick Douglas Balfour. *Ataturk: A Biography of Mustafa Kemal, Father of Modern Turkey*. New York: William Morrow, 1965.

————. *The Ottoman Centuries: The Rise and Fall of the Turkish Empire*. New York: William Morrow, 1977.

Knight, Oliver. *Fort Worth Outpost on the Trinity with an Essay on the Twentieth Century by Cissy Stewart Lale*. 1953. Revised, Fort Worth: Texas Christian University Press, 1990.

Leach, William. *Land of Desire: Merchants, Power, and the Rise of a New American Culture*. New York: Pantheon Books, 1993.

Lewis, Bernard. *The Multiple Identities of the Middle East*. New York: Schocken Books, 1998.

Longrigg, Stephen Hemsley. *Syria and Lebanon Under French Mandate*. London: Oxford University Press, 1958.

Mackey, Sandra. *Passion and Politics: The Turbulent World of the Arabs*. New
  York: Dutton, 1992.

Makarem, Sami Nasib. *The Druze Faith*. Delmar, NY: Caravan Books, 1974.

Mango, Andrew. *Ataturk: The Biography of the Founder of Modern Turkey*.
  New York: Overlook Press, 1999.

Ma'oz, Moshe. *Ottoman Reform in Syria and Palestine 1840–1861: The Impact of
  the Tanzimat on Politics and Society*. Oxford: Clarendon Press, 1968.

———. *Syria and Israel: From War to Peacemaking*. Oxford: Clarendon Press,
  1995.

Marcus, Stanley. *Minding the Store: A Memoir*. Boston: Little, Brown, 1974.

Mariott, Alice, and Carol K. Rachlin. *Oklahoma: The Forty-sixth Star*. Garden
  City, NY: Doubleday, 1973.

Mathews, John Joseph. *Life and Death of an Oilman: The Career of E. W.
  Marland*. Norman: University of Oklahoma Press, 1951.

Moore, Richard R. *West Texas After the Discovery of Oil: A Modern Frontier*.
  Austin, TX: Jenkins, 1971.

Morris, Juddi. *The Harvey Girls: The Women Who Civilized the West*. New
  York: Walker, 1994.

Morrow, Pete, and Gene Monnig. *A Monnig Family History: The Descendants
  of Bernard Joseph Monnig and Katharina Henriette Stuckmann*. Mendota
  Heights, MN: Media Computer Enterprises, 1990.

Naff, Alixa. *Becoming American: The Early Arab Immigrant Experience*.
  Carbondale: Southern Illinois University Press, 1985.

Najjar, Abdallah. *The Druze*. Translated by Fred I. Massey. American Druze
  Society, 1973.

Namias, June. *First Generation: In the Words of Twentieth-Century American
  Immigrants*. 1978. Revised, Urbana: University of Illinois Press, 1992.

National Geographic Atlas of the Middle East. Carl Mehler, project editor.
  Washington, DC: National Geographic, 2003.

The New Handbook of Texas. 6 vols. Austin: Texas State Historical
  Association, 1996.

Newsom, D. Earl. *Drumright: The Glory Days of a Boomtown*. 1983. Reprint,
  Perkins, OK: Evans Publications, 1987.

Niepage, Martin. "Memoirs and Diaries: The Armenian Massacres."
  www.firstworldwar.com/diaries/armenianmassacres.htm.

Noel, Thomas J., and Cathleen M. Norman. *A Pike's Peak Partnership: The
  Penroses and the Tutts*. Boulder: University Press of Colorado, 2000.

Oklahoma: A Guide to the Sooner State. 1945. Revised, Norman: University of
    Oklahoma Press, 1957.

Olien, Roger M., and Diana Davids Olien. *Life in the Oil Fields.* Austin: Texas
    Monthly Press, 1986.

———. *Wildcatters: Texas Independent Oilmen.* Austin: Texas Monthly Press,
    1984.

Orfalea, Gregory. *Before the Flames: A Quest for the History of Arab
    Americans.* Austin: University of Texas Press, 1988.

The Oxford Companion to American History, edited by Paul S. Boyer. Oxford:
    Oxford University Press, 2001.

Palmer, Alan. *The Decline and Fall of the Ottoman Empire.* New York: M.
    Evans, 1992.

Pate, J'Nell. *North of the River: A Brief History of North Fort Worth.* Fort
    Worth: Texas Christian University Press, 1994.

Pavlowitch, Stevan K. *Anglo-Russian Rivalry in Serbia, 1837–1839: The Mission
    of Colonel Hodges.* Paris: Mouton, 1961.

Peterman, V. M. "Pete." *Pioneer Days: A Half-Century of Life in Lamb
    County and Adjacent Communities.* Lubbock: Texas Tech Press, 1979.

Poling-Kempes, Lesley. *The Harvey Girls: Women Who Opened the West.* New
    York: Paragon House, 1989.

Quilliam, Neil. *Syria and the New World Order.* Reading, UK: Ithaca Press,
    1999.

Rand McNally Goode's World Atlas, 17th ed., edited by Edward G. Espenshade Jr.
    Chicago: Rand McNally, 1986.

Reeves, Pamela. *Ellis Island: Gateway to the American Dream.* New York:
    Barnes & Noble Books, 2002.

Rizk, Salom. *Syrian Yankee.* New York: Doubleday, 1943.

Rosenberg, Leon Joseph. *Sangers' Pioneer Texas Merchants.* Austin: Texas State
    Historical Association, 1978.

Rundell, Walter, Jr. *Oil in West Texas and New Mexico: A Pictorial History of
    the Permian Basin.* College Station: Texas A & M University Press, 1982.

Shirk, George H. *Oklahoma Place Names.* 1965. Revised, Norman: University
    of Oklahoma Press, 1974.

A South Dakota Guide. Compiled by the Federal Writers' Project of the Works
    Progress Administration. Sponsored by the State of South Dakota, 1938.

Speranza, Gino C. "Victims of Fraud and Deceit." In *The New Immigration*,
     edited by John J. Appel, 43–53. New York: Pitman, 1971.

State Farm Road Atlas. Skokie, IL: Rand McNally, 2001.

Stowe, Estha Briscoe. *Oil Field Child*. Fort Worth: Texas Christian University
     Press, 1989.

Syrian and Lebanese Texans. James Patrick McGuire, principal researcher. San
     Antonio: University of Texas at San Antonio, Institute of Texan Cultures,
     1974.

Tibawi, A. L. *A Modern History of Syria, Including Lebanon and Palestine*.
     London: Macmillan, 1969.

Van Steenwyk, Elizabeth. *Saddlebag Salesmen*. New York: Franklin Watts, 1995.

Wakin, Edward. *The Lebanese and Syrians in America*. Chicago: Claretian
     Publications, 1974.

Walbridge, Linda S. "Middle Easterners and North Africans." In *A Nation of
     Peoples: A Sourcebook on America's Multicultural Heritage*, edited by Elliott
     Robert Barkan, 391–410. Westport, CT: Greenwood Press, 1999.

Wallach, Janet. *Desert Queen: The Extraordinary Life of Gertrude Bell,
     Adventurer, Adviser to Kings, Ally of Lawrence of Arabia*. New York:
     Anchor Books, 1996.

Wassef, Ceres Wissa. *Egypt*. New York: Harper & Row, 1983.

Weatherford, Doris. *Foreign and Female Immigrant Women in America,
     1840–1930*. New York: Schocken Books, 1986.

Webster's Guide to American History. Springfield, MA: G & C Merriam, 1971.

Weir, Ben, and Carol Weir, with Dennis Benson. *Hostage Bound, Hostage Free*.
     Philadelphia, PA: Westminster Press, 1987.

Wolf, Martin L., ed. *A Treasury of Kahlil Gibran*. Translated from the Arabic
     by Anthony Rizcallah Ferres. Secaucus, NJ: Citadel Press, 1974.

Ziadeh, Nicola A. *Syria and Lebanon*. Beirut: Lebanon Bookshop, 1965.

GOVERNMENT DOCUMENTS

Dallas, Texas. *City Directories, 1925–1933*. Dallas Public Library.

Dawson County, Texas. Marriage License of Ed Aryain, Miss Etta Stone, May
     14, 1925.

Drumright, Oklahoma. Court Records, 1922. Office of Court Clerk, City Hall.

Fort Worth, Texas. *Obituaries*. William Monniq. Fort Worth Public Library.

Fort Smith, Arkansas. *City Directories, 1914, 1918–22, 1925–26, 1928–29.* Fort
Smith Public Library.

Newkirk, Oklahoma. Kay County, Oklahoma County Criminal and District
Court Records, 1923. Office of Court Clerk.

Sapulpa, Oklahoma. Court Records, 1922. County Courthouse.

Seminole, Texas. *City Directories, 1965, 1974.* Gaines County Library.

Seminole, Texas. *Obituaries.* Ed Aryain. Etta Aryain. Gaines County Library.

State of Oklahoma. The Criminal Court of Appeals of Oklahoma. Case of A.
Francis, A-3619, 1922–23.

———. Superior Court of Creek County. Drumright Division: Criminal Cases
Roll No. 1-2555. Case of John Francis and Alex Francis, 1918–21.

United States. Certificate of Citizenship. Ed Aryain. May 16, 1939. No.
4482648.

United States. List or Manifest of Alien Passengers for the United States. *SS
Niagara* sailing from Havre [LeHavre, France] June 7, 1913. Manifest Line
Number 30. Mohamed Aryen [*sic*].

INTERVIEWS

Aryain, Eddie (son of Ed and Etta Aryain). Telephone interviews with J'Nell
Pate. Los Angeles, California. July 17, 2003, March 17, 2004, August 13,
2005, and others.

Aryain, Jameil, and Pat Aryain (son and daughter-in-law of Ed and Etta
Aryain). Interview with J'Nell Pate. Seminole, Texas. July 16–17, 2003.
Also numerous telephone conversations.

Caldwell, Tom. Telephone interview with J'Nell Pate. Drumright, Oklahoma.
June 3, 2003.

Cothes, Reeves. Telephone interview with J'Nell Pate. Seminole, Texas.
September 3, 2003.

Crow, Herman. Interview with J'Nell Pate. Hurst, Texas. July 5, 2003.

Ehlmann, Arthur J. Interview with J'Nell Pate. Fort Worth, Texas. August 1,
2003.

Elam, Dayton. Telephone interview with J'Nell Pate. Seminole, Texas. August
4, 2003.

Gill, Jimmie E., DVM. Interview with J'Nell Pate. Haltom City, Texas. August
14, 2003.

Kelsey, Michael (Temple Public Library, Temple, Texas). Telephone interview with J'Nell Pate. August 11, 2003.

Roark, Carol (manager of the Texas/Dallas History and Archives Division, Dallas Public Library). Interview with J'Nell Pate. August 15, 2003.

Sahliyeh, Emil. (Associate Professor of Political Science, University of North Texas, Denton). Telephone interview with J'Nell Pate. February 9, 2006.

Sullivan, Glen. Interview with J'Nell Pate. Seminole, Texas. July 17, 2003.

———. Telephone interview with J'Nell Pate. July 26, 2003.

LETTERS

Aryain, Badih Jameil, to Jameil Aryain, August 8, 2000. In possession of Jameil Aryain.

Aryain, Etta. Letter to son Eddie. No date (1973).

Aryain, Jameil. Letter to the editor, *Seminole (TX) Sentinel*, May 17, 1987.

Bair, Billie (Fort Smith, Texas, Public Library Genealogy Department), to J'Nell Pate, July 14, 2003.

Lambersen, Sharon (Hannibal Free Public Library, Hannibal, Missouri), to J'Nell Pate, July 9, 2003.

Roark, Carol (manager of the Texas/Dallas History and Archives Division, Dallas Public Library), to J'Nell Pate, August 19, 2003.

Wallen, Harvey, and Nan Wallen. Letter to editor, *The Seminole Sentinel*, May 6, 1987.

NEWSPAPERS

Drumright News. Drumright, Oklahoma.
Lamb County Leader. Littlefield, Texas.
The Seminole Sentinel. Seminole, Texas.
Terry County Herald. Brownfield, Texas.

Index

· · ·

Arab Bureau, n. 223
Arab countries, 181
Arab home, 6; hospitality in, 192
Arab immigrants, 90 percent before 1914
  are peddlers, xxxi
Arab language newspapers, xxx
Arab proverb, xxxi
Arabic-speaking immigrants, xxxi
Arab world, n. 233
Arabic writing, 11
Arabs, 85; attacked Aqaba, n. 224; in
  refugee camps, 168
Arabs revolt, n. 223
arak, 37
Arbeely, Joseph, xxviii
Armenian Christians, n. 216
Armenian massacre, 44, 169
Armenian quarter of Beirut, 188
Armenian service, 167
Armenians, xxx
Armistice, 84
Arnold, Paul, 164
Aryain, Adel, 161, 193
Aryain, Amy (*see also* Carpenter, Amy),
  xxxviii, 149, 165–66
Aryain, Assam, 160–61
Aryain, Badih Jameil (great-nephew), n.
  214, n. 232
Aryain, Biriki, 18, 25
Aryain, Dwight (Chip), xxxviii, 149, 166
Aryain, Ed, began peddling in Midwest,
  xxxiii; birth of, 3; came to U.S. in 1913,
  xxviii; certificate of citizenship, n. 230;
  changed name to, 49; church attendance of, xxxvi; credit manager complimented, 123; death of, xxxvii;
  description of, xxxix; detailed journey,
  xxxvi; didn't know Libya not democratic, n. 214; didn't live to see civil war, n.
  235; emigration from homeland, xxix,
  39–46; and family moved to
  Brownfield, n. 230; had blue eyes, xxv;
  health of, xxii; helped by Syrian network, xxx, 47–52; his famous ancestor,
  n. 214; in Beirut airport, 153; leaving
  Brownfield, n. 231; lived to see grandchildren, xxxviii; marriage to Etta,
  xxxiv, 112–13; mentions Abdul Hamid,
  xxiii, 8; mentions Druze religion, xxiv,
  6, 9, 13, 19, 26, 28, 37, 161; mentions

1860 massacres, xxv, 26–28; mentioned
  scar, xxxii; persuasions to move to
  Beirut, 190; pride in ancestor, xxv,
  18–24, 160; a relative of Hameeds, n.
  227; saw Statue of Liberty, xxx, 42, 199;
  selling consumer goods, xxxi; visited
  Beatrice, Nebraska, n. 216, 48–49, 51;
  visited millinery wholesaler, 114,
  120–21, 129, n. 230; writing in 1973, n.
  215
Ed and Etta, n. 232, n. 235
Aryain, Edward (Eddie), xxi, xxii, xxxvi,
  xxxviii, xxxix, 131, 133, 135, 139, 152,
  159, 171, 200; birth of, 119; graduated
  from high school, 146
Aryain, Etta, xxii, xxxiv, xxxviii; a Baptist,
  xxv; church attendance of, xxxvi; death
  of, xxxvii; wrote down Ed's story, xxi
Aryain family, n. 215
Aryain, Hameedie (*see* al-Baraki,
  Hameedie), 171
Aryain, Hassim, 4
Aryain, Hussian, 4, 33
Aryain, Jameil, xxii, xxxvi, xxxvii, xxxviii,
  133, 135–36, 149, 152, 159, 171, 200, n.
  232; birth of, 122; graduated from high
  school, 148; has Ed's citizenship certificate, n. 230; saw KKK, xxxv
Aryain, Jameil (cousin), 153–54, 180,
  192–93
Aryain, Linda (*see also* Robins, Linda),
  xxxviii, 148, 166
Aryain, Mohammed (*see also* Aryain, Ed),
  xxi, 4, 34, 73, 132, 154, 174, 192, 199;
  arrived in America, 42; got new clothes,
  48; changed name, 49; left Syria, 39;
  ship's manifest concerning, xxx;
Aryain, Mr. and Mrs. Jameil, 148
Aryain, Mrs. Shebly, 162
Aryain name associated with Druze, 28
Aryain, Ollie (*see also* Aryain, Uncle Ollie),
  72
Aryain, Patricia (Pat, *see also* Denton,
  Patricia), xxxvii, xxxviii, 149, 152
Aryain, Pam, xxxviii
Aryain, Safaka, 4, 151, n. 232
Aryain, Shebly (senator), 25, 153–55, 159,
  173, 183–84, n. 232; and Mrs. Shebly,
  160
Aryain, Shebly (*see also* al-Aryan, Shibli),

Denton, Texas, 148
Denton, Troy Lee, xxxvii
Denver, Colorado, 70–71, 164, n. 218, n. 221
"Depression," 125–26, 131, n. 217
"Dink" (*see* Jameil Aryain), xxxvi
discrimination, contributing factors to, xxxv
Dixon, Billy, xxii
Dixon, Olive King, xxi
Djedie, Lebanon, 155–57, 169, 177, 191–93
Dodge City, Kansas, 58, 80, n. 218
Dome of the Rock, 164, 166
Dr. Austin's Arch Support Shoes, n. 228
Drhbe, 12–13
Drumright, Aaron Hatcher, n. 222
Drumright, Oklahoma, 86–87, n. 223; began store partnership in, 82; had Christian Syrian friends there, 28; met man from, 100; named for landowner, n. 222; oil boomtown, 58, 80; oil boom waned after World War I, n. 223; streets filled with people, 81; there when World War I ended, 84
Druse (*see* Druze), xxiv
Druze, xxii, xxv, xxvi, 6, 9, 13, 19, 26, 28, 37, 161, n. 213; attack, n. 215; army, n. 215; beliefs, practices of, xxiv; blamed Christians, 27; books, n. 214; cemetery, 174; character traits of, 7; children, 7; combined with Bedouins, xxvi; gave up arms, 30; had trouble with Moslems, 29; leader Walid Jumblatt, n. 232; massacre of Christians in 1860, 185; in name only, 35; officer at Bsharri, 183; origin of, xxiv; practices, xxv; population, 7, xxiv; religion of Ed Aryain originally, xxviii; supplier, n. 220; thorn in Turks side, n. 215; villages, 14, 147
Druze Arabs, xxxi; have blue eyes, 122
Druze man or men, actions of, 7; dress of, 6; married outside of faith, xxv; wanted armed escort of, 183
Druze people, 14–15; buried on mountaintop, 174; in Lebanon, 158; suffered under Turks, 11
Druze religion, xxiv, 36–37; association of calf with, n. 215; question of calf worship, 34–36

Druze woman or women, activities 7; couldn't emigrate, xxv; dress of 6; keep face veiled, 194; wear veil, 39
dry goods store business, 3
Dunn and Bradstreet, 123
Dusseldorf, Germany, 153

early Christians, persecuted, 176
East Beirut, Christian section, n. 235
Easter Sunday, 163–66
Egypt, xxiii, xxv, xxvi, 19–20, 85, 151, 180, 191, 193, 196–97, n. 214; Ed and Etta's trip to, 235; headquarters in Damascus, 22; Syrian emigration to, xxiv
Egyptian army, 20–21
Egyptian Museum, 197
Egyptians, Shibli al-Aryan fought, n. 214
1860 massacres, xxvi
Eighteenth Amendment, n. 226
Eisenhower, President [Dwight D.], 156
Ellis Island, xxix, xxx; Mohammed Aryain at, 42–44; experiences at, xxx
Empire State Building, 198
English, 142
Erdman, Loula Grace, xxxiii
Essexes, 65
Estacado High School, xxxviii
Europe, days sailing from, xxvii
Exxon, n. 225

Fair Store, The, xxxvi, n. 230
Faisal I, n. 223–24
Farrar, Fred and Pauline, 138
father of Turkey, n. 231
"Father Turk," n. 231
fez, adopted in 1828, n. 216; Ed threw into ocean, 42; remembered, 199; signifies one's religion, 6
Field, Marshall, xxxiii
Finns, xxx
fire in Navarro, 109–10
First Baptist Church, xxxvii
first Syrian immigrant, xxviii
First United Methodist Church, 147
First World War (*see* World War I), 142, 169
Ford or Fords, 65, 72, 76, 119
foreign-born merchant, 130
Fort Concho, Texas, n. 227